P9-BYG-085

Solving Thorny Behavior Problems

How Teachers and Students Can Work Together

CALTHA CROWE

NORTHEAST FOUNDATION FOR CHILDREN

© 2009 by Northeast Foundation for Children, Inc.

All rights reserved. No part of this book may be reproduced in any form or by any electronic or mechanical means, including information storage and retrieval systems, without permission in writing from the publisher, except by a reviewer, who may quote brief passages in a review.

ISBN 978-1-892989-32-1

Library of Congress Control Number: 2008943115

Cover and book design by Helen Merena
Cover and interior photographs © Alice Proujansky, Jeff Woodward, and Peter Wrenn. All rights reserved.

Thanks to the teachers and students of Bronx Charter School for Better Learning, Bronx, New York; Hart Magnet Elementary, Stamford, Connecticut; Kensington Avenue School, Springfield, Massachusetts; Regional Multicultural Magnet School, New London, Connecticut; and Six to Six Interdistrict Magnet School, Bridgeport, Connecticut, who welcomed Northeast Foundation for Children to take photos in their classrooms.

Northeast Foundation for Children, Inc.
85 Avenue A, Suite 204
P.O. Box 718
Turners Falls, MA 01376-0718

800-360-6332
www.responsiveclassroom.org

14 13 12 11 10 09   7 6 5 4 3 2 1

ACKNOWLEDGMENTS

This book rests on a firm foundation built by the work of many educators. More than twenty years ago, my friend and colleague Nancy Kovacic introduced me to the work of Jane Nelsen. Jane Nelsen's writing about exploring children's motivations, encouraging children, and helping children work together has informed my teaching since that day.

Reading *Teaching Children to Care* by Ruth Sidney Charney taught me about many of the strategies that I describe in this book. Other colleagues from Northeast Foundation for Children (NEFC), developer of the *Responsive Classroom®* approach to teaching, have helped me think about the strategies described herein, especially my coach, Chip Wood, and my colleague Paula Denton. My dear friend and teammate Sarah Spencer accompanied me to my first *Responsive Classroom* workshop and supported me in my first attempts to implement the approach.

I would like to thank all my colleagues at Kings Highway School in Westport, Connecticut. Maria Castellucio, principal at Kings Highway, created a climate in which I was able to practice the strategies described in this book. She believes in the power of community and supports taking time to nurture it, even in these challenging times. Anne Nesbitt and Catherine Carmona, assistant principals, consistently supported my work by providing time and conversation as well as working side by side with me in the classroom. Michele Cunningham, Kelly Harrison, Carmela DiStasio, Jessica Carey, and Deborah Philips were true teammates, providing day-to-day reflection and an openness to try new strategies.

Many educators read drafts of this book, gave me helpful feedback, and provided examples from their own classrooms. Among them are Kelly Harrison, Jessica Carey, Janet Adams, Valerie Babich, Melanie Carroll, Karen Feiss, Lisa Garsh, Amy Glaser, Marty Kennedy, Barbara Klein, Kaye McHugh, Nicole Perham, Karrie Sadler, and Caron Stebinger. Some of these names appear in the text; others have been changed to protect the privacy of their students. I want to especially thank Suzy Stark for those long walks around the pond as we discussed particularly thorny classroom dilemmas. Lauri Bousquet, Kathy Brady, Roxann Kriete, Suzi Sluyter, and Tina Valentine read the entire text and provided invaluable feedback, strengthening the book immeasurably.

I want to thank the entire publications team at NEFC. I especially want to thank Alice Yang for her superb editing. She respectfully helped me organize my thoughts and hone my words to make my meaning clear. Elizabeth Nash added precision and polish to my writing. Mary Beth Forton, in her inimitable way, had creative solutions for dilemmas that emerged as I wrote. Helen Merena turned a stack of manuscript pages into a book that is easy to use and beautiful.

I appreciate proofreader Janice Gadaire Fleuriel's attention to detail. She caught errors that escaped everyone else.

I want to thank my mother, Frances Crowe, for encouraging me to take on this project when I found it daunting. I want to thank my life partner, Jerry Allison, for encouraging me every step of the way, even when he might have preferred that we both go climbing rather than staying at home so that I could write. I also want to thank my daughter, Rosa Crowe-Allison, for inspiring me to believe in the power of young people and their ability to be strong, independent people who make ethical decisions about their lives.

CONTENTS

Introduction

Teaching is challenging work. I have found this to be true whether teaching in the inner city or in the suburbs, whether working with preschoolers or fourth graders. As educators, we need to present interesting and well organized lessons, keep students motivated, help children get along, create a nurturing community, and give them structures for working productively together—all while sharing an often small space with upwards of twenty-five unique individuals all day long.

Teaching is also satisfying work because this effort pays off. When we take steps to create a positive classroom climate, the days generally go smoothly, our class enjoys being together, and children make progress academically and socially.

A reality of teaching, however, is that even in the best of climates, children will sometimes have problems. They'll argue with each other, exclude classmates, form cliques, "forget" to do homework, refuse to share, refuse to do work, play too roughly, and mishandle each other's belongings—as all children are wont to do on occasion simply because they are children.

Such problems, although not unusual, can be frustrating roadblocks to joyous learning. They can impede progress for the students immediately involved and for the class as a whole.

This book is about what to do when these sorts of common but learning-disrupting problems come up in the classroom. It offers practical, classroom-tested strategies for addressing different types of difficulties: ones involving individual students, ones involving the whole class, anticipated problems, and problems that have already occurred and have persisted despite the usual array of teacher interventions.

Over the years, I've seen these strategies help children of all elementary grades.

- When first graders Randy and Amira got into a yelling fight over who would get to use the blue crayon, they marched off to have a first-grade version of a conflict resolution meeting.

- A second grade class learned ways to be safe on the playground through an age-appropriate role-play about careful ways to play tag.

- Angela, a fourth grader with a history of defying teachers, *finally* began to improve her behavior when she started using an individual written agreement after all other problem-solving methods failed to bring any change.

- After a chaotic day with a substitute teacher, a group of fifth graders used a class meeting to plan how to treat substitute teachers respect-fully when their teacher needed to be away in the future.

- Through a problem-solving conference with her teacher, sixth grader Marlena finally created a system for getting homework assignments written down in her assignment book.

You'll learn about all these strategies from this book. For each strategy, I break down the steps, pull out keys to success, and show instances of the strategy being used in various grades with suitable modifications.

As just one example of an age-appropriate adjustment, the student-to-student conflict resolution protocol described in Chapter Three calls for students to learn to resolve their conflicts independently. The chapter describes how kindergarten teachers can give even their very young students a taste of conflict resolution by teaching the children to express feelings and listen without interrupting, while supervising and helping the children resolve the conflict. Thus these young students learn basic social skills that will prepare them for the full conflict resolution protocol once they are developmentally ready.

The strategies in this book can become an important part of your teaching whether you teach in urban, suburban, or rural schools. They can be used in conjunction with the special education plans for children who need such extra supports, and they work for children who are more typical learners.

These strategies will help you if you're a beginning teacher. They're also tools that you might add to your repertoire if you've been teaching for many years. As Jon Saphier and Robert Gower point out in *The Skillful Teacher*, teaching is a complex endeavor that calls for constant learning on the part of the practitioner (Saphier & Gower, 1997).

Gaining Skills

I want to emphasize, as Saphier and Gower do in their book title, the word skillful. When you read this book, you'll gain skills. What can help make teaching satisfying, indeed joyful, is skill—the teacher learning practical methods for handling the smooth and routine moments of teaching as well as the bumpy and tricky ones. It is the teacher's skill, not luck or charisma, that makes the most difference to successful teaching.

This is one of the most important lessons I have learned over my career in education. I began teaching elementary school in a third grade classroom in New Haven, Connecticut. I had few skills in classroom management and thus fumbled my way through that first year.

Because I was unsure how to set limits, Delores argued with me about whether or not to do her math work and Jackson refused to write. Since I didn't yet have the skills to build a caring community, Nicole and Shanesha formed a clique and wrote mean stories about the other children. Every day there was a dispute, a tantrum, or an unkind act that exhausted me and detracted from the children's learning. My principal suggested that I observe a more experienced teacher.

Barbara Lanier's classroom was an oasis of peace. Ms. Lanier stated directions softly and kindly. Her students responded by being cooperative and purposeful. When a problem flared up, she restored order with a few words and a calm gesture or two. When George threatened Mikal, for example, she redirected them into a brief conversation to respectfully resolve their differences.

Not that things were perfect in her room. Not all problems were resolved smoothly and completely. But the overall climate was decidedly one of cooperation, friendliness, and fruitful learning.

As I observed Ms. Lanier's class, I wondered, *How does she achieve this?* I was pretty sure she didn't just have "all the good kids." *What did she do that I didn't do?*

As time went on and I gained more teaching experience, I began to see the answer to that question. Ms. Lanier took steps to create a safe, cooperative, and respectful learning community. She assumed nothing about her fifth graders' knowledge of how to navigate their school environment. Instead, she taught them the routines for each part of the day. She established classroom rules with them to build their sense of ownership, modeled expected behaviors, and gave the children opportunities to practice. She used positive teacher language and responded to misbehavior firmly but respectfully.

And for those times when children had trouble despite being immersed in such a positive climate, she was prepared with a range of problem-solving strategies that fit the situation, strategies like the ones I describe in this book.

I first learned these strategies when I took a *Responsive Classroom*® course many years ago. Since then, I've practiced the strategies and discussed them with colleagues. In the course of my career as a teacher in several elementary grades and school settings, I've always kept in mind that I must refine and adapt each strategy to meet the needs of my students.

I share these strategies explicitly in this book so that you won't be like me watching Ms. Lanier: knowing that she was doing *something* but not quite seeing what it was. The liberal use of examples from real classrooms and the breaking down of each strategy into concrete steps are meant to help you see the skills behind the success—exactly what it is that teachers do to achieve peace and productivity in their classrooms.

What Makes These Strategies Work?

The strategies in this book work because they do the following:

Bring out the best in children

The strategies in this book assume that children want to and can learn, want to treat each other with consideration, and want to be treated by others with consideration. From problem-solving conferences to individual written agreements, these strategies bring out and build on children's positive intentions and abilities. For example, when teachers use language such as "Let's see if we can solve this problem so that we take care of each other," the phrase "so that we take care of each other" builds on children's desire to be cared for and their ability to see that others would like to be cared for as well.

Position the teacher and student as collaborators

In all the strategies, the teacher and students work together to address obstacles to the children's learning. The teacher gathers the children's ideas about what's causing the problem and what can be done about it and combines these ideas with his or her own understandings. With their combined wisdom, the teacher and children then use the problem-solving structures to support the children in behaving more peacefully and productively.

Build on relationships: teacher and student, student and student

For collaborative problem-solving to be successful, the parties involved must have a good relationship. The strategies in this book recognize that fact. As Chapter One explains, if these strategies are to work, the teacher has to create a caring classroom community that nurtures positive teacher–student and student–student relationships. When class members then use the problem-solving strategies to address difficulties that come up, the power of those relationships works to their advantage. The trust and understanding they've built helps them empathize with each other in the face of a problem and makes them more open to each other's ideas for solving it.

Look for the underlying cause of the problem

Teachers using the problem-solving strategies in this book search for possible causes of a child's problematic behavior. Rather than assuming a cause, they recognize that each child is unique and look for clues about what's causing that particular child's difficulty.

Clues may come from the child's classroom interactions, previous teachers, and school records. They may come from what the teacher knows about the child's family life and from conversations with the child herself. When an accurate cause is identified, problem-solving is naturally more effective.

Teach children specific problem-solving skills

The approach presented in this book puts children at the center of solving their own problems. It also teaches children the skills they need to do this problem-solving well, skills such as listening, empathizing, speaking, and compromising. This explicit focus on skill-building not only helps ensure that the immediate problem-solving experience will be productive and emotionally safe, but also makes the children better problem-solvers in the future.

Aim for reasonable improvement, not perfection

Our students are real human beings who are imperfect, just as we teachers are. Like many things in life, the knotty problems that we work with students to untangle often have no easy fix. Given this truth, the problem-solving strategies in this book don't aim for easy fixes. Instead, they'll help you communicate clearly with your students and help your students communicate clearly with each other. They'll give all class members a format for listening to and perceiving each other's feelings. They'll help you and your students collaborate respectfully.

Some solutions may resolve a problem once and for all; other times, a solution works for a while and then unravels. In any case, you and your students will have taken steps of improvement.

These steps are actually no small thing. They can mean the difference between a recess spent scowling and kicking gravel at other children and a recess spent playing happily. They can mean the difference between a writing block spent pecking randomly at computer keys and a writing block spent productively composing. Over time, these incremental successes add up to larger growth.

Avoid one-size-fits-all

These strategies provide a framework for teachers and children, but they allow for tailoring to fit individual situations. Because children vary enormously in their concerns and their needs, the questions we ask and the potential solutions we and our students explore must be based on our knowledge of the individual children involved. Observing children carefully, listening to their unique concerns, and paying attention to where they are developmentally are all central to the strategies in this book.

The Teachers We Want to Be

The problem-solving strategies I share in this book have allowed me to become the teacher I wanted to be when I observed Ms. Lanier's classroom. I encourage you, as you read this book, to think about which strategies you might add to your repertoire.

The wonderful thing about our profession is that there is always more to learn, always a new challenge. So go slow. Try one strategy at a time. Don't feel that you need to use every strategy. Think about which ones might work with your students. Seek support and encouragement from colleagues. You'll gradually grow more skillful as you observe students, learn from your colleagues, and gain knowledge from the accumulated wisdom of the teaching profession.

If you're an experienced teacher, use this book to hone your practice. If you're a new teacher, keep this book at hand and return to it again and again to add to your skills. In time, you, too, will be the teacher you want to be.

CHAPTER ONE

Getting Ready

M y first year of elementary school teaching was a chaotic one. I was hired the Friday before Labor Day to start teaching the following Tuesday. That Friday, I walked down the hall to see my new classroom and found it empty—no tables or chairs, no books, no paper or markers. Somehow I managed to scrounge some basic furniture and supplies and began a semblance of teaching on Tuesday.

Equipped mostly with good intentions, I wasn't prepared to create a sense of order and predictability in my classroom and thus spent the year putting out fires. Arguments between children were the norm. Children refusing to listen to me or their classmates was commonplace. There was so much chaos that even if I'd known the problem-solving strategies described in this book, I still would not have had time to address all the problems. If I could relive that year, I'd start with the strategies that I'm about to describe, strategies for creating a safe and orderly classroom climate.

Why Classroom Climate Is So Important

Even in a safe, respectful, and appropriately challenging class, problems will inevitably arise in the course of the year. Students will find themselves in conflict; some will feel excluded; some will refuse to do hard work. These are the facts of classroom life.

But a positive classroom climate makes the handling of classroom problems easier. It reduces the number of problems that arise, making the need for problem-solving the exception rather than the norm. When problems do arise, they tend to be less severe. And the rules, routines, and skills that children learn when they're immersed in a positive classroom climate make them better problem-solvers when issues do arise.

The story of Patrick illustrates these points.

Patrick arrived in his new third grade class in February, eager to learn and make friends. In Morning Meeting on his first day, Ms. Lyons had the class do a greeting that would welcome him and help him get to know his new classmates: Each child picked a name card, greeted the person whose card was picked, and made a positive statement about that person. For example, "Rachel loves puppies and helps kids with their math." "Luke is a wiz at basketball." "Ming greets everyone who comes into the room when it's her turn to be classroom hostess." Later in the meeting, the class played a rousing singing and clapping game, with lots of partner changing.

Ms. Lyons orchestrated many other deliberate steps to help Patrick thrive in his new environment. She observed him carefully and took opportunities to get to know him. She met with his mother to hear her insights about his learning style and his past schooling. She had Patrick's new classmates tell him about their class routines: how to sign out for the boys' room, where to put his snack, and where to keep his independent reading book.

All of Patrick's new classmates wore nametags during the next few weeks so he could learn their names. Ms. Lyons assigned Patrick a buddy to play with at recess and sit with at lunch. She carefully modeled many expected behaviors over the next couple of days so that Patrick learned such procedures as how to get in line and how to take down his chair, as well as more complex processes such as how to write about his thinking as he solved a math problem.

Patrick adjusted easily to his new class and quickly became a lively member of this orderly, child-centered community.

A few weeks later, Ms. Lyons called Patrick's previous third grade teacher. "Oh, you have Patrick now," Ms. Weintraub said. "Good luck. I tried to help him. We put him on an individual written agreement but it didn't help." As the two teachers talked, it became clear that in his previous class Patrick had had many behavior issues.

What accounted for Patrick's dramatic behavior change? The answer was that in his previous classroom, expected behaviors had not been explicitly taught. There wasn't much opportunity for children to move around the classroom, something that children need at this stage in their development. Nor did Patrick have structured ways to get to know his classmates.

Without such clear and developmentally appropriate structures, Patrick had not thrived academically or socially. He had acted out, sometimes explosively, interfering with classmates' learning. The individual written agreement hadn't worked because Patrick was still expected to sit still for long periods of time, something he was developmentally unable to do. He didn't interact well with his classmates and didn't follow routines because he didn't know how. He hadn't been taught.

Patrick's new third grade teacher found that when she taught him the expected behaviors, he was able, for the most part, to succeed in third grade. Of course there were times when he had conflicts with classmates or had difficulty maintaining self-control, as happens to all children. At such times, Ms. Lyons used some of the strategies described in this book to help him. Because of his comfort and success in this environment, the strategies helped Patrick get back on track.

Patrick's case is not unusual. In classroom after classroom, children do better when teachers take the time to know them as individuals and consider where they are developmentally. They have fewer problems if teachers explicitly teach how to follow school routines and how to work and play with classmates. When problems do arise, the problem-solving strategies teachers use are more likely to be successful if the classroom atmosphere is safe, caring, and respectful. Effectively addressing the inevitable difficulties that come up in classroom life must therefore begin with creating a positive classroom environment.

It is beyond the scope of this book to describe in detail all the steps in achieving such a climate. I include below a brief summary of the most important steps. A number of books explain these processes in greater detail. I recommend the following:

- *The First Six Weeks of School* by Paula Denton and Roxann Kriete

- *The Morning Meeting Book* by Roxann Kriete

- *The Power of Our Words: Teacher Language That Helps Children Learn* by Paula Denton, EdD

- *Rules in School* by Kathryn Brady, Mary Beth Forton, Deborah Porter, and Chip Wood

- *Teaching Children to Care: Classroom Management for Ethical and Academic Growth, K–8* by Ruth Sidney Charney

- *Yardsticks: Children in the Classroom Ages 4–14* by Chip Wood

Getting to Know the Students

It's August and, along with most other teachers in this country, I'm in my classroom getting ready for the students. Teaching is so much about relationships, about that trust and that sense of knowing and being known between teacher and student. If I know well the children who will soon fill the room, I'll feel empathy for them, and we'll all have a better chance at getting off to a good start. If I like my students, and they know that I like them, we'll be more likely to work smoothly together. The more I understand the individuals who will fill this classroom, the better I'll do at helping them solve the problems that will, inevitably, come up.

Before school starts

Getting to know students as individuals

I start getting to know students before school even starts. I read over their records. I talk with their former teachers. I learn which strategies worked and which didn't with the children who struggled socially or academically. Chloe needed a brisk walk around the classroom before the day began. Pete benefited from recording comments on the white board during whole-class lessons. It kept him focused.

The school nurse and the PE, art, and music teachers are all rich sources of information. The nurse knows who has frequent illnesses and who drops in for a little TLC. PE, music, and art teachers teach everyone and have often known students for a few years. They see skills and strengths that other teachers may miss. A student who has been diagnosed with learning disabilities may be a gifted artist or athlete.

If I hear any complaints about students, I take them seriously but also with a grain of salt: I know that many circumstances contribute to a child's doing poorly in any particular classroom, and that sometimes we teachers can fall into griping about children whose needs we haven't been able to meet.

Families are also a source of information about students. Before school starts I send home a questionnaire asking such simple questions as "What does your child like to do at home?" and "What are your hopes for your child this year?"

Completed questionnaires show me who loves to play outside, who prefers to watch TV, whose parents aren't home much, which families report struggles over routines. This information will help with problem-solving when a child is, for example, having difficulty completing homework or learning classroom routines.

Family questionnaires also give me glimpses into the cultural milieu of the family. I notice who mentions relatives in other countries. I make note of who volunteers to come into the classroom to share a family holiday observance. I tuck this information away, reminding myself that learning from the family and being sensitive to their culture are crucial in preventing and solving problems involving their child. I take note if a parent's written English is limited. This information alerts me to the fact that the student may need extra homework support. By providing or arranging for this extra help, I can prevent possible problems around homework completion.

Knowing where students are developmentally

Making sure school life fits children's developmental stages is one of the most fundamental steps in achieving a positive classroom climate. This includes considering the developmental fit of routines, expectations, assignments, schedules, and the physical room setup.

To begin, I study the class list and write down students' names and birth dates in birthday order. I notice the ages that will predominate in September and review the common developmental qualities of that age group. Because it sometimes takes a few months for children to grow into the characteristics of their age, I review the common characteristics of children one year younger as well.

I remember the August that I was preparing to teach first grade after having taught third the previous year. I read about how physically active most six-year-olds are, how they talk, hum, and whistle as they go through their days. I certainly couldn't expect the level of quiet that sometimes prevailed in my third grade room. I read about the way six-year-olds fall off their chairs. I would have had a frustrating year if I'd treated that behavior as something I needed to control. I read about six-year-olds' constant tooth eruption and decided that a tooth graph would be just the thing for an ongoing math graphing experience. By the time the students arrived, I was ready to relate to them as the six-year-olds they were.

The first six weeks of school

On the first day of school, some children come bursting into the classroom, full of noise and energy. Others are quieter, checking things out before they get involved. Some come in with friends, others alone.

Despite the bustle of the first day, between making sure everyone knows what to do and silently practicing their names, I try to step back and observe the students. Who approaches whom? Who hangs back? This information will be invaluable later as the predictable complications of life set in and children have problems to solve.

In the next few weeks, as the students begin to relax and come together as a group, I have even more opportunities to learn about them. Who plays with whom at recess? Who has difficulty finding someone to play with? When children are having difficulty getting along, who comes to the rescue?

In February, when Alyssa struggles with asking someone to play with her on the playground, I'll remember back to the first week of school when she sat on the bench and chatted with the teacher on recess duty. This memory, a clue that Alyssa is perhaps more comfortable with adults than with peers, will provide important context as she and I look for solutions to her problem.

During these first weeks of school, I also notice after-school arrangements. Which students travel together to the same library program on Tuesday afternoons? Which children play in a soccer league together? Which students go to the same YMCA after-school program? This information gives me insights into children's relationships and alliances. I tuck it away.

Later in the year, when we're sorting out conflicts and social challenges, I'll pull out this information to help me puzzle through what exactly is going on and what we might do about it. I notice Julius, small and awkward, going off after school to play football. I have some context when later I see Liam, the football star, teasing him. Tracy is a pro at getting all of the children in her religious education class organized to walk there together. Perhaps she can be encouraged to ask Alyssa to join their Four Square game at recess.

The rest of the year

Throughout the school year, we have so many opportunities to keep learning more about our students. We should observe them, meet with them privately about an assignment, and check in one-on-one about how lunch or recess went. We should keep in touch with their parents.

We also have so many other responsibilities. We need to teach required curriculum, keep our classrooms lively and engaging, and make sure the children are treating each other kindly, to say nothing of completing paper work and attending staff development sessions. How can we do it all?

My experience is that it's well worth giving up something in exchange for making time to observe children and meet with them individually. For example, periodically, rather than teaching a new skill, I have children practice previously learned skills independently or with partners. I spend the period walking around, quietly observing and taking notes, and sometimes meeting with students privately. The information I glean helps me teach new skills more efficiently in subsequent weeks, and it lets me stay more attuned to the students' school life in general.

As I meet with Ron in preparation for his family–teacher conference, I learn for the first time that students are teasing him on the bus. When I sit back and watch the class during a transition time, I notice that Marty waits for others to put away the supplies while Sue applies herself busily to cleaning the paint brushes. When I check in with a quick phone call to Nikki's parents, I discover that Nikki, seemingly so sunny in school, cries every night over her homework. All this is important information that allows me to help the children address obstacles that are keeping them from learning at their best.

Establishing a Safe and Orderly Environment

Children want to learn. They want to feel safe. They want to be treated respectfully, and they enjoy treating others respectfully. When their classroom environment allows these things—allows them to learn, feel safe and respected, and know how to treat others with respect—their school days are smoother and more productive, and their difficulties fewer and less severe.

Here are some important ways to establish this kind of environment.

Teach routines

Starting from the first day of school, children need to know what the routines are. Our clarity about where they are to sit, what kind of academic work we expect them to do, and how we expect them to treat each other helps them relax and focus. They take a deep breath of relief. *Yes. This classroom is a safe and orderly place.*

A crucial basic routine to teach is listening for and responding to the teacher's signal for attention. I use a melodious hand-held chime as the signal. This sound establishes a tone of calm and respect. Within the first half hour of school, I explain to the children that when I play the chime, their job is to stop what they're doing, look at me, and listen.

Then we practice. I ring the chime and watch the children stop and listen. I congratulate them on their quick response. We continue to practice the signal throughout the day.

As we practice, I time the children's response in a friendly and playful way, noticing improvement and saying "Oops, we need to practice again" if they are slow to get quiet. They respond faster with each practice until they quiet down instantaneously. At that point, we're ready to use the chime in our daily life together.

This routine, so simple yet so powerful, is the first step in establishing a classroom climate conducive to learning and working together through the challenging moments that are sure to come up.

During the first weeks of school, I teach many other routines that will help us work and play well together. I teach each one explicitly, whether it's how to sign out for the restroom or where to hang our coats. For each routine, the children practice until their behavior is smooth and habitual.

Create ownership

Children need to know that their contribution to the group is expected and valued. All too often, children feel that the classroom belongs to their teacher, not to them. This can lead children to believe that the reason to behave appropriately is to please the teacher, rather than to be true to their own understanding of what's helpful and appropriate. My goal is to build student ownership in our shared community so that children want to take responsibility for their work and behavior.

When students arrive on the first day of school, the classroom is relatively bare. It's clean and organized, but except for the materials that children will need for making name tags and labels for their table and cubby, most everything else is still packed away. I show the first few students how to make these tags and labels. As those students finish, they show subsequently arriving classmates how to complete these simple yet satisfying tasks. Soon the entire group is busy labeling cubbies and drawing a design that "represents them" on their table name tags.

Over the following weeks, the class organizes the classroom library, labels the art supplies, and arranges the math materials so that they're accessible and attractive. All this is done with my guidance but also with significant input from the children. As we complete these tasks together, the children are learning that this is their classroom, not just the teacher's. This feeling of ownership will serve all of us well through the smooth and the rocky times of the year ahead.

Help children know and be known by each other

A class has the potential for being a community. It also has the potential for being a collection of cliques and isolated, lonely individuals. I use a range of methods to help children know and be known by each other so that the classroom becomes a friendly place where cliques are minimized and kindness prevails. This atmosphere of inclusion and cooperation is crucial both in preventing problems and addressing problems effectively when they do arise.

For example, my classes begin each day with Morning Meeting, a whole-group gathering that offers the children a safe, predictable structure for learning about each other and building community.

We begin each Morning Meeting with children greeting each other by name—"Good morning, Cassie," "Hello, Terrance!"—and doing a small activity such as shaking hands, singing, or gently passing a Koosh ball to the person they're greeting. Then children share information about themselves in a safe and structured way, while classmates respond with respectful questions and comments. Next comes a lively cooperative game that allows us to laugh together while reviewing academic content. Finally, the children read the morning message, a short letter from me that serves as a community builder, further practice of academic content, and a warmup for the day ahead. (To learn more about Morning Meeting, see Appendix A.)

The academic blocks of the day offer lots of opportunities for children to interact and get to know each other. For example, I assign partnerships and small working groups for tasks such as partner reading, peer editing, and math problem-solving. During whole-class lessons, I spotlight children's thoughts as much as possible by giving them ample chances to speak, and I hold children accountable for listening to each other's ideas. "Everyone think about Jason's suggestion" or "Let's all try to remember Kirstin's idea about that," I frequently say.

Throughout the year, and especially during the first weeks of school, I also create structures and teach skills that help children develop positive relationships during the social times of their day. Students take turns inviting a classmate to eat lunch with them, for example, with the emphasis on getting to know new friends. As a class, we discuss and practice ways to have a conversation with someone you don't yet know very well. The assumption, often stated and regularly practiced, is that everyone will work and play cooperatively with everyone else.

Ensure emotional safety

Children need to feel safe emotionally if they are to take the risks necessary for learning and solving problems together. To feel safe emotionally, they need to feel respected.

We teachers spend a lot of time telling students to "be respectful." So often, however, students don't know what being respectful means. We need to teach them.

I find that one of the best ways to teach respect is by example. When we treat students with respect, they are more likely to treat each other with respect. We are powerful models for children, who learn more from what we do than what we say. When I include Sam, a student diagnosed with a behavior disorder, as a full member of our class and use friendly words and body language with him, his classmates are more likely to do the same.

We also send a strong message when we hold students accountable for respectful behavior from the first day of school. When Laura says, "Eww, I don't want to sit next to Mala! She's a dork," I quietly tell her that in this class we're friendly and caring toward everyone. Whenever we see an unkind side comment, eye rolling, or a knowing look between two students when another is talking, it's important to address it, for these seemingly small acts can poison the climate of the room, leading children to think that increasingly malicious acts are alright, too. Ultimately, all class members appreciate the expectation of kindness as they begin to feel the power of community.

Pay attention to physical comfort

If children are not comfortable physically, they're not ready to learn. I know from my own experience in faculty meetings that if I've been sitting still too long or if I need a drink of water or a snack, I lose my focus and soon have no idea what we're discussing. If the room is overheated, I'm lulled into wanting a nap.

Children's needs for exercise, food, water, and fresh air are even greater than ours because they're growing and developing. In fact, children's behavior problems often are a result of these needs being unmet.

Movement is perhaps the most overlooked of children's physical needs. Sufficient exercise keeps the blood moving and the brain active. I make an effort to give students frequent "energizer" breaks, when we stand up and take two minutes to play a round of a familiar game such as Head, Shoulders, Knees, and Toes. When such energizers are a regular routine, children calm down quickly afterwards and are more available for learning.

For a slightly longer movement break, I take students outside for a five- or ten-minute organized whole-class game. It's a sad fact that many teachers feel they can't do this because it takes time away from academic learning. I find, though, that a quick outdoor game makes students more alert and attentive, resulting in increased learning.

Moreover, even outdoor games can be an opportunity to review academic content. My ever resourceful colleague Nancy Kovacic has devised a way to turn the childhood classic Red Light, Green Light into practice in estimating lengths. She asks children, "How many feet do you think it is to the leader?" or "How many more giant steps to the leader?"

Even climate control and lighting can affect children's learning and behavior. I remember well one morning when the whole class seemed restless. No one was paying attention. I realized that one of the children had turned out the lights. It had been a bright, sunny morning, so I hadn't noticed much difference. But when the sun went behind some clouds, the children's behavior deteriorated. I turned on the lights and suddenly, able to see, the class became attentive again.

When children are inattentive or misbehaving, it pays to think about whether the physical environment needs some adjustment. Think about fresh air. Do you need to open a window? Think about food and water. Do the children need a snack, a drink, or a bathroom break? Think about movement. Does the class need to do an energizer or go outside for a brisk five-minute game? Sometimes by simply meeting these physical needs, we can ensure more problem-free days.

Know children's developmental readiness

A few weeks ago, I was taking a walk with a colleague. She was describing some boys in her kindergarten class who had taken to throwing themselves on the floor, kicking and screaming, during whole-group lessons. "I know it would be different if they had more time to play," my colleague said.

Five-year-olds need time for physical, imaginative play. It's an important part of their development. Five-year-olds also have trouble sweeping their vision from left to right. This means it's hard for them to sit still and read words on a page.

Yet this is what we so often demand of them in our attempt to teach them to read. This makes about as much sense as forcing out-of-shape, far-sighted middle-agers to read without their glasses while running a 10-K race.

What makes much more sense is to immerse five-year-olds in active play that teaches early literacy and eventually leads to reading. This same colleague assures me that her whole class is most attentive when she reads aloud to them. As she engages her students in listening to a developmentally appropriate story, they are learning to love literature, the foundation for joyful literacy. As her students play simple drama games, acting out the parts to favorite nursery rhymes, they're using their bodies to reinforce crucial pre-reading phonemic awareness skills.

Although we've seen in the past few years that it is possible to teach five-year-olds to read, I believe there are costs associated with this practice. In my experience, some children, often boys, learn these new skills only with enormous effort, if at all. These children miss out on the experience of joyful literacy acquisition. They're often the ones who are still rebelling against literacy at eight, nine, and ten.

My colleague with the struggling kindergartners decided to put out storybook character puppets as a literacy choice so that some of her students will be able to play at reviewing story elements.

Applying the same principle to math learning, she decided to open the block area during math time, knowing that building with blocks will provide her students with practice in understanding spatial relationships and still meet their need for play.

Older children, too, need teachers to understand their developmental needs. While planning the first six weeks of school for her new sixth graders, a friend mentioned to me that she was going to start the first day with some challenging math "brain teasers." Although this would be a terrible first-day activity for younger children, who need familiar, reassuring tasks early on so they won't feel overwhelmed, it's a great way to start off a sixth grade class. As this astute teacher knew, eleven-year-olds prefer meeting new challenges and learning new skills over perfecting old ones. She would have had some unhappy and rebellious students if she'd started sixth grade with "boring" review.

When things aren't going well with a class, one option we have is to recheck the students' ages and what children are typically capable of at those ages. Classroom problems often dissolve or become less severe when we adjust our expectations to meet children where they are developmentally.

Design engaging learning tasks

Children are more attentive and ready to learn, and less likely to act out, when we present them with appropriately engaging academic challenges. When school work is slow and repetitive, children find ways to create their own excitement. When it's too hard, they find other ways to feel good about themselves. Think of the class clown, the child who generates her own fun when work is too hard, too easy, or just plain not engaging enough.

I look around my classroom and see children curled up in corners or sprawled on the rug, reading books of their choosing. Fallon is reading *Dragon Rider* by Cornelia Funke, and Hank is reading *Commander Toad and the Planet of the Grapes* by Jane Yolen. Each child is reading a just-right-book, and each is absorbed and content. Soon they'll get together with assigned partners of similar skill level to share thoughts about their books. Once a week they'll write letters to me about their reading.

In contrast, a few years ago, caught up in test-prep fever, my team ordered a set of test-prep workbooks from a national company. The stories that the children read were out of context and not particularly aligned with their interests. The questions were confusing to them. Misbehaviors abounded.

We've since learned that we can teach the skills needed to respond to those predictable test-prep questions based on students' own reading of their just-right books. With this new strategy, one built on student engagement, behavior has improved and so have test scores.

This is not to dismiss the pressures teachers feel in the face of standardized tests and mandated curricula. The point is that we can, with some creativity, design learning tasks that are engaging for children and help them do well on the tests.

Take a positive approach to rules

Having classroom rules that everyone knows and understands is a key part of creating a positive classroom environment. But not just any rules.

Think of those long lists of rules handed down from some faceless, nameless authority, all beginning with "No." "No running in the hall," "No hitting," "No pushing," "No cutting in line," "No writing on desks," "No talking back to the teacher," "No talking." Such rules lead to resentment and rebellion. They inspire sayings such as "Rules are made to be broken."

When I learned the *Responsive Classroom* approach to teaching, I began to use, and help children use, classroom rules in a different, positive way. During the first weeks of school, all the children articulate their hopes and dreams for the year's learning. The children and I then come up with rules that will allow all class members to achieve their hopes and dreams. I help the children state their rules in the positive—"Don't yell" becomes "Speak quietly," for example—and we consolidate the long list of rules into a few general ones that encompass all the specifics the children name.

The result is classroom rules that embody the children's ideals for working and playing as a community. The rules are also few in number so the children can remember them. One typical year, my third grade class ended up with these as our rules:

> We will listen to the teacher and classmates.
> We will be kind.
> We will take care of everything in our room.

But it's not enough to establish the rules. When I first started teaching, the class created their rules, I put them up on the wall, and none of us ever mentioned them again.

I've learned through experience that if students are to live the rules, I need to teach them how—by modeling the rules for them and helping them notice what it would look and sound like to follow their rules in different situations. I've learned that I need to keep the rules front and center in students' attention by talking about them frequently.

For example, we're about to have peer writing conferences. First we talk about what our rules "Be kind" and "Help each other learn" would look like during writing conference time. Or, it's time to get ready for lunch. Before we move from our seats, we discuss how we can follow our rule "Take care of our environment and everything in it" during our lunchtime transition. These reminders help keep behavior on track.

I know this consciousness-raising is working when a visitor arrives in our classroom and one of the students says, "Let's tell him about our rules."

I also refer to the rules when our classroom life inevitably hits bumps in the course of the year. "One of our rules says 'Be kind,'" I might say. "How can we solve this problem in a way that's kind to everyone in the class?" By referring to the rules this way, I give the children a compass for the sometimes complex business of problem-solving.

(For more about the *Responsive Classroom* approach to creating and teaching rules, see Appendix B.)

Respond to rule-breaking with logical consequences

No matter how assiduously we use proactive strategies, children sometimes break the rules. They forget, they lose control, they test limits. But if we respond to rule-breaking with logical consequences—consequences that enlist children's cooperation and help them learn from their mistakes—we take major steps toward creating a community where children follow the rules most of the time.

We also show, by example, that in this classroom, when something goes wrong, we take a reasoned, caring approach to making it right again. This mentality will serve the children well as they themselves engage in problem-solving in their day-to-day classroom life.

What gives logical consequences this positive effect—and what distinguishes them from punishment—has been articulated as "the three Rs." Logical consequences are *related* to the misbehavior, *respectful* of the child, and *reasonable* for the child to do, as well as in proportion to the child's mistake (Nelsen, 1981, p.86).

For example, when Naomi and Greg initiated a food fight in the cafeteria, they made amends by helping the custodian clean up the cafeteria after lunch. This consequence was related to their food fight because they were cleaning up the mess that they had made. It was reasonable and in proportion to their mistake because Naomi and Greg weren't asked to clean the cafeteria for a week or to clean the whole school by themselves. It was respectful because the children weren't publicly humiliated. They cleaned the cafeteria after the other students had left the room, not in full view of the entire grade. As a result, Naomi and Greg gained a greater understanding of why food fights are destructive, and they didn't repeat that behavior.

One logical consequence that has played a crucial role in bringing a climate of calm learning into my classrooms is the use of time-out for small misbehaviors. So many of the disruptive behaviors that teachers need to deal with in the moment are behaviors caused by children's losing control. Marla chats with Desiree during a lesson, and soon most of the students are chatting with their neighbors, the lesson lost in a sea of conversation. Derek pokes Janine as students get in line, a single behavior that quickly escalates into a class-wide pushing match.

By quickly removing a student from the group as soon as we notice the initial behavior, we prevent small things from escalating into major disruptions. So I quietly and respectfully tell Marla to "take a break" (what we called time-out that year) as soon as she starts chatting with Desiree. And I tell Derek to do the same the moment he pokes Janine.

The challenge is to use time-out in such a way that children feel it's supportive rather than punitive. I have found that if I introduce time-out as a helpful tool that we all use sometimes, then nearly all students will come to see it as a way to regain self-control rather than a technique for punishment and humiliation.

I tell them I use time-out myself and demonstrate how to use it by calmly walking over to the time-out chair, sitting for a moment, breathing deeply to collect myself, and then walking back to the group. Then I use the time-out chair for real when the classroom is getting chaotic and I'm afraid that I'm about to slide into teacher behaviors that I'd rather not use, such as raising my voice. I encourage children to follow my example and use our time-out spot voluntarily when they notice that they're losing self-control.

Using Positive Teacher Language

Our language—what we say to children and how we say it—conveys powerful messages. It can tell children that we believe they can learn or that we doubt they can. It can show children what a community feels like or encourage social hierarchy and division. It can establish a climate of safety and predictability or one of anxiety and chaos. With our language we can show children that adults make all the decisions or that children's contributions are expected and appreciated.

In many ways, then, teacher language is the tool that makes all our teaching strategies, from Morning Meetings to classroom rules, work at their best. The skillful use of language helps us create an environment in which children usually follow the rules and the need to use problem-solving strategies is the exception rather than the norm.

Here are some of the most important goals to keep in mind when choosing our words and tone.

Foster shared responsibility

When I first began teaching, I often said things like "I like the way Denise is getting ready for lunch" when I saw behavior that I wanted to see more of.

Although this way of talking sometimes controlled students' actions, it had the unintentional yet insidious effect of conveying that my approval was the currency of our classroom. It led students to feel that ensuring an orderly classroom was my job, rather than a shared responsibility between all of them and me. It also sowed seeds of division among the children by publicly holding Denise up above all others as an exemplar.

Later I learned to spend a few days having students practice our lunch-prep procedure and asking questions such as "What have you noticed about our lunchtime preparations?" Asking what children noticed conveys that the group has the power and the responsibility to work toward an orderly transition. And honoring all the children's perceptions conveys that all of them are valued members of the community.

Reinforce desired behavior

"You've all read for half an hour today. That's ten minutes more than yesterday." When I see children practicing desired behavior, I reflect it back to them using this kind of language, language that names the specific behavior in a matter-of-fact way. This specificity allows students to know exactly what they're doing well so that they can keep doing it or build on it.

Equally important, by placing the focus on their behavior, rather than my approval of it, this language helps children measure their own growth toward an ideal. It again encourages them to take responsibility for their own learning.

Remind children of expected behavior

Before children go into a potentially tricky situation—for example, before recess at the beginning of the year, before an all-school assembly, or before an independent work period—we can use language to remind them briefly of the expected behaviors for that situation.

"Remember how we practiced walking to assembly and sitting quickly?" or "What do you need to do before we start independent reading?" or "How did we agree to pick teams for kickball?" we might say. Assuming that the expected behaviors have been taught and practiced, the use of such short reminders is good proactive teaching that reduces the likelihood of problems.

In addition, rather than repeating all the instructions, short reminders show our faith in children's ability to recall the expected behaviors themselves. When they actively do the recalling, they're more likely to practice the behavior.

Redirect children when behavior goes off track

When children begin to misbehave, our language can help them refocus and get back on track. Simply saying "Classroom rules" in a kind and firm voice can remind students that we all agreed to be kind to each other.

When children cross the line and are out of control, we can calmly give a simple, clear statement: "Stop. Walk." This lets them know, without confusion, what the expectations are.

Well Positioned to Solve Problems

You're getting to know students well. You're watching them as they work and play, and you're learning about their families and home cultures. You're showing that you like each of them as an individual. You've created rules with students and taught them how to follow the rules through modeling, and when students lose control, you're using logical consequences to teach them more appropriate behaviors.

Even so, problems will still arise in your classroom, as they do when any group of human beings spend time in close proximity.

By being proactive, however, you'll be limiting the number of problems to a sum that you can deal with. Rather than being overwhelming, the problems will seem manageable. You'll have the time and energy for problem-solving.

CHECK THE FOUNDATION

Establishing a positive classroom climate will help you use the strategies in this book successfully when problems come up.

But before using a strategy, ask yourself, "Have I laid the foundation for a positive climate well enough?"

Only when you know the foundation is solid should you go on.

Use this checklist to see whether certain aspects of this foundation need to be reinforced. Jot down observations and any further actions you might take.

First, define the problem.

Be specific. Describe the behavior rather than labeling the child's character. For example, "During small-group independent work time, Charlene either sits idly or bothers neighbors with games or non-assignment-related talking."

Now check the foundation.

Knowing the child

What do you know about the child as an individual? What do you know about the child's developmental stage, family, and home culture?

Does the child know that you like her?

Classroom routines

Does the child understand the routines? Do you need to reteach any routines?

Sense of ownership and community

Do the children feel ownership of their classroom? Are there things you could do to deepen their sense of ownership?

Are the children friendly and respectful toward each other? What do you know about their relationships? What can you do to help them know each other better and treat each other with greater respect?

Physical environment

Do the children have enough opportunities and room to move?

Is the temperature comfortable? Is the lighting bright but not glaring?

Do the children have opportunities to eat and drink?

Developmental fit

Are classroom expectations and activities developmentally appropriate for this child?

Do you need to make changes to help this child engage more deeply with learning?

Rules and expectations

Does the child understand and respect the rules? Have you modeled expected behaviors? Have you given the class opportunities to practice?

Do you need to reteach any rules or expectations?

Responses to rule-breaking

Have you used logical consequences to allow the child to fix mistakes, make amends, and learn more constructive behaviors to use the next time a similar situation comes up?

Have you taught students how to use time-out in a positive way?

Do you use time-out for small things before they escalate to bigger problems?

Teacher language

Is your teacher language respectful and clear?

Do you notice and reinforce appropriate behaviors? Do you name the specific behavior in a matter-of-fact way?

Do you briefly remind this child of expected behaviors before a potentially tricky situation? Do you prompt this child to recall the behaviors?

Do you use words to stop and redirect the child firmly and quickly when misbehavior begins?

CHAPTER TWO

Problem-Solving Conferences

Andrew, a verbally articulate special education student with learning disabilities and ADD, fell apart every time he was asked to write.

He sulked, argued with teachers, and sometimes threw full-blown tantrums on the classroom floor. During the daily writers' workshop in our third grade class, he would lie on the floor, kick his feet, and refuse to write. I would sit beside him and offer support in getting started, but that didn't help.

At a time when he was calm, I asked Andrew to a private one-on-one conversation with me to see if we might together figure out a way to make writing go better for him.

I began by affirming his skill in expressing his ideas when speaking, then stated matter-of-factly that I noticed he had trouble getting his good ideas down on paper. Andrew, perhaps relieved by my tone, agreed quickly. "Yep, it's hard for me," he said. I explained why it was important that he learn to write well and invited him to work with me to become a better writer.

Talking together for a few minutes, we identified a likely cause of his difficulty: When I asked whether it's because he never has energy at writing time, he confirmed that he gets "really, really tired."

Together we brainstormed for possible solutions and decided on one to try. Because Andrew was most energetic early in the day, we'd create a time first thing in the morning for him to write. After a conversation with his parents, we decided that three days a week, Andrew's dad would bring him to school before the other children arrived. Andrew would sit at the reading table and write while I prepared for the morning.

We tried this. It didn't solve all of Andrew's writing problems, but for the first time in several years, Andrew did begin to do some productive writing.

This conversation with Andrew took about fifteen minutes and is an example of a problem-solving conference, a strategy for helping individual students overcome a persistent problem they're having at school. It's a private, structured conversation about what's creating the difficulty for the child and what might help him overcome it.

Purpose: Building an Alliance to Solve the Problem

In a problem-solving conference, the teacher builds an alliance with the student to solve a problem. The teacher opens up discussion with the child, listens to her, and makes the problem a mutual issue. The teacher and child then together identify a likely cause of the problem and together decide how to address it.

Problem-solving conferences rest on a foundation of rapport between the teacher and student, a rapport established before any problem-solving is attempted. They build on children's natural desire to belong and to learn. Conducted well, these conferences work because when children feel accepted and trust that their teacher cares about them, they're generally eager to work with their teacher to become more successful in school.

Sometimes these conferences quickly solve the problem—the teacher and student successfully find a solution, and the student's behavior changes. Other times the problem is more complex, perhaps requiring the involvement of colleagues, special educators, or child mental health professionals. The problem-solving conference may then represent the beginning of a conversation, providing helpful information to the teacher and any other adults involved.

While the immediate reason for a problem-solving conference is to address a current difficulty, this strategy can have far-reaching effects. It can enhance the teacher's relationship with the student, helping the student see that the teacher cares about him as a person and about his success in school.

Moreover, in guiding students to think about possible causes of their problem and what they can do to solve it, we teach them to be self-reflective. We teach them to take responsibility for their behavior. These are habits and skills that will serve them well now and in their adult lives.

When to Use Problem-Solving Conferences

A problem-solving conference is a strategy for addressing one persistent problem involving one student.

One persistent problem

Children with challenging behaviors usually act out in multiple ways. But asking them to work on all of their problems at once is likely to overwhelm them. A more productive approach is to choose one problem to address in the conference. This increases the chances that the student will succeed. That success then gives the child the confidence and interest in working on other needed improvements.

It's also important to reserve problem-solving conferences for persistent issues. Many classroom problems are occasional and fleeting. Elizabeth gets angry at her friend Michaela and tells Michaela she won't spend time with her at recess, but the next day the two fifth graders are back on good terms. Deagan, usually a productive sixth grade writer, today can't figure out how to add details to his reader's notebook entry and sits sucking on his pencil. For these kinds of problems, a reminder about classroom rules or a quick reference to ideas for getting past writer's block, rather than a problem-solving conference, might be an appropriate teacher response.

By contrast, Savannah habitually calls out during Morning Meeting, barely letting her fellow first graders make comments. Reminders, more modeling of raising hands and waiting, redirections, and use of logical consequences have had no effect. Because these routine interventions have not worked to help Savannah gain control of her calling out, a problem-solving conference would be an appropriate strategy to try.

A problem involving one student

Problem-solving conferences are designed to address a difficulty that one child is having rather than a problem involving the interplay between two or more students. Other strategies—possibly conflict resolution (see Chapter Three)—are more suitable for issues that involve more than one student.

Admittedly, classroom problems often fall in a gray area between involving one student and involving several. The teacher's task is to discern whether there is one child whose behavior is essential to the interactions. Christopher often argued with classmates. The arguments would escalate as each student reciprocated with sharper and sharper barbs, but I could see that it was Christopher who initiated them with cutting teasing. "You're a dork," he would whisper to Sean. "Your pants are high-waters." Sean, mortified about the pants that had seemed fine just a few minutes ago, would whisper back, "You're mean," and the argument would be on its way. A problem-solving conference with Christopher thus seemed to be the appropriate response.

Behaviors that might be addressed through problem-solving conferences

Academic problems *(Examples: difficulty getting started on or completing assignments, doing careless work, not being thoughtful)*

Problem-solving conferences can be a way to explore children's behavior problems around academic work. Silvie rushed through her assignments. Daniel seemed unable to settle down to read. Conferring with each gave me insight into the reasons for the student's academic struggles. Once we had a common understanding of the reasons, we could work together to create a plan that would enable the student to be a more successful learner.

Behaviors that interfere with others' learning
(Examples: calling out, demanding constant teacher attention)

Some of the thorniest classroom problems are those that arise from so many people spending all day together in one room. Mitchell talked incessantly during kindergarten group discussions, preventing other children from speaking. Third grader Rachel followed Ms. Harrison around the room, calling "Teacher, Teacher," preventing Ms. Harrison from attending to the other children.

It takes great self-control for children to hold back their impulses so that everyone can learn. For those who consistently have trouble, problem-solving conferences can be a way to heighten awareness of the need for self-control and to set up a structure for the teacher to give reminders and monitor the child's improvements.

Behaviors that alienate other children *(Examples: tattling, speaking in a mean way, being a bad sport, initiating exclusive cliques)*

Some children, although they desperately wish for friends, are their own worst enemy "in the friends department" as Michelle, a student I taught, used to say. Michelle kept choosing Raven as a partner, even as Raven backed further and further away from her. Ruby was only interested in working with Mia and wanted Mia to work only with her, despite Mia's interest in making new friends in their fifth grade class.

There are many possible causes for such problems, from how a child treats classmates, to children's perceptions of who or what is "cool." A problem-solving conference can be a vehicle for exploring reasons and solutions and coaching children in mastering more successful social behaviors.

Defiance toward the teacher
(Examples: ignoring directions, arguing with the teacher, rude looks or remarks)

When children, on occasion, choose to ignore or defy teacher directions, logical consequences usually remedy the problem. Some children, however, are chronically oppositional. Lisa was such a student.

On the second day of school Lisa had a tantrum during a math lesson on sorting and categorizing "ways that we use math in the world." For homework the night before, the children were to find examples of math use in objects from their homes. Lisa refused to group her examples with any other student's. On the third day of school she threw some base ten blocks at me when I restricted the number of blocks she could use.

Even though each incident was fleeting, Lisa showed a pattern of defiance. This told me that I needed to have a problem-solving conference with her right away to establish basic classroom expectations. (See "Lisa, defiant toward the teacher" on page 71.)

Steps in a Problem-Solving Conference

A problem-solving conference consists of specific steps that establish a tone of respectful collaboration and ensure clarity about the goals of the meeting. Though there are several steps, some are quite quick, so the entire conference usually takes only ten to twenty minutes. The steps are:

1. Establish the purpose of the conference.

2. Reaffirm teacher–student rapport.

3. Talk about the problem area: what the teacher notices, what the student notices.

4. Name the behavior as a problem and why it's a problem.

5. Invite the student to work with the teacher on the problem.

Teacher Intention in Problem-Solving Conferences

Positive teacher intention is paramount to the success of problem-solving conferences. The effectiveness of this strategy is determined, at least in part, by our open-hearted willingness to collaborate with a student who is exhibiting behaviors that are self-defeating and may be irritating to others. A problem-solving conference will not be effective if we feel blame or anger toward the student, and our feelings will come through even if we think we're masking them.

To make sure I'm on the child's side, I spend time thinking about his behavior before the conference, trying on different perspectives, reflecting about what his point of view might be. A colleague's fresh eyes and ears can be helpful. One day I sat down with another teacher to talk through my plans for a conference with a student who wasn't doing his homework. I thought I was giving a balanced and objective recounting of the child's actions. My colleague listened and said, "It sounds like you're angry at him."

She was right. I realized that my feelings of helplessness about getting the student to do his homework had led me to feel irritated with him. Through talking with her, I was able to reframe my own thoughts and feelings so that I was ready to ally with the student. Only then could he and I work together to make appropriate modifications to his homework and a plan for completing it.

6. Explore the cause of the problem.

7. Articulate a clear, specific goal to work on together.

8. Generate solutions and choose one to try.

9. Set a time for a "How are things going?" check-in.

In the next pages, you'll see what these steps looked like in a conference I had with a third grader named Erica.

The youngest in a family of high achievers, Erica was a happy-go-lucky child who loved to laugh. She arrived at school every morning with a big smile, ready to give school her all. Despite the fact that she was the youngest in our class, with a December birthday, she got along well with classmates and had lots of friends.

Erica's problem was with reading and writing. Choosing a "just-right" book was a struggle for her. She chose thick books with small print and challenging words, and then "read," flipping through the pages rapidly without comprehension. When it came to writing, Erica rushed. She covered many pages with unpunctuated nonsequiturs, her scrawled handwriting wandering all over the paper. She routinely misspelled words that I knew she could spell correctly.

I believed that Erica could do a lot better if she just slowed down. A problem-solving conference seemed like the right strategy to try. Of Erica's two problematic academic areas—reading and writing—I decided to focus on writing for the moment.

One morning as the children were arriving, I quietly asked Erica if she'd like to have lunch with me. I said that I'd like to discuss her writing and it would be nice to do so over lunch. She agreed. At lunchtime, Erica went to get her food, and then arrived in the classroom with her lunch tray. I already had my sandwich out. We sat down together at the reading table.

Step 1. Establish the purpose of the conference

The first step is to establish clearly what the conference will be about. I wanted to reiterate that our conversation would be about her writing, and I wanted her to know that I cared about what she thought. I began by asking how she felt things were going so far.

Misunderstanding, she launched right into how things were going with friends. "I like to play with Jenny. Trent called me 'dumb face' one day when you were out at a meeting."

Refocusing and clarifying, I asked how she thought things were going with her writing.

She paused and then replied hesitantly, "Okay."

Step 2. Reaffirm teacher-student rapport

It's vitally important that we've already built a positive relationship with the student before attempting a problem-solving conference. Reaffirming this rapport usually helps the student relax and become thoughtful, allowing the teacher and student to collaborate.

I list this as the second step, after establishing the purpose of the conference. But it can just as easily come before establishing the purpose if that feels more natural. That's what I did in the conference with Andrew that opens this chapter.

We can reaffirm rapport in different ways. We can note positive behaviors we've observed in the student, to remind the child that we see her competencies and have faith in her ability to succeed in school. Or we can just chat briefly about something the student likes or is happy about—a hobby, for example—which shows the child that we notice and care about her interests.

With Erica, I noted her positive learning behaviors. "I've been noticing that you listen carefully during lessons and contribute your thoughts during group discussions," I said. I chose these behaviors because they showed that Erica had the motivation to be a good student. I might have simply asked about her birthday party the previous week. Either way, a positive and friendly tone is crucial.

Step 3. Talk about the problem area: What the teacher notices, what the student notices

Now the teacher turns the conversation to the problem area. But this is not the same as saying that the behaviors are a problem and why—that comes next. First, the teacher simply states some specific behaviors she has noticed aren't working. Then she asks what the student has noticed. Before they can solve a problem together, the teacher and child have to establish which behaviors are under question, and the two need to agree that the student is indeed exhibiting those behaviors.

With Erica, I brought up these problem behaviors using an objective tone. I wanted her to see these as problems to solve rather than as an attack from me. "I've noticed that when you write you often forget your punctuation and miss spelling words that I know you know. I'm wondering if you're rushing to finish quickly. What have you noticed?"

My question reflects the fact that this is a collaborative strategy and Erica's views were a key to the collaboration. It was important, therefore, that I ask Erica what she had noticed. Erica readily agreed that she rushed with written work.

Step 4. Name the behavior as a problem and why it's a problem

Only now, when the teacher and student have agreed on the facts, does the teacher assert why the behavior is a problem that needs to be solved.

With Erica, I simply stated, "It's important that we find a way to have you do your best work in school, and that means careful work so that you can learn to be an even better writer."

Step 5. Invite the student to work with the teacher on the problem

In this step, the teacher specifically invites the student into the problem-solving process as a partner. This invitation serves the dual function of guiding the child to take responsibility and allowing the teacher to gauge the student's readiness to confront the issue.

"Would you like to work together on finding ways you can be careful with your written work? I'd like to help you with this, if you'd like to work on it," I said to Erica. I knew that she might or might not want to work with me, but if this problem-solving was to be successful, her cooperation would be important.

By this point in the conversation, Erica trusted that I truly wanted to help her do her best, and she agreed to work with me.

This is a place to abandon the conference and simply state classroom expectations if the student doesn't see her behavior as a problem or doesn't want to collaborate with the teacher. If Erica had said no to my invitation to work together, I would have accepted her answer. I would have simply stated that our class rules say she is to do her best and that I would monitor her writing carefully. If a student isn't ready to take responsibility for her work and learning, the teacher needs to take responsibility for it.

Step 6. Explore the cause of the problem

Part of working together on a problem is coming to a shared understanding of its cause. But simply asking children why they're doing something often gets a shrug or an "I don't know," so prompting them with possible explanations is helpful. To keep my position neutral, I phrase these prompts as questions starting with "Might it be," "Could it be," or "Why do you suppose," rather than as assertions.

"I'm wondering why you rush when you write," I said to Erica. "Could it be that you want to be like your older sister, Melissa, and you think that she writes quickly?" I had thought of this as a possible cause when planning for this conference.

Erica's reply surprised me. "No," she said. "I know that Melissa works carefully. It's just that when I'm working I feel like I'm in a danger zone and I have to work fast to get out of it."

"Hmm, what do you mean by 'danger zone'? What does it feel like?"

With some prompting, Erica explained that by "danger zone," she meant the work is hard and it feels scary. She wants to hurry so that she'll be done as soon as possible.

Then, as children sometimes do in a problem-solving conference, Erica volunteered information that revealed a deeper issue than the specific problem at hand. She said, "I was supposed to be in second grade right now. My mom thought I could work harder so I started kindergarten when I was four. Third grade is pretty hard."

Erica's grade placement wasn't something I could realistically control, so going down this conversational path risked opening a can of worms. Still, for the sake of understanding what she was feeling, I took a chance and asked, "Do you wish you were in second grade?"

"Yes," Erica responded.

Even though we weren't going to put Erica in second grade or retain her for another year in third grade, the conference helped me to realize that Erica, a young third grader, needed a lot more academic support than I was giving her. I made a mental note to talk with the principal about getting some extra help for Erica from a retired teacher who was volunteering in our school.

Step 7. Articulate a clear, specific goal to work on together

For now, I refocused on how to help Erica with her writing. I brought out her writer's notebook and opened it to a rare high-quality entry I had previously identified. It was one with a drawing of Erica and her dad fishing. I thought that looking at this successful entry would motivate her to work toward consistently producing quality pieces.

I asked if the picture had helped her to gather her thoughts.

She responded by saying, "Fishing is one of my favorite things to do. I took the whole thing from my mind and pasted it on the paper."

"I see that you remembered your punctuation and spelled words from our class 'no excuses' list correctly," I said. I pointed out that she'd written in complete sentences and that her sentences made sense. "I see that you can do quality writing in your notebook," I said.

I then made a list that described the quality work I saw in the "fishing" entry:

- Spelled "no excuses" words correctly

- Put end punctuation at the end of each sentence

- Wrote in complete sentences

- Wrote sentences that made sense

I could have suggested that Erica try to accomplish all these things every time she wrote. But now that I knew that writing felt scary to her, I realized it would be overwhelming for her to try to meet all of these goals at once. I had to collaborate with Erica to find a manageable goal and a way to achieve it. She needed success.

"I want to help you do quality writing every time you write in your notebook," I said. "Which of these areas might be a good place to start?"

"I know how to spell lots of words. I think I can remember to spell my 'no excuses' words correctly. I can remember periods and question marks, too," Erica responded.

"Okay, let's start with those. Later on we can work on sentences that make sense," I said.

I wrote down *Erica will check for punctuation and spelling whenever she writes. She will spell "no excuses" words correctly and put end punctuation at the end of each sentence.* She and I both signed the paper, and I wrote the date at the top.

Step 8. Generate solutions and choose one to try

In a problem-solving conference, the student plays a role in coming up with solutions to try. It's helpful, however, for the teacher to be ready to suggest some potential solutions in case the student can't think of any. Chances are if the child knew of a solution, she would have tried it already.

It's also important to be ready to switch to a whole other set of suggestions if the cause of the problem turns out to be something other than what the teacher had guessed. This was the case with Erica. The solutions I had prepared were ones for slowing down, which were no longer applicable. What Erica needed were strategies for feeling safer and more successful when writing.

So I shifted gears in the moment, suggesting some strategies that had helped other struggling writers feel safer. I asked Erica if it would help to use her personal spelling dictionary each time she wrote. And I suggested that she might be able to remember end punctuation if she read her pieces aloud to herself and listened for the pauses.

Erica suggested that if she had a writing buddy, the buddy could help her check for punctuation and correct spelling.

After we generated this list of possible solutions, I invited Erica to choose one to try. She chose her idea: working with a writing buddy. We both agreed that this would be a good start and that we might discuss adding another strategy at a subsequent conference.

Step 9. Set a time for a "How's it going?" check-in

In our busy teaching days, it's easy to feel relieved that a problem is solved and we can cross it off our to-do list. But for problem-solving to be successful, we need to schedule regular check-ins to monitor progress toward the goal. I know that for me, when a problem-solving conference has not been successful, it's often been because I've let the ball drop and haven't kept up the regular check-ins.

"Let's try this strategy and meet again next Monday at lunchtime to see how things are going," I said to Erica.

The conference had taken about twenty minutes, and it was time to pick up the rest of the class from the lunchroom.

During the week I kept a close eye on Erica's writing, and on Monday, she and I compared observations about whether the week's writing had gone better. Together, we decided she should continue working with a writing buddy a little longer.

Meanwhile, I thought about Erica's reading. The problem-solving conference addressed her writing, but her reading was still an issue. How could I help her choose appropriate independent reading books? I decided to talk with my colleague Ms. Reilly to get her opinion. Ms. Reilly taught second grade and was knowledgeable about literacy, often leading staff development sessions for all the second grade teachers in the district.

After hearing my description of Erica, Ms. Reilly said, "It sounds like she wants to look like everyone else when she reads. Maybe you need to limit her choices." At Ms. Reilly's suggestion, I prepared a book basket for Erica, filled with books that Ms. Reilly helped me pick for someone of Erica's age and reading development. When Erica was ready for a new book, she'd choose from her basket.

Erica actually seemed relieved to have her choices limited. Soon she was happily reading, and comprehending, books that were right for her.

Keys to Success in Problem-Solving Conferences

Problem-solving conferences will be most effective if you do the following:

Set a classroom climate of respect and reflection

A problem-solving conference will be most effective if the teacher has already established some rapport with the child. Critical to this rapport is a safe, caring classroom filled with mutual respect between the teacher and students, where the teacher knows and cares about each child. Does the child with whom I want to hold a conference know that I like and respect him? Do I show that I'm happy to see him in the morning? This is the basis for our work together.

Also, a problem-solving conference asks the student to be reflective. Children are more likely to be reflective if we nurture the habit and skills of reflection at other times in the day. I ask myself, "Am I asking open-ended questions in math, reading, and science? Am I honoring children's responses to these questions, whether or not they're the ones that I would give?" If children are expected to think for themselves in math, reading, and science, they will be more likely to be thoughtful and honest when looking at their own behaviors.

Take time to plan before a conference

Teacher planning is a critical part of the conference process. Here are the important areas to think about while planning.

A way to reaffirm our positive relationship with the student

Beginning a conference by reaffirming our positive relationship with the student helps the student relax and get into a constructive problem-solving mode. Before going into a conference, I think about how I might do this. Are there positive behaviors I can point out in the student? How else might I show my faith in his ability to succeed in school? Or should I simply chat a little about the student's favorite baseball team or what he did over the weekend?

There's no one right way to reaffirm rapport. It depends on the student. The important thing is to choose something that the student cares about and to be truthful. If we decide to name a positive behavior, it's important to name only the behaviors the student has truly shown, rather than stretching the truth just to be complimentary. The goal is to remind the child of the genuineness of our relationship with him, of the fact that we notice and value him.

I often redouble my efforts at observing the child when I plan this aspect of the conference. For example, with Erica in the preceding example, I knew there were a lot of positive behaviors that I could name. To refresh my mental list, I spent a day noticing again what she did well. She was friendly and caring to all. She put lots of energy into assignments, getting right to work and producing volumes of writing. She joined group lessons with enthusiasm and contributed her ideas readily. I planned to articulate some of these strengths during the conference.

Which one behavior to focus on

A successful problem-solving conference focuses on one main behavior. When a child has multiple behavior problems, it's best to start by addressing just one of them.

Often it helps to think about which behavior is predominately interfering with success in school. Seven-year-old Clayton crawled around on the floor during lessons, left mountains of paper scraps all over his work area, and was occasionally defiant of me. I decided that until I could be sure that he would respectfully respond to teacher directions, it would be hard for us to work on anything else. So I chose to focus on the defiance in our first problem-solving conference.

Sometimes it helps to think about which behavior the child is probably most able and motivated to change. Nathan, age nine, argued with teachers, whined, and swept papers and books onto the floor during math, refusing to do the math work. I thought that with targeted support he might become successful at doing at least one problem each math period. The other behaviors seemed less surmountable at the moment. Once he was actually doing some math, I reasoned, the other behaviors might be moderated because he would feel more successful academically and therefore less frustrated.

Once I've chosen a behavior, say "responding respectfully to the teacher" or "do more math," I think about a couple of very specific goals that fit under that category. These are behaviors that both the teacher and child would be able to see or hear. By monitoring these specifics, both would be able to agree easily whether there has been progress. Erica and I could agree whether she included periods and question marks. Clayton and I could agree whether he was going to time-out without arguing. Nathan and I could both see whether he completed at least one problem each day in math.

Here are some questions to consider in choosing which behavior to focus on:

Which behavior is getting in the way of success in school?
Which behavior is most irritating to the other children?
Which behavior is interfering with the feeling of community in the classroom?
Which behavior, left unaddressed, might become entrenched and habitual?
Which behavior is the student most able and motivated to change?

Possible reasons for the student's difficulty

As mentioned previously, it helps to come to a conference ready to suggest some possible causes of the student's difficulty. I begin by thinking about my own teaching. Are my expectations for the child reasonable and developmentally appropriate? For example, am I expecting a seven-year-old to function as part of a small group when she is still in an inward and moody stage of growth?

Next I think about every child's basic human need for a sense of belonging and significance. Might the child be thinking mistakenly that her behavior is a way to achieve these goals? Trish followed me around the classroom, asking me for constant feedback on her work. Was she feeling that she wouldn't belong without my constant attention? To test this hypothesis I might work on giving her important classroom jobs that could help her feel needed by the community.

Speaking with a colleague helps enormously as well. Often, in the thick of things, I lose perspective. I get stuck in reacting simplistically to students' behaviors or self-concepts. A student feels discouraged, so I feel hopeless. A student becomes mired in the need for power; thus I feel defensive. A student keeps rushing, so I just want her to slow down. A heart to heart with a trusted colleague can move me out of the box.

In the case of Erica, for example, I spoke with her previous teacher. "I feel frustrated," I told Ms. Perham. "Why is Erica's work so lacking? I think I'm making my expectations clear, and I've modeled careful work, but she just rushes through. Did this happen in second grade? How did you handle it?"

"I checked her work pretty carefully, every fifteen minutes," replied Ms. Perham. "Otherwise she'd just start writing anything on the page."

Just talking with Ms. Perham helped me feel less frustrated. I still didn't know for sure the cause of Erica's work style, but I learned that it had a long history. My best guess was that Erica wanted to be a good student and that she hurried because she saw her older brother and sister working quickly and thought that was what good students did. I planned to prompt her with this thought as a possible cause of her rushing.

Sometimes our guess at the cause turns out to be wrong, as was the case with Erica. That's okay. Positing an explanation often helps draw out of students the correct explanation.

Some potential solutions to suggest

In planning potential solutions to suggest, I consider what I know about the child and what has worked and not worked for him in relevant situations, as well as solutions that have helped other children who've had similar difficulties.

Potential solutions might be something that the teacher will do, something that the student will do, or something they'll do together. It's important to be flexible about these potential solutions though. A problem-solving conference is a collaborative process, and the child may have ideas of his own.

For Erica's conference, I decided that if she needed prompting, I would suggest that I give her a reminder to slow down, that she use her personal spelling dictionary to check her spelling, or that we have a brief check-in during each writing time.

Of course, some of the solutions we plan to suggest may become irrelevant if—as was the case with Erica—our guess at the cause of the problem turns out to be off. During Erica's conference I discarded my idea of reminding her to slow down, for example, once I understood that she hurried because writing felt scary. Rather than being told to slow down, she needed strategies for feeling safer when writing. So I articulated only those strategies that might increase her sense of safety.

Where and when to meet

I always try for a private time and place to meet, away from the listening ears of classmates. Seven-year-olds, for example, can be anxious and moody and need protection, and eight-, nine-, and ten-year-olds are so social and interested in what's going on that they love to listen in on conversations that sound important. Knowing that our conversation is confidential encourages students to lower their guard and be honest, open, and thoughtful.

It's tempting to hold the conference in the classroom while the class is working, since we have so little time alone to plan and prepare as it is. But I've tried that and found that students don't share as honestly with me.

Some kindergarten teachers have told me they're able to hold conferences right in the classroom while classmates are focused on their own play during choice or an activity time. They explain that as long as children are deeply engaged and aren't listening in, the conversation can feel very private. I suggest that you use your own judgment about which setting will feel most private to your student. The important thing is to make sure the conference environment feels safe for the student so that she will be open and honest.

Erica loved to play with her friends at recess, so holding the conference then didn't seem like a good idea. I decided to hold it during lunch because I thought she might enjoy eating in the classroom with me, away from the bustle of the lunchroom.

I invite students to conferences in a friendly yet low-key way, mentioning the problem but not dwelling on it. And if the meeting time we suggest doesn't work for the student, I look for another time. For example, if Erica had said she had plans to eat lunch with a friend, I would have scheduled a different time to talk with her about her writing. Whether or not to meet with me isn't a choice, but when to meet is.

Use careful teacher language

As with all aspects of teaching, choosing our words and tone of voice carefully makes a big difference to the success of problem-solving conferences.

Use a matter-of-fact tone

Children who have difficulty controlling themselves, getting along with others, or doing their school work are probably used to being talked at in angry or pleading tones and often have had years of experience in tuning out adult words. By using a neutral tone that implies that these are issues everyone struggles with and we're here to help, we allow the children to relax, listen, and participate.

Keep teacher talk to a minimum

Early in my career, I'd often "have a chat" with a student who was misbehaving. These chats entailed me talking and the child acting like she was listening. Then the child would happily run off, ready to continue the behavior that I had so articulately chatted about.

When I learned about problem-solving conferences, I realized that our goal should be to enlist children in the work of solving problems, forging a partnership with them. To do this, we need to give them the space to think and talk, to actively engage in finding a solution. Keeping our own talk to a minimum allows them to do this.

Be specific

Being specific when describing problematic behaviors allows the child to understand what exactly isn't working. "Your reader's notebook entry has no periods" is clear and direct. "You're always careless with your work" is too general, leaving the child to guess at what we mean. Such generalizations may also sound like accusations, making the child feel attacked and therefore defensive. This destroys the collaborative tone we hope to establish.

When we name the goal as one or two specific behaviors, the child knows what is expected. It's okay to include a general goal statement such as "Erica will do quality writing" as long as "quality writing" is defined with some specifics. In Erica's conference, we included the two specifics of spelling "no excuses" words correctly and using end punctuation in each sentence.

Use words and phrases that empower the child to reflect

Using the phrase "I've noticed"—as in "I've noticed that you don't let others play the game"—helps us avoid making a value judgment about a child's behavior. It thus allows the child to examine the behavior for himself rather than become defensive.

"Might it be?" or "I'm wondering if"—as in "Might it be that you really like Justin and want to play with him" or "I'm wondering if it's because you want to have as much time to play with Justin as possible"—are phrases that imply that we, the teachers, have an idea but we're enlisting the child in considering its validity. We might also say, "I'm going to throw out some ideas here. One might sound right to you. Let's try and see."

"Sometimes kids … " is another phrase that allows us to suggest an idea without being overbearing. For example, "Sometimes kids don't let others play a game because they want more time to play with their best friend." A child can then decide whether he is one of those kids. It's important that we allow students to explore their thoughts and feelings, not the thoughts and feelings that we think they have or should have.

Use positive language that helps the child see a new way

If we use phrases such as "control of your body," "doing careful work," or "being a good friend," we show the child what she may be able to achieve. To say that "Erica will do quality writing" encourages Erica to imagine herself as a quality writer. In contrast, "Erica will improve her writing" focuses on a more negative image of Erica as a problem writer. With our words, we help children envision a way to be their best selves in the classroom.

Stay open to surprises

In problem-solving conferences, we share our thoughts and listen to the student's thoughts. In this way, we team up with the child and reflect together. Often, we learn things we didn't know before. Being open to children's ideas is vital in successfully solving the problem with them.

Without Erica's crucial insight about writing being a "danger zone," for example, she and I might have wandered down a path of trying one solution after another that didn't address the true cause of the problem.

In another example, Rachel followed her third grade teacher around the classroom asking questions all day long. Because Ms. Harrison knew that Rachel was the youngest child in a large and busy family, she thought that Rachel was trying to get more attention. She tried to offer this attention when Rachel wasn't acting so demanding by inviting Rachel to have special lunches with her. But it didn't work. Rachel didn't want to have special lunches with Ms. Harrison.

Then Ms. Harrison met with Rachel using the problem-solving conference format and asked, "Might it be that you want me to pay more attention to you?"

Rachel's response surprised Ms. Harrison. "Oh no," Rachel explained, "I don't want any teachers noticing me. I want to blend in. It's just that sometimes I don't understand how to do my school work." Once Ms. Harrison realized that what Rachel wanted was academic help, she was able to give her that support.

Children can also surprise us by suggesting great solutions to their problems. Eric was a first grader who talked all day long. During class meetings and group discussions he called out constantly, interfering with other children's learning. During a problem-solving conference, Eric and his teacher brainstormed possible solutions. When Ms. Adams said that one possibility would be for Eric to raise his hand to speak, Eric said, "We keep trying that, and it hasn't worked. Why don't we try Popsicle sticks?"

At Eric's suggestion, Ms. Adams gave Eric three Popsicle sticks at the beginning of each class discussion. Every time he spoke, Eric gave Ms. Adams a Popsicle stick. Once the sticks were gone, Eric had made his contributions to the discussion. This system reminded Eric to stop and think, before he opened his mouth, whether what he wanted to say was really important. That pause also gave him time to remember to raise his hand to be called on.

Bring outside information to the conference

It's important to be open to children's ideas, but it's also important to prepare some working hypotheses of your own before the conference. Classroom observations, information from colleagues and parents, knowledge of child development, and educational theories can all help. This information helps us to think on our feet during the conference and to provide appropriate follow-up after the conference.

Classroom observations

Through observing our students we have an "opportunity to wonder and learn," as early childhood educators Judy Jablon, Amy Laura Dombro, and Margo Dichtelmiller put it (Jablon, Dombro, & Dichtelmiller, 2007, p.7). Wondering and learning involves collecting information through our eyes and ears, thinking about what that information might mean, and constructing hypotheses about student behavior accordingly.

In one fourth grade class I taught, students were creating objects to show what they learned during our recent field trip to the Nature Center. Carlos was making a meticulous forest scene out of clay. The leaves on the trees were shaped to look like oaks, maples, and sycamores. No detail was omitted.

Later in the day, at writing time, Carlos had one sentence on his paper. He was paralyzed, unable to move forward with his story. This writer's block showed up in other writing situations as well. By the second month of school, Carlos's writing had ground to a halt.

On the basis of many classroom observations of Carlos, like the one of his work on the forest scene, I surmised that his perfectionism was holding him back as a writer. When we met for a problem-solving conference, I asked, "Might it be that you think your writing has to be perfect the first time?" Carlos readily agreed that he did want his work always to be perfect. This opened a conversation about writing as a process. It allowed me to take the first steps in helping him break writing into manageable steps so that he could become a more fluent writer.

Observing our students gives us an opportunity to know them better and thus have tools to forge a vital alliance, to become the adult who will help the child grow.

Information from parents

Children spend a long day in school, but their day continues at home. Parents can supply crucial information about after-school play, sibling relationships, and weekend interactions among friends.

Tony was a bright and charming fourth grader. He loved to read and would arrive each morning eager to tell me all about the chapter of *Harry Potter* that he'd read the night before. I could count on Tony to contribute thoughtfully to math discussions, sharing a strategy that others might not have thought of. Other students loved to work with him because of his creative ideas.

But Tony had a problem with homework. By mid-October he had turned in few assignments. The class had practiced doing "homework" in school, brainstormed the best places to do homework at home, and reviewed what to do if they got stuck. Most of the students were completing their nightly homework with pride. Tony, on the other hand, always had an excuse: "Last night we had a special birthday for my grandmother" or "I had to go to my sister's basketball game."

Logical consequences such as finishing homework during a portion of Morning Meeting weren't working. Tony was missing too much of Morning Meeting. I called home to discuss Tony's homework but quickly realized that Tony's parents, who both worked long hours, weren't able to supervise Tony's homework. I also thought that since Tony was a fourth grader, homework should be his responsibility. So I asked Tony to meet with me to discuss the problem.

Before we met, I looked at the parent/guardian questionnaire that Tony's mother, Mrs. G., had responded to in September. Could anything there provide clues to why Tony did so little homework? "Tony is our oldest child and our only boy. He is our 'little prince,'" Mrs. G. had written. "His sisters do everything for him. They fix him snacks, do his chores, and give him their toys."

Although this didn't solve the mystery around Tony's homework problem, it did help me recognize that there might be differing expectations of Tony at home and at school. I kept Mrs. G.'s words in the back of my mind as I prepared for the conference. To forge an alliance with Tony, I needed to be empathetic toward him, and his mother's observations helped me gain that empathy.

When Tony and I met, we noted things that were going well in school. Then we looked at my record of his homework completion and noticed the many boxes without checks. I explained that homework was an important part of fourth grade and I wanted to help him do his homework independently. In a friendly and empathetic tone I said, "Sometimes kids just don't feel like doing their homework. Might that be true for you?" I told him a true story about how I hid my homework in the bushes when I was in school.

Tony immediately lit up. He quickly agreed that he'd much rather watch TV than do his homework. My acceptance of the fact that he just didn't feel like doing his homework seemed to help Tony accept that despite his feelings, he had to do his homework. Together we began to shape a homework plan for him. We agreed that Tony would do his homework right away, as soon as he got home from school, before he turned on the TV. Tony's homework habits began to turn around.

Knowledge of child development

Knowledge of child development can help us consider realistic objectives for a student and strategies for reaching them. It can even help us decide whether a problem-solving conference is appropriate.

Megan's mother left a message for me. "Megan didn't sleep at all last night. She was so worried about the big math test today. Could you give her a little reassurance this morning?" I wracked my brain. What math test? What could Mrs. K. be referring to? I quickly called Mrs. K.

As we talked I realized that the day before, I had said that I was going to start quizzing students in this third grade class informally on their addition facts to see what they remembered from second grade. Megan, a seven-year-old, had worried about this quizzing all night.

Seven-year-olds tend to be perfectionists. They can become tense and overwhelmed by feelings of inferiority. I guessed that Megan's bad night was a developmentally expected bump in the road. In a quick chat with Megan as the students were arriving in the morning, I explained that I didn't expect her to remember all of her addition facts, that kids forget things in the summer. I also quizzed her on some easy addition facts and congratulated her on knowing them. Such reassurance is much needed by seven-year-olds and goes a long way with them. Sure enough, Megan went skipping off, once again confident of her math abilities.

If Megan were a generally confident eight-year-old, I might have seen her worries differently because eight-year-olds, unlike sevens, tend to be energetic and eager to take on big challenges. If an otherwise self-assured eight-year-old were having math anxiety, I would have guessed that anxiety to be a symptom of true difficulty. I would have begun to pay careful attention to her attitudes toward math, thinking about a possible problem-solving conference if the problem were to persist.

Educational theories

Information from educational thinkers can help us understand our students. Andrew, the child with learning difficulties and ADD whose story began this chapter, actually had many unsuccessful problem-solving conferences with me throughout the fall before we had that breakthrough conference. In each of the unsuccessful ones, we easily agreed upon the problem—that Andrew got stuck when it was time to write. He even agreed that he would like to work with me to get better at writing.

Our conferences, however, always broke down at the "exploring the cause of the problem" stage. None of the ideas that I floated using "Might it be … ?" questions seemed right to Andrew, and when I asked for his ideas, he would just say "I dunno."

Because we didn't know why getting his ideas down on paper was so hard for him, I only had rather formulaic strategies to suggest, such as "I could make a mark on your paper, and then come back to check whether you've written to that mark." The strategy in Andrew's special education plan, that he use the computer to write, was no help at all. Andrew would just play with the computer keys and change the fonts over and over.

Hoping to get some direction, I read *A Mind at a Time* by pediatrician Mel Levine (2003), an authority on behavioral and learning problems in children. Levine wrote that some children with ADD have difficulty controlling their mental energy. These students, he writes, "show signs of mental fatigue more often and with greater severity than others" (p. 61). Sometimes such children also have difficulty controlling their "sleep–arousal" cycle.

I thought of how Andrew's mother had reported that Andrew had difficulty falling asleep at night and getting up in the morning. I decided to try another problem-solving conference.

In this conference (the one described at the opening of this chapter), I asked him, "Might it be that when it's time to write, you feel too tired to get your ideas down?" For the first time, I saw that look of recognition in Andrew's eyes. "I get really, really tired and writing is hard for me," he said.

"Are there times when you aren't as tired?" I asked Andrew.

"I'm full of energy first thing in the morning."

From there we quickly agreed that Andrew should have a special writing time in the morning. After a conversation with Andrew's parents, we also agreed that to make that happen, his dad would drop him off at school on his way to work.

Gradually give the student more responsibility

Many effective teachers teach children to read using a "gradual release of responsibility" model. First the teacher directly instructs the whole class. Then children practice the new skill in a small group under the teacher's watchful eyes. Once the skill is partially mastered, the children might practice the skill more independently with partners. Finally, they practice the skill as they read by themselves.

In the same way, as children are practicing new social skills or new work habits, they begin with maximum teacher supervision and then move on to greater independence.

Eric started practicing self-control by giving his teacher a Popsicle stick whenever he spoke in the group. Gradually he and Ms. Adams moved toward Eric's taking more responsibility for turn taking, giving up the Popsicle stick method.

Ultimately, we want to teach children age-appropriate social skills. Nudging the child to move, as he is ready, from more supervision to less supervision allows for this learning.

Questions from Teachers

What if the student doesn't see his behavior as a problem?

A problem-solving conference doesn't mend every difficult situation. Not every student is ready to be self-reflective. If that's the case with a student, it's best to simply state the classroom rules and redouble your efforts to use logical consequences consistently to reinforce those rules.

For example, Mason teased other children mercilessly. When I made this observation during our conference, he said, "But they're annoying." Further conversation only led to more blaming of others rather than reflections about his own behavior.

Given Mason's intransigence, I decided to abandon the conference. I reframed the meeting and set clear limits. I reminded Mason that one of our classroom rules was "Be kind" and told him that if I heard him teasing he would be separated from the group so that the other students would not have to endure his unkindness.

Not every student is open to collaboration, either. Children who are engaged in a power struggle with their teacher, for example, are not usually ready to collaborate. In that case, it's better not to try a problem-solving conference but rather to withdraw from the conflict and begin to build a different relationship with the child.

For example, Shanesha refused to do her math work. When work was assigned, she loudly announced "You can't make me" and proceeded to sit passively throughout the math period.

I found myself feeling provoked, as if I wanted to make her, and recognized this as a symptom of a power struggle. Shanesha was right, I couldn't make her. Rather than attempting a problem-solving conference, I used logical consequences, simply telling Shanesha that math time was for math and she'd have to make up any missed work either during Quiet Time or for homework. I didn't discuss it with her.

Meanwhile, I worked on building a positive relationship with Shanesha during other times of the day. On the playground I twirled the jump rope while she and her friends jumped. I found ways to give her positive power. I invited her to teach some other children how to fold the paper airplanes she was so skilled at creating. Slowly Shanesha began to relax and trust me. Then we were ready for a problem-solving conference.

What if the teacher and student agree on a strategy, but it doesn't help?

Some conferences lead to an effective strategy right away. With Erica, the writing buddy solution and the extra academic support that I arranged from Ms. Fraser, a retired teacher, did in fact help. Erica's work improved and her confidence in her academic ability grew.

Other conferences lead to strategies that are effective only for a while. Andrew, for example, wrote productively for a couple of months after we instituted the special early morning writing time. But when I raised the bar and expected more writing, Andrew dug in his heels and refused to write anything.

Sensing that a different approach was now needed, I met with Andrew again and introduced an individual written agreement, a structure for giving external incentives for behavior change when a child needs intensive support. (See Chapter Six to learn about individual written agreements.)

Occasionally, a strategy that a student and teacher agree on is completely ineffective. Ruby and Mia ate together every day at lunch. The two fifth graders walked around the perimeter of the playground every day at recess, making it hard for others to be with them. Ruby was the one "in charge," and Mia's mother reported that Mia felt resentful because she wished she could play with other children.

The teacher met with Mia, hoping to give her support in making some additional friends. The two agreed that Mia would invite others to join them at recess. But Ruby responded by calling the other children names. Their teacher quickly realized that the strategy she and Mia had crafted wouldn't be helpful without Ruby's cooperation. Her next step was to use a different strategy, a conflict resolution meeting between Ruby and Mia. (See Chapter Three to learn about conflict resolution.)

I have several students who could use problem-solving conferences. I don't have time for so many. What should I do?

If you have more than one or two students in the problem-solving conference process at one time, it may be beneficial to look at other aspects of your classroom. Are you using encouraging teacher language? Modeling and practicing expected behaviors? Assigning academic work that the children can do?

Also keep in mind that a problem-solving conference should be reserved for a child's persistent, rather than occasional, problem. When the classroom community is safe, friendly, and purposeful and the work is at just the right challenge level, persistent problems should diminish.

If you're doing all these things and multiple students are still having difficulties, next think about whether all those students need a one-on-one conference. Is there a small group of students who have continual conflicts with each other? Perhaps those students would benefit from a conflict resolution meeting (see Chapter Three) or a small group meeting using the class meeting format suggested in Chapter Five.

Once you've tried or ruled out these other problem-solving strategies, if you still have too many students who need a one-on-one problem-solving conference, I suggest starting with the one or two students whose behaviors are most troublesome. Success with them will bring a measure of peace to your classroom and allow you to make time for another conference.

Examples of Problem-Solving Conferences

EXAMPLE 1
Saul, who bit and scratched

Saul, a first grader, had trouble making friends. His most worrisome behavior was that he scratched and bit other children. Classmates avoided him and their parents complained, "If only Saul weren't in the class."

Saul's teacher, Ms. Thomas, was determined to help Saul become part of the classroom community. She knew that she would need to work with the other students to help them be more accepting of Saul, but first she needed to help Saul with the behaviors that were particularly bothersome to his classmates.

Ms. Thomas spent a few days observing appealing things about Saul. She noticed that Saul tried to do his best school work. He loved to write and happily spent stretches of time covering pages with sentences about trucks (TRKS) and Power Guys (PR GIs). Saul was anxious to please and wanted to show his teacher his work as soon as it was completed.

Ms. Thomas also paid attention to her own relationship with Saul. She made sure that she greeted Saul warmly each morning, checked in with him during independent work times to make sure that he understood directions and was working comfortably, and helped him join the tag group at recess.

For their problem-solving conference, Saul and Ms. Thomas met during lunchtime. Ms. Thomas started by warmly smiling at Saul and saying that she was pleased to have lunch and chat with him. Saul grinned widely, happy to have some time alone with his teacher.

Ms. Thomas said she knew that Saul really wanted to have some friends and that she'd like to help him make friends.

"Yup," Saul responded. "Yesterday you got the boys to let me play tag with them."

"I've noticed that the kids often don't want you to join them," continued Ms. Thomas. "One of our rules is 'Be kind to everyone,' so they need to let you play. Why do you suppose they don't want you to play?"

"Because they're mean?" suggested Saul.

"Remember when you scratched Justin when he cut you in line?" asked Ms. Thomas. "When you scratch other kids while they're standing in line, they don't want to stand next to you."

"They're mean to me. That's why I scratch and bite," Saul replied.

Ms. Thomas knew it was important for Saul to be assured that his teacher would protect him from exclusion, just as the teacher would protect the other students from Saul's scratching and biting. "It's important that they be kind to you. That's our rule," said Ms. Thomas. "I'll work on helping them learn to be kinder. It's also true that the kids will want to work and play with you if you learn to be gentle with them. Would you like me to help you with that?"

Saul looked up at his teacher a little teary-eyed and said, "Okay."

Ms. Thomas wrote down the goal: *Saul will be gentle with his classmates.*

Saul and Ms. Thomas then brainstormed some strategies that might help him remember to be gentle. They agreed that Ms. Thomas would give Saul a private, nonverbal reminder, a tap on the shoulder, before he got in line, sat in the circle, or went to PE—all of which were his predictable trouble spots.

They also agreed that after one week they would meet again to compare observations on how things had gone during the week and think about where to go from there.

Throughout the week, Ms. Thomas gave Saul gentle reminder taps. This close support helped him refrain from hurting his classmates.

Meanwhile, Ms. Thomas was using other strategies such as a whole-group reflection on the class rules and a class meeting (see Chapter Five) to help the other children be kind to everyone, including Saul. She also spoke with the other first grade teachers so that they would be alert on the playground, helping Saul to join group games. The classroom community was beginning to include Saul, and Saul was beginning to feel a sense of belonging.

THINGS TO NOTE in Saul's conference

- *Teacher–student rapport:* Saul knew from Ms. Thomas's warm greetings, check-ins during independent work time, and support on the playground that she liked him.

- *Specificity in describing the problem:* "When you scratch other kids while they're standing in line, they don't want to stand next to you."

- *Reference to classroom rules:* "One of our rules is 'Be kind to everyone.'"

- *Positive language that helped Saul envision a better way:* "The kids will want to work and play with you if you learn to be gentle with them."

- *Writing down the goal:* This way Saul and his teacher could both refer to it later.

- *An exciting goal:* Saul was motivated to achieve his goal because it would help him make friends.

- *Respect for Saul's privacy:* Ms. Thomas and Saul established a nonverbal reminder for him to be gentle.

- *Follow-through:* After the conference, Ms. Thomas consistently gave Saul the reminder taps.

- *Work with the entire class:* Ms. Thomas used several strategies to strengthen the atmosphere of inclusion, respect, and trust in the class.

EXAMPLE 2
Lisa, defiant toward the teacher

On the second day of fourth grade, Lisa argued bitterly with me during a whole-class lesson on ways we use math in the world. She was so intent on having things her way that she lay on the floor kicking and screaming, effectively bringing an end to the math lesson for everybody.

The third day of fourth grade, during another math lesson, this time about base ten blocks, she threw her blocks at me. This time I called an administrator, and she was sent home for the rest of the day.

Even though we'd only been in school a few days, Lisa was showing a pattern of defiance. This told me that I needed to have a problem-solving conference with her right away to establish basic classroom expectations.

Lisa was an appealing child with an off-beat sense of humor. I was happy to see her when she arrived in the morning and looked forward to her funny contributions in classroom conversations. After only a few days of school, I could tell that she knew I liked her. Lisa was a bright, articulate child with a strong sense of self. I had a feeling she'd have a lot to say at a problem-solving conference.

Lisa arrived on the fourth day of school with an apology note that her mother had helped her write during her afternoon at home. I had had plenty of time to calm down myself and was ready to greet her in a friendly manner.

"I can see that you're sorry," I said in a friendly voice. "I do think that we need to talk. How about meeting today at lunchtime? We need to figure out together how to make sure events like the one yesterday don't happen again."

I purposely phrased my invitation as a question. To avoid confusing children, I don't ask when I mean to tell. But this invitation was truly a question. If Lisa had wanted to have lunch with friends, I would have arranged a different time. But Lisa said yes to my invitation, and we met at lunchtime, sitting at her table, each eating our sandwich.

"Lisa," I said, "You have so much to contribute to our classroom community. You've shared thoughtful ideas as we've begun to create our classroom rules. You've offered thoughts about why listening is important and why we all need to be kind to each other."

Lisa responded, "In third grade some kids really bugged me. That's why we need a rule about being kind." Her words didn't surprise me. After only a few days of school, I was beginning to see how she viewed the world.

"There's one thing we need to talk about, though," I said. "You know that in school kids need to listen to teachers and do what they say," I added. "You even contributed some ideas about that as we were working on the class rules." Just to make sure that she understood, I added, "When kids argue with teachers during lessons, it keeps everyone from learning. No one learned much math during our lesson yesterday or the day before."

Lisa rolled her eyes a little in a knowing way and said, "Well-l-l, I know I'm supposed to listen to teachers. I just get so mad sometimes. I wanted more blocks yesterday. I had a really good idea about what to do with them."

In that sentence, Lisa acknowledged that she did need to listen to teachers and also explained the reason that it was hard for her. I could skip the step of searching for the causes of the problem, because Lisa had revealed the cause.

"So, sometimes it's hard for you to control yourself when you have important ideas?" I asked, to make sure that I understood her.

"Yeah."

"Would you like to work on this problem with me?" Everything she had said implied that she did want to work on the problem, but I felt that it was important to ask formally and obtain her agreement. Knowing we might have hard times ahead, I wanted us to have this moment to refer back to.

"I know I should listen and I shouldn't argue, but I just can't stop myself," Lisa responded.

"What if we thought of some strategies that might help you stop yourself?" I asked.

"Okay," she answered in a reluctant tone. Lisa clearly knew that arguing with teachers wasn't helping her or her classmates learn, but I could see that the goal of controlling herself was a daunting one for her. It was enough that she agreed to work with me, however reluctantly. We could build on that.

"Lisa, it's fine if you disagree with teachers. It's helpful to all of us when you share your thoughts," I said. "But if you feel yourself losing control, you need to find a way to first calm down and then talk to me later, after the lesson." I wanted her to feel free to engage with the lesson but not to disrupt and bring learning to a halt. "What might we do to help you notice when you're losing control?" I asked.

"You could give me a sign that the other kids wouldn't know about, and I could go sit at the reading table," Lisa suggested. I hadn't yet introduced positive time-out to the class, but Lisa had experienced this strategy in other grades.

"You could sit right next to me during lessons, and I could give you a gentle tap when I see you starting to argue, just to remind you," I suggested.

"We could keep a chart like I had in second grade, and I could get stars for staying in control," Lisa added.

"Which of these would you like to try first?" I asked. I knew that Lisa needed to feel in control of this process. If she chose the strategy, it was more likely to be effective.

"Let's try you giving me a sign, and I'll go and sit at the reading table to calm down," Lisa said. "You can pull on your ear. That's what my third grade teacher did." Lisa had experience with many possible strategies!

I wrote down our agreement: *When Lisa starts to lose control and argue with her teacher, Ms. Crowe will pull on her ear, and Lisa will go to the reading table and sit there while she regains control. She will discuss her disagreement with Ms. Crowe after the lesson is over.* I wrote the date and we both signed the paper.

"Let's meet next week to talk about how things are going," I said. Lisa was excited about another private meeting with me. She wrote next Friday's date on two sticky notes, putting one on her table and one on my plan book.

The next day, when Lisa started to argue during a science lesson, I gently pulled on my ear. Lisa quietly got up and went to the reading table to calm down.

As the year progressed, Lisa continued to struggle with maintaining self-control in various areas, but we had together come up with an effective way to address the specific problem of her arguing with me. That proved a critical starting point in her ongoing learning.

THINGS TO NOTE in Lisa's conference

- *Teacher–student rapport:* The children and I, as a group, had begun to build a positive classroom climate during the first few days of school. Furthermore, I'd had lots of friendly and personal interactions with Lisa during these few days, and she knew that I liked her.

- *Calm teacher and student demeanor:* The meeting took place after both parties had had time to calm down after the second incident.

- *Positive language:* I used words that helped Lisa envision a better way. Examples are "some strategies that might help you stop yourself" and "first calm down and then talk to me later, after the lesson."

- *Pacing and flow:* It's important to include all steps in a conference. But when Lisa spontaneously identified the reason for her arguing, there was no need to explicitly search for reasons. I went right to the next step in the conference.

- *Respect for Lisa's privacy:* I gently pulled on my ear to let her know it was time for her to leave the group.

- *Building on past success:* Lisa and I borrowed from strategies that had worked for her in other grades.

- *Writing down the goal:* Lisa and I could both refer to it later as needed.

- *Follow-through:* I used the strategies that we agreed on, and we met a week later to discuss how things were going.

Making it work for you

Use this sheet as you plan and conduct a problem-solving conference.

Write down your ideas ahead of time in **pencil**, paying particular attention to the language you'll use. (Suggested phrases are included in italics.)

Then, during the conference, use **pen** to record what happens.

That way you'll be prepared to use positive and collaborative language, and you'll have a record of the conference to look back on later.

Student: _____

Date, time, and place: _____

Reaffirming rapport

For example:

You work so hard at math time.

Yesterday I saw you helping Melanie find her independent reading book.

Talking about the problem

For example:

I noticed that when you write, you often forget punctuation and spelling that I know you know. What have you noticed?

Teacher	Student

Naming the behavior as a problem and why it's a problem

For example:

When I see you poking kids in line, I notice that they get annoyed.

It's important to keep your papers in your own area so that your tablemates will have space to work.

It's important that you read a just-right book so you can learn to be a better reader.

Inviting the student to work on the problem

For example:

Would you like to work on this together?

I'd like to help you with this, if you'd like to work on it.

(If the student declines your invitation to work together, abandon the conference, restate the rules, and redouble your efforts to use logical consequences consistently.)

Suggesting possible causes of the problem

For example:

Might it be that you think kids will want to be your friend if you snatch their hats and run away?

Sometimes kids forget their homework because they think it's too hard. Could that be what's happening here?

Articulating a clear, specific goal to work on

For example:

Your classmates will want to work with you more if you share your thoughts calmly and respectfully. What if we thought of some ways for you to do that?

Which one of these three goals would you like to work on first?

Suggesting possible solutions for working on the problem:

For example:

What might help you remember to wait your turn to speak in a group discussion?

The solution the teacher and student agree to try:

CHAPTER THREE

Student-to-Student Conflict Resolution

"Teacher, he won't play with me."

"Teacher, she cut me in line."

"Teacher, he took my book."

"Teacher, she let Clemmy sit in my seat in the lunchroom."

Conflicts between classmates are a familiar part of elementary school life, and words such as these fill our days as teachers. For many years, resolving students' conflicts sapped my energy, engaged too much of my attention, and took time that otherwise would have been used for teaching.

Conflict is a natural part of life. We all have differences with friends, family, and colleagues. But children seem to have more conflicts, or at least more overt ones, and it's no wonder: They spend their days in a small space with a lot of people. They're socially inexperienced. They mirror the competitiveness of our society.

But children can also work out their everyday conflicts equitably, if we teach them how. I realized this after learning about student-to-student conflict resolution and teaching it to my classes. At first, the children used the protocol with my guidance; eventually they used it on their own. As students got better and better at this method, conflicts were resolved much more quickly, to the greater satisfaction of all parties, and with less need for my direct involvement.

Educators have developed a variety of conflict resolution protocols for use in school. In this chapter I offer one protocol that I've found effective for the myriad ordinary clashes that crop up in everyday classroom life: arguments around sharing, taking turns, cutting in line, name calling, being excluded. It's a protocol that can be adapted for most elementary grades.

Here's how two first graders used it in the spring, after practicing conflict resolution skills since the beginning of the year:

Randy was sitting at his table drawing a picture of the class's upcoming family picnic. He turned to Amira, who was concentrating deeply on her own drawing, and said, "I need the blue crayon!"

"No, I'm using it," Amira responded.

Frustrated, Randy shouted, "I need it now!"

"No, I need it!" Amira yelled back.

Randy got up from the table, walked around the classroom taking deep breaths, and returned, saying to Amira, "I have an I-statement for you." The two children moved to a table in a corner of the room.

Randy took a deep breath, a technique the class had learned for calming down, and addressed Amira. "I felt angry when I heard you say I couldn't have the blue crayon. I needed that crayon to draw the sky."

Amira answered, "You wanted the blue crayon, but I was using it to draw the sky in my picture. I'll let you use it when I'm done."

"Okay," said Randy, taking another deep breath. "You'll finish your sky, and then I'll color in my sky."

Randy and Amira shook hands and returned to their table. Randy sat, eyeing Amira, waiting impatiently for her to finish with the blue crayon but managing to maintain self-control.

Despite their earlier frustration with each other, Randy and Amira were able to resolve their differences peacefully using the student-to-student conflict resolution protocol and calming-down techniques they had learned in their class. Although their conversation may seem too smooth to be true, it is what conflict resolution can look like when we carefully teach children the steps and give them plenty of opportunities to practice.

Purpose: Teaching Skills for Independent Conflict Resolution

The immediate purpose of student-to-student conflict resolution is to take care of the problem at hand fairly and with minimal disruption to classroom functioning. But there's also a longer-term purpose: for children to resolve future conflicts in a way that is fair and acceptable to both parties and to do so independently.

Such independence is possible because the strategy involves teaching children concrete skills for showing consideration of another's needs and desires as well as their own. In practicing conflict resolution, children are learning to express themselves assertively, honestly, and kindly. They're learning to listen to others with respect, come up with possible solutions, weigh the possibilities, and agree on a solution that is acceptable for both parties. Instead of taking time from learning, children's conflicts then become opportunities for them to develop important social competencies.

Because of the independence that conflict resolution ultimately asks of children, I suggest that you try this strategy if you teach grades two through six, or if you teach fairly mature first graders. If you teach younger children, you can give them an introduction to some of the steps described in this chapter. (See "Modified Conflict Resolution in Kindergarten" on page 89.) With teacher supervision and support, even five-year-olds can practice skills that will serve them well in their relationships with classmates and teachers.

Teachers often say, "But how much time does all this take?"

It does take time to teach children all the skills for independent conflict resolution, but it takes just as much time, if not more, to solve their conflicts for them. Ignoring the disagreements also ends up taking more time, as does sending children off to deal with conflicts alone before we've taught them the requisite skills. The disputes inevitably siphon energy from learning, or they're pushed underground in a way that damages the atmosphere of safety in the classroom.

When to Use Student-to-Student Conflict Resolution

These guidelines will help you decide whether to use student-to-student conflict resolution for any given dilemma.

Use it for ordinary conflicts

The protocol described in this chapter is for ordinary disputes among children: when they use minor unkind words, disagree about sharing supplies or choosing partners, refuse to take turns, and the like. It is not appropriate for serious infractions such as hitting, cruel teasing, or bullying. Those infractions require adult intervention and a response based on the school's discipline policy.

Let students use it alone only after ample coaching

Expressing oneself assertively and listening to others respectfully are crucial to conflict resolution. But they're hard behaviors to adhere to, especially in the middle of a conflict. It takes careful and sometimes repeated teaching and coaching from an adult before children will be able to sustain these behaviors on their own.

It's easy to relinquish supervision of students' conflict resolution too early. When I first learned about conflict resolution, I taught it to the class and, relieved that I would no longer be solving all their conflicts for them, announced that anyone who wanted to use it could do so. But the children didn't have the needed skills yet. They argued and interrupted each other. They became bossy and vengeful. I had to backtrack, breaking the skills down, teaching them step by step, and supervising and observing the children's conflict resolution meetings. Only when I was sure they could handle these responsibilities on their own did I allow them to hold the meetings independently.

Use it for children with equal power

Even in the strongest of communities, children can hold varying amounts of power. In encouraging children to use conflict resolution, be careful not to set less powerful children up for cruel teasing, or worse.

Liam was a sixth grade sports star, a natural at football, baseball, and basketball. He was handsome and confident. Julius was small and awkward. When Liam loudly announced to Julius in the lunchroom, "You can't sit here. You're a nerd," his teacher, Mr. Toms, knew he had to handle this one delicately. Allowing the statement to stand would be painful to Julius and damaging to the community. Yet embarrassing Liam publicly or expecting Julius to handle the insult independently would surely backfire, resulting in more teasing and exclusion out of adult sight.

Instead of student-to-student conflict resolution, Mr. Toms chose to meet with Liam privately to restate classroom rules and let him know that the way he had treated Julius was unacceptable.

He also held a class meeting to discuss with the whole group a plan for inclusiveness in the lunchroom. During the meeting he didn't use names or refer to the incident between Liam and Julius. Students involved knew which incident had precipitated the discussion, and many subsequently took responsibility for being kind to Julius. Liam at least modulated his behavior and was friendly, if not friends, with Julius. (See Chapter Five to learn about using class meetings as a process for problem-solving.)

Steps in a Conflict Resolution Meeting

A conflict resolution meeting, known in my classroom as a "Peace Talk," consists of specific steps. Each step is crucial, but most are also quick, so once children have had some practice, the meetings usually take five to ten minutes.

1. The children cool off.

2. First child (aggrieved party) thinks of an I-statement and asks the other child for a meeting.

3. First child says the I-statement.

4. Second child states his or her understanding of what was said.

5. Second child states his or her point of view.

6. First child states his or her understanding of what was said.

7. The process continues until both children feel they have been fully heard.

8. Both children brainstorm possible solutions.

9. The children together choose a solution to try.

10. The children make a plan and shake hands.

The following pages show how these steps looked in an incident between Suzanne and Tobey, two students in a fourth grade class I was teaching.

It was a rainy spring day. The children had been indoors all week, and everyone's frustration level was rising. As the children walked upstairs from lunch, Suzanne was kicking Tobey's feet. I looked at her in surprise. "Well," said Suzanne, "he took my seat in the lunchroom, and I was going to sit with Melissa."

This class had been practicing Peace Talks for months. I knew that once prompted, Suzanne and Tobey would be able to take responsibility for resolving their conflict themselves assertively and respectfully.

"One of our rules says 'Be safe.' How might you take care of your feelings and live by our classroom rules?" I asked Suzanne.

"Well, we could have a Peace Talk," she replied.

Step 1. The children cool off

"It looks like you could use a little cool-off time," I said to Suzanne. "Find a different place in line, and let Tobey know when you're ready with an I-statement."

Disgruntled but cooperative, Suzanne stepped to the end of the line. We returned to the classroom, where she spent five minutes of Quiet Time fiercely pinching a ball of modeling clay.

Step 2. First child (aggrieved party) thinks of an I-statement and asks the other child for a meeting

An I-statement consists of a couple of sentences that tell the listener how we feel and what we'd like. In my classroom, children construct their I-statement by filling in these blanks:

I feel/felt _____ when I see/saw (or hear/heard) _____

because _____. What I would like is _____.

Suzanne sat in her seat, pinching the clay, periodically glancing up at the chart on the wall with the fill-in-the-blank sentences. At the end of Quiet Time, she walked over to Tobey and said, "I have an I-statement for you. Let's go to the Peace Talk place."

In our classroom, the spot behind the easel chart stand is set aside for Peace Talks. A large poster of the steps in a Peace Talk hangs on the back of the chart stand. Two copies of the ground rules for Peace Talks are stored in a basket under the stand.

Tobey and Suzanne sat down facing each other. They each picked up a ground rules card and read it over: "Listen respectfully. Work to solve the problem."

Step 3. First child says the I-statement

Suzanne said to Tobey, "I felt angry when I saw you sitting in my seat in the lunchroom because I couldn't sit with my friends. I would like you to let me sit in the seat where I put my things when we go into the lunchroom."

Step 4. Second child states his or her understanding of what was said

This is the magical step. Often we are so focused on our own hurts or needs that we don't truly listen to the person we're in conflict with. Requiring children to paraphrase what their partner said forces them to listen and leads them toward understanding their partner's point of view. It also helps the partner feel heard.

"You didn't like it when I sat next to Zach," Tobey said to Suzanne. "You thought that was your seat." He looked at Suzanne to confirm that he'd understood her. Suzanne clarified her point by saying, "It *was* my seat. I put my jacket on it."

Step 5. Second child states his or her point of view

Now it was Tobey's turn. He had been able to listen carefully when Suzanne was talking, in part because he knew his turn was coming. Tobey had the option of also using an I-statement to explain his feelings or of simply stating a fact to clarify the situation. He decided to state a fact. "I sat there because there weren't any other seats left that were next to boys. I wanted to sit with one of the boys in our class, so I sat next to Zach. Anyway, you weren't sitting in the seat. You shouldn't have gotten up if you wanted to sit there."

Step 6. First child states his or her understanding of what was said

Just as Tobey was expected to listen and state what he understood Suzanne to have said, Suzanne was expected to do the same for Tobey. "You wanted to sit with Zach," said Suzanne. "You think that I shouldn't have gotten up." She looked at Tobey, waiting for confirmation that she had understood him. Tobey nodded. This step of confirming the accuracy of the paraphrasing is important. Without it, misunderstandings may persist.

Step 7. The process continues until both children feel they have been fully heard

Suzanne offered further explanation for her action. "Ms. Z. called kids having hot lunch to get in line. That's why I got up. I left my jacket on the chair."

Now it was Tobey's turn again. "So, you left your jacket and went to get hot lunch. I really wanted to sit by Zach, and I didn't see your jacket," he said.

Both children were careful to continue restating their understanding of what the other had said before further giving their own point of view.

Now that Suzanne and Tobey had both had their full say, it was time to find a solution.

Step 8. Both children brainstorm possible solutions

"Next time you could find a chair without a coat on it," said Suzanne.

"You could put your coat right on the seat, not just on the back, so that I can see it," offered Tobey.

Both Tobey and Suzanne were using self-control to keep from saying what they thought of each other's ideas. It's important that brainstorming be a free exchange of suggestions without judgment. Once children start evaluating the ideas, one or both of them may become defensive, short-circuiting the process.

"I could make sure that the kids sitting next to me know that it's my seat if I have to get up to get hot lunch," suggested Suzanne.

"I could plan ahead who I'm going to sit with," offered Tobey, "and we could get into the lunchroom early so we can get two seats together."

"We could ask Ms. Z. if we could have a boys' table and a girls' table in the lunchroom," added Suzanne.

Step 9. The children together choose a solution to try

Children first rule out ideas they know won't work and then narrow the list down to one solution both can live with.

"I don't think Ms. Z. would agree to a girls' table and a boys' table," said Suzanne. "Besides, we don't have an equal number of boys and girls. That's why this happened. Almost all of the other boys were sitting together at one table, and there weren't any spaces left there."

"Well, I could be more careful about finding a chair without a coat," said Tobey.

"I could be more careful to put my coat right where people can see it," Suzanne responded.

"That sounds okay," Tobey said.

Step 10. The children make a plan and shake hands

In this step, children move from agreeing on a solution to making a concrete plan for implementing it. Without this step, the solution may never actually happen.

"Okay, so, next time I'll put my jacket in a place where I'm sure someone can see it," said Suzanne. "And I'll look and make sure there's no jacket on a seat before I sit there," Tobey added.

The meeting closes with a simple ritual that seals the agreement. In my classroom students shake hands and say "Peace." Suzanne and Tobey performed this simple ritual.

Then, before getting up to rejoin the class, Tobey blurted out, "I'm sorry I took your seat. I wasn't looking for coats because I wanted to sit near Zach."

"Okay," said Suzanne. "I can see that you're sorry."

Modified Conflict Resolution in Kindergarten

Kindergartners, still egocentric in their world view, usually aren't ready to learn how to resolve conflicts fairly without teacher intervention. They can, however, learn some important skills that will enhance their relationships with classmates and give them a taste of how to be both assertive and cooperative when they have disagreements with peers.

Modified I-statements

It's the second week of school. Ms. Bowen and her assistant, Ms. Fox, have gathered the class in a circle on the floor. "Sometimes children have arguments. Sometimes they have trouble sharing or following our rule to be kind," begins Ms. Bowen. "Today we're going to practice what to do when children have trouble sharing or being kind." The children are listening. Some of them have already experienced these difficulties.

"Let's pretend that Ms. Fox and I are looking at books in the library area," says Ms. Bowen. "Ms. Fox has the book that I want. It's *Where the Wild Things Are*, the book that the teacher read to us yesterday. I really like that book. I grab *Where the Wild Things Are* away from Ms. Fox. I didn't follow our rule that says to be kind. What can Ms. Fox do?"

Ms. Fox says, "I can say, 'I didn't like it when you grabbed the book away from me.'"

"In this class, if someone does something we don't like, we'll say to them, 'I don't like it when you do that,'" explains Ms. Bowen. "If you want a teacher to come with you while you say that to your friend, you can ask us, and we'll go with you."

Over the next few days, the children practice saying "I don't like it when _____" as part of simple role-plays as well as in real-life situations. As the year progresses, the class adds to their bank of modified I-statements with "I feel angry when _____" and "I feel sad when _____."

For example, while reading *Alfie Lends a Hand* to the class, Ms. Bowen stops and asks, "How did Min feel when Bernard popped the bubble on her sleeve?"

Lori raises her hand and says, "She feels sad."

"What could she say to Bernard?" asks Ms. Bowen.

"She could say, 'I felt sad when you burst the bubble on my sleeve,'" contributes Lori.

Thus, another modified I-statement is added to the class repertoire.

The children are learning to express their feelings clearly and assertively. Some children need a teacher nearby to support them as they make their modified I-statements. That's fine; the important part is that the children are practicing saying the words themselves.

Listening without interrupting

In addition to learning to speak assertively about their concerns, kindergartners can also learn to listen without interrupting. This is a skill they're already practicing in many situations in school—for example, as part of Morning Meeting (in classrooms using that *Responsive Classroom* routine), as they discuss the book their teacher just read aloud, or as they create little "plays" to dramatize a math story problem.

"Mr. Rosen, Danny keeps saying that I have to be the baby," complains Ron. "I was the baby yesterday. It's his turn today."

"Ron, tell him how you feel about that," replies Mr. Rosen. Mr. Rosen accompanies Ron to the housekeeping corner and says, "Danny, Ron has an I-statement for you. It's important that you listen to him without interrupting."

"I don't like it when you keep saying I have to be the baby. I want to be the dad today," says Ron. Mr. Rosen sits next to Danny, ready to remind him to listen without interrupting if he starts to forget.

"Okay, Danny, you listened without interrupting," says Mr. Rosen. "Now it's your turn to tell Ron how you feel. Ron, it's your job now to listen without interrupting."

Knocking over the block building: A modified kindergarten conflict resolution talk

Wes, full of energy after a long morning indoors, began zooming around his kindergarten classroom, making train noises as he went. He chugged through the block area, bumping into the intricate castle that Grace had been working on for the past fifteen minutes. The castle collapsed as Grace looked on, horrified.

Ms. Stephen, the teaching assistant, redirected Wes. Meanwhile, Grace sought out the teacher. "Teacher, teacher," Grace said, "Wes knocked down my building."

"Did you tell Wes how you feel?" asked Ms. Stark.

"Noooo," replied Grace.

"Will you tell Wes on your own, or do you want me to come with you?" Ms. Stark asked.

"I want you to come with me."

"Let's practice first. What are you going to say to Wes?"

"It made me mad when you knocked over my castle. I worked hard on that castle," stated Grace, using one of the modified I-statements that this class was learning.

Grace and Ms. Stark walked over to Wes, now energetically pouring water at the water table.

"I have something to tell you, Wes," said Grace. She took Ms. Stark's hand for courage. "It made me mad when you knocked over my castle. I worked hard on that castle."

Wes looked at Grace and said, "I didn't see your castle. I didn't know it was in my way."

"Wes, how can we help Grace feel better?" asked Ms. Stark. Ms. Stark wants to raise the children's awareness about making amends. Because this situation is pretty straightforward—Wes clearly was the one who made the mistake when he knocked down Grace's castle— Ms. Stark is asking Wes how he might fix his mistake, rather than asking both children for ideas on how to solve the problem.

"I could help her fix her castle," offered Wes.

"That's okay, I'll fix it myself," answered Grace.

Wes went back to measuring and pouring the water and Grace headed off to the block corner to rebuild.

Teaching Conflict Resolution

Student-to-student conflict resolution demands of students a set of sophisticated skills—skills that teachers must explicitly teach. Successful Peace Talks such as the one between Suzanne and Tobey described earlier are the result of such teaching followed by months of practice under the teacher's guidance. Because ultimately students will need to conduct conflict resolution by themselves without adult supervision, it's important to invest effort up front to make sure they develop these skills solidly.

I begin introducing conflict resolution during the first weeks of school using a combination of teaching methods. What this teaching looks and sounds like depends on the children's age, but it always covers the crucial skills of cooling off, making assertive statements, listening respectfully, and agreeing on a solution.

Teachable moments: Introducing a simplified version of conflict resolution

Right from the first week of school, students have predictable conflicts about sharing materials, choosing work partners, or deciding whom to play with. These are teachable moments, when teachers can informally model a simple version of the conflict resolution protocol and send a message about how disagreements will be handled in this class.

One such conflict arose on a beautiful fall day one year when I was teaching second grade. It was recess, and the playground was full of second graders running, swinging, climbing, and tossing balls. Emily came running over to me, saying, "Teacher, teacher, Joanne wouldn't let me play."

Emily and I went to find Joanne, and the three of us sat down together on a bench, Emily and Joanne side by side.

In the ensuing conversation, I coached the children through the following steps, which foreshadowed what the class would be learning formally in the weeks to come.

The first child (aggrieved party) states the issue

"Emily, tell Joanne what you told me. Make sure you look at her," I said.

Emily started to blurt out, "She wouldn't let me play."

Immediately I let the children know that this was not going to be business as usual: I wasn't going to solve the problem for them. Instead, they were going to talk to each other. "Emily, look at Joanne and talk to her," I said.

Emily looked at Joanne but didn't speak. She needed a sentence starter. "You could start with 'Joanne, when … ,'" I said. To the other child, I said, "Joanne, it's your job to listen carefully."

"Joanne, you wouldn't let me play, and I wanted to," said Emily.

I didn't expect Emily to use an I-statement at this point. That would come later, after I had taught the whole class about I-statements. I-statements are not the most natural way to talk, and they take some practice. It was enough at this point to learn and practice listening and restating.

The second child listens and restates what he or she heard

Joanne was defensive, ready to explain how she was in the right. "It wasn't …" Right away I stopped her. "Joanne, first let Emily know that you understood her by telling what you heard. You might begin by saying, "I heard you say that …"

"But I was just…," Joanne persisted. I stopped her again. "You don't have to agree with Emily. Right now you just need to let her know you heard her by telling what you heard."

Often children can't state their understanding because rather than listening carefully, they were busy preparing their defense. Sometimes they need to have their partner repeat.

"Emily, tell Joanne again what you said." Emily repeated her statement, which Joanne heard this time.

"I heard you say that you wanted to play, and I didn't let you," Joanne said.

"Emily, did Joanne hear you accurately?" I asked. Emily nodded.

If students haven't had much practice listening carefully to others, they may need to paraphrase a few times before they get the gist of their partner's statement.

The second child states his or her point of view

"Joanne, now it's your turn to tell Emily your point of view about what happened," I said. "Emily, you're going to listen carefully."

"I'd already planned to play with Valeria," Joanne said eagerly. "We didn't see each other all summer, and I wanted to be alone with her."

The first child listens and restates what he or she heard

"Emily, it's your job now to tell Joanne what you heard her say. Later you'll get a chance to say whether you agree with her."

"But it's not fair …" Emily interjected. Clearly Emily also needed help suspending the urge to argue her case. "Remember, Emily, right now you're letting Joanne know that you understood her, just what you understood her to say," I coached.

"You and Valeria wanted to play alone together," Emily stated simply.

"Emily, now check with Joanne to make sure that you heard her accurately." Emily looked at Joanne, and Joanne nodded.

The process continues until both children have been heard

"Joanne, do you have anything more to add?" I asked. Joanne shook her head.

"Emily, do you have anything more to add?" Emily shook her head.

The children had begun to learn a powerful lesson about getting along with others. With coaching, they had listened to and understood each other. At this point in the school year, this was the most important thing for them to learn about resolving differences. They would continue to practice this crucial skill as our year unfolded.

The children reach a solution

At this early stage I don't introduce the process of brainstorming for solutions. Brainstorming is the naming of multiple ideas without concern for their appropriateness or feasibility. Its purpose is to encourage creative thinking. That's a great exercise, but too much for this first experience. For now I skip to agreeing on a solution, normally the step that comes after brainstorming.

"Emily, do you have any ideas about what you and Joanne might do to solve this problem?" I asked. "Joanne, do you have any ideas?"

"We could play together tomorrow," Emily suggested.

"That's okay with me," said Joanne.

The two girls ran off to enjoy the rest of their recess.

Whole-class lessons: Explicitly teaching conflict resolution skills

While children are practicing listening and perspective-taking as conflicts arise, I use whole-class lessons to teach the full range of skills they'll need when they try the formal conflict resolution protocol later.

I set aside a thirty-minute block each week early in the year for this direct instruction. The lessons I describe on the following pages usually take about eight separate teaching segments spread out over one to two months. Your timing may be different, depending on your students' maturity, their previous experience with conflict resolution, and your inclination.

How soon students can go off to do conflict resolution on their own after these lessons also varies. On one end of the spectrum, some first grade teachers have told me that they continue teacher-guided practice throughout the year. On the other end, some fifth and sixth grade teachers send their students off to use conflict resolution as soon as they've finished the whole-class lessons and demonstrations.

Cooling off

We do our best thinking when we're calm. Our ability to think and listen is so improved when we're calm, and so compromised when we're not, that I emphasize cooling off as a specific first step when teaching conflict resolution.

MAKING SURE CHILDREN KNOW WHAT IT MEANS TO FEEL CALM

I begin by making sure students know what "calm" feels like. With children seated comfortably in a circle, I tell them that we all get angry sometimes. "Think about a time when you were really angry," I say. "Put yourself there. What do you see? What do you hear? How does your body feel?"

The children turn to their neighbors to talk briefly about this. I keep this segment short so we can spend more time thinking about being calm than about being angry.

Now the children think about a time when they were relaxed and comfortable. With young children, this might be a time when they were lying in bed while an adult read to them. With older children, it might be a time when they were at a beach or another beautiful place. Again I prompt students to remember how their bodies felt and to chat with a neighbor about it.

DISCUSSING WHY COOLING OFF IS IMPORTANT

Once I'm confident that students understand what it means to be calm, it's time to discuss why cooling off is important.

Brain research shows that the amygdala, the part of the brain that processes the strong emotions we feel when we're in a conflict, triggers the release of stress hormones such as adrenalin and cortisol. These hormones impede logical thinking. Emotional stress also triggers a drop in serotonin, and that drop is associated with increased aggression (Jensen, 1998). To resolve our conflicts logically and peacefully, then, we need to take a step away and wait for our body chemistry to return to normal.

I share this information with students in a way that's appropriate for their age. To third graders, I say, "When we're angry, our brains release substances that keep us from thinking clearly. It's important to do our best thinking when we're sorting out disagreements with classmates. So we need to cool off first." Third graders seem satisfied with this explanation. Younger children will want a less sophisticated explanation and older children a more sophisticated one.

SHARING TECHNIQUES FOR COOLING OFF

Next we discuss techniques for cooling off. When I was a child and conflicts erupted in the classroom, my teachers would suggest a short walk down the hall for a drink of water. This is an example of conventional teacher wisdom being, in fact, wise: Exercise and hydration both reduce stress. Deep, cleansing breaths also calm and restore our best selves, as yoga practitioners teach us.

"When you're upset, what do you do to calm down?" I ask students. As students contribute ideas, I write them on a chart, making sure that deep breathing, exercising, and getting a drink of water all make it onto the list. We post this list of "Ways to Keep Your Cool."

One technique that is helpful and easy to practice with students is deep breathing. I teach students to breathe slowly through their nose, filling their lungs all the way to their diaphragm. "Now let your breath out gradually through your mouth," I say. Third and fourth graders often enjoy making posters with directions for "yoga breaths." As they create these posters they cement their learning and also provide the class with a handy reference.

Finally, because children learn more from what we do than what we say, I try using stress-reducing techniques myself during those inevitable stressful times in the classroom. For example, in those moments of chaos when everyone wants to ask me the same question at the same time, I try simply closing my eyes and taking a couple of yoga breaths. That has impact—for myself and the children.

Making I-statements

We come to understand each other best when we remain open and nondefensive. To set this tone for conflict resolution, I teach children to open their conversation with an I-statement that begins with "I feel/felt ____" rather than the "When you _____" that some conflict resolution formats call for.

I have found that when children begin by expressing their feelings, their partner is more likely to interpret the communication as a request for help. By contrast, if children begin with "When you _____," or worse, the dreaded "You always ____" or "You never _____," the listener is likely to feel attacked and become defensive.

FEELING THE DIFFERENCE BETWEEN I-STATEMENTS AND YOU-STATEMENTS

With the children seated in a circle, I say, "Pretend that I've just walked into the classroom, and art supplies are everywhere. Markers are lying on the floor with their tops off, and bits of clay are ground into the rug. I'm worried that the markers will dry out and that Mr. Evans won't be able to vacuum the rug."

I continue, "Pretend I say to you, 'You never put the art supplies away.' How do you feel when you hear me say that?" The children turn and talk with their neighbor. Then some of them share their reactions with the whole class. Mike, directing his comment toward me, says, "I feel mad at you. I do put the art supplies away. Why are you talking that way?"

"Okay, let me try saying it a different way," I tell the class. I rephrase my concern using an I-statement: "I felt frustrated when I saw the art supplies all over the floor because I was afraid that our beautiful supplies would be ruined and that Mr. Evans wouldn't be able to vacuum the rug. What I want is supplies put away safely."

I pause a bit to let children feel the difference, then ask, "How does that make you feel?" The children certainly do feel the difference. "I want to help take care of the supplies now," says Gretel.

When I use a you-statement, the children feel attacked and want to retaliate. When I use an I-statement, the art supplies become the issue, and the children feel much more willing to clean them up.

TRYING SOME EASY I-STATEMENTS

For most of us, children and adults alike, I-statements don't come naturally. To help the children practice them, I take out some sentence strips that I prepared ahead of time:

I feel/felt _____

When I see/saw (or hear/heard) _____

Because _____

What I want is _____

The class tries out various ideas for filling in the blanks. I start, using positives and keeping things light. "I feel good when I see you smile because I think that means you're happy. What I want is for you to keep being happy."

The children suggest more positive ideas, such as "I feel interested when I hear you tell me about a great book because I like books. What I want is to read that book myself" or "I feel happy when I hear you ask me to play because I don't have anyone to play with. What I want is to have friends at recess."

EXPRESSING STRONGER FEELINGS

Next, using literature the class is familiar with (see the box "Teaching I-Statements with Children's Literature"), I introduce stronger feelings. For example, using characters from *Tales of a Fourth Grade Nothing* by Judy Blume, one class made this statement: "Peter felt angry when he heard that Fudge had swallowed his turtle because he loved his pet. What he wanted was to get his turtle back."

"Now put yourself in Peter's shoes," I said. "If you were Peter, how might you express your feelings to Fudge using an I-statement?" The children easily converted the "Peter-statement" to "I felt angry when I heard that you swallowed my turtle because I love my pet. What I want is to get my turtle back."

Using examples from literature this way keeps the feelings just one step removed from real life, which makes practice more comfortable.

PRACTICING WITH SCENARIOS

Once students have had some practice using literature, they're ready to practice using scenarios like those they often encounter in real school life. "Let's suppose you asked your friend to save you a seat in the cafeteria, and she doesn't do it," I said to a fifth grade class. "What's an I-statement you can say to her?"

Because such scenarios are so true to life and often stir up genuine feelings in students, it's easy for them to revert to you-statements as they try different wordings, especially if some time has passed since their last lesson on I-statements. Knowing that we all remember what we've practiced, however, I want to make sure they construct I-statements, not you-statements. With this fifth grade class, then, I reviewed a few I-statements before sending them off in pairs to come up with ideas for the cafeteria seat example.

Here are some other scenarios suitable for this practice:

- Your tablemates take all the pencils.

- Another student takes the book you're reading and starts to read it.

Teaching I-Statements with Children's Literature

The world of children's books offers abundant opportunities for children to practice making I-statements. Here are just a few examples:

Frog and Toad Are Friends by Arnold Lobel (chapter one)

Toad wanted his friend Frog to leave him alone so that he could continue his winter sleep. Children might practice making I-statements that Toad could say as well as I-statements that Frog could say.

Little Bear by Else Holmelund Minarik (Birthday Soup)

It's Little Bear's birthday and it seems to him that Mother Bear is making birthday soup, not birthday cake. Little Bear wants a birthday cake for his birthday. What could Little Bear say to Mother Bear?

Ramona the Brave by Beverly Cleary (chapter one)

Ramona's sister Beezus (Beatrice) wishes Ramona wouldn't call her "Beezus" in front of the boys at the playground. What could Beezus say? What could Ramona say?

Bridge to Terabithia by Katherine Patterson (chapter three)

Jess has always been the fastest runner in fifth grade until Leslie moves to Lark Creek. Leslie joins the boys' footraces at recess and beats Jess. Jess wishes that Leslie wouldn't run in the foot races and, especially, that she wouldn't beat him. Children might enjoy making I-statements from Jess's point of view and from Leslie's point of view.

- Your snack is missing, and you see a friend eating something that looks like your snack.

- Your partner does all the writing when you want to do some of it.

- Your classmates leave you out of the kickball game.

- A classmate calls you a silly name.

- Two kids, busy playing, walk away from you when you thought you were playing with them.

- Someone bumps into you while you're standing in line.

- A classmate says, "You can't sit at our table."

- Some kids on the bus make fun of your clothes.

- Your parents are learning to speak English. You hear a classmate making fun of the way they talk.

- Your friend's family doesn't celebrate Halloween. Another friend says to you, "It's stupid not to celebrate Halloween."

MAKING A "FEELINGS BANK"

Being able to express their actual feelings is crucial to children's success with conflict resolution. But children don't always know the words to describe their feelings. To help, the class can keep and post a bank of feelings words that classmates have used in the course of constructing their practice I-statements. Such words as "angry," "frustrated," "sad," and "nervous" often appear in the bank. Older children might enjoy picking feelings words out of their independent reading—words such as "puzzled," "snubbed," "glum," and "offended."

When children who are just learning to make I-statements come to me reporting a conflict, I still coach them through it by using a simplified conflict resolution protocol (as in the earlier Joanne and Emily example). But after I-statements are taught and practiced, I expect the aggrieved party to start the conversation with an I-statement.

Listening respectfully

Conflict resolution cannot be successful without respectful listening. Learning cannot be rigorous or joyful, and the classroom community cannot be strong, without respectful listening. All this makes respectful listening one of the most important skills to teach.

INTERACTIVE MODELING

I begin this teaching with interactive modeling. The students sit in a circle so that everyone can see and participate equally. I've asked a student ahead of time to help with the modeling by telling about something fun she did over the weekend. To the rest of the class, I say, "I'm going to listen respectfully to Gina. I'm going to show her with my face and with the rest of my body that I'm listening. Notice exactly what I do to listen respectfully to Gina."

While Gina speaks, I turn to face her, look at her with interest, and nod my head as I murmur "umm."

When I ask students what they noticed, they name my body posture and facial expression and the small sound I made. I ask for other ways to show respectful listening and record students' ideas on a T-chart:

Respectful listening

LOOKS LIKE	SOUNDS LIKE
A friendly face	Listening-sounds such as "umm"
Turn body toward person	Statements such as "Wow, really?"
Look at the person	Silence, no interruptions

Sometimes children say "Make eye contact" as a way to show respectful listening. Eye contact is tricky though. It's not respectful in all cultures to look someone right in the eye. Also, for children with certain neurological conditions, making eye contact is difficult. If a child names eye contact as something she noticed in my modeling, I prefer to rephrase by saying, "I did look at Gina," which names a behavior that is more inclusive of students' diverse backgrounds and abilities. At another time, I might explain to my class that eye contact is hard for Max or that some families don't think eye contact is polite.

After this discussion the children partner up and take turns listening respectfully to their partner. I give them simple prompts such as "Tell your partner what your favorite color is (or favorite ice cream flavor or favorite dinner food) and why." I circulate, reminding children to turn toward their partner, coaching them on keeping an interested expression, and noting the careful listening I see.

Fourth, fifth, and sixth graders often enjoy getting into foursomes, with two members of the group talking. The other two observe, tallying the number of times they see interested expressions and respectful body language. Then the students switch roles.

As I continue to coach students' conflict resolution in the following days and weeks, I watch for and reinforce their efforts to listen respectfully. I also comment on respectful listening in other interactions, such as during Morning Meetings and class academic discussions. It helps to name the specific behaviors by saying, for example, "I noticed you looking at your partner as he told you what he was upset about." The specificity lets students know exactly what they're doing right and should keep doing.

SPECIAL ATTENTION TO SARCASM

When teaching respectful listening, it's valuable, particularly with older children, to address sarcasm and put-downs directly. According to Webster's New World Dictionary (1982), "sarcasm" originates from a word that means "to tear flesh, like dogs." Yet this type of humor is so prevalent in our culture, especially in TV shows about school, that many students think it's acceptable.

But sarcasm is not acceptable in school. Responding to someone's comment with a put-down, no matter how funny it might seem, takes our attention away from the speaker's concerns, usually hurts the speaker, and discourages harmonious conflict resolution.

A colleague of mine, a sixth grade teacher whose students were trying out sarcasm and put-downs, addressed the issue by gathering the class for a discussion. Mr. Browne asked the students to think about a time when someone put them down. "How did it feel?" he asked them.

"The other kids laughed and I was embarrassed," said one student. "I pretended I thought it was funny, but that's not how I felt," added Toni. "Harsh," chimed in Sarah.

These sixth graders then thought about a time when they'd used sarcasm on someone else. My colleague, knowing how easily embarrassed eleven-year-olds can be, had them keep these memories private.

"The next time you think of making a sarcastic remark to a friend, remember how you felt when someone made one toward you," Mr. Browne said.

Paraphrasing

Student-to-student conflict resolution calls for children to paraphrase what they understood their partner to have said before giving their own point of view. Paraphrasing like this doesn't come naturally to any of us, yet it's the step that makes conflict resolution so effective.

I start with the many academic applications of paraphrasing. During Morning Meeting I might ask children to restate the morning message in their own words. They practice first with partners and then share their ideas with the class. As I read aloud from a chapter book such as *Poppy* by Avi, I might ask children who would like to restate what Poppy said to her father when he told her to go on a dangerous quest.

As I coach students through conflicts about teams and playmates, sharing and turn taking, I consistently ask them to restate what they heard their partner say. I find that when I ask, "What did you hear _____ say?" children understand what is expected. I next check with the partner. "Did Sal state your idea accurately?" If the answer is "Yes," we go on to next steps. If the answer is "No," I have the students try again.

A crucial step, paraphrasing ensures that students are listening to each other carefully. It deserves careful teaching and may take quite a bit of coached practice for some children. If you teach younger children and find that paraphrasing is difficult for them, try having them simply echo their partner's words.

Brainstorming and narrowing ideas

I teach the solution-generating portion of student-to-student conflict resolution as two distinct steps: first, brainstorming; second, narrowing down the brainstormed ideas.

In the first step, brainstorming, participants share their ideas freely without worrying yet about how good the ideas are. All ideas are accepted without comment and treated as equally valuable.

This is important because often children in a conflict each see only one solution to the problem. In fact, their limited vision is probably a big reason they're in conflict. The purpose of the brainstorming step, then, is to open up their thinking. Naming ideas without judging them often frees children, leading them to creative solutions they never would have thought of otherwise.

Only when the children have a long list of ideas do they go to the next step of narrowing them down, weeding out the less feasible ideas and agreeing on one to try.

INTRODUCING BRAINSTORMING

I introduce brainstorming by using it with topics that aren't likely to be emotional for the children—some academic content or some fun aspect of classroom life, for example. This lets children get familiar with the process without the distraction of emotional tension.

"We're going to practice brainstorming," I say. "We'll create a storm of ideas from all of your brains. As classmates share, we'll listen to all ideas. We'll see how many ideas we can come up with. Afterwards we'll discuss and evaluate the ideas."

"How many characters can you think of in literature who have an important friend?" I ask them.

Frog and Toad (from *Frog and Toad Are Friends*); Charlotte and Wilbur (from *Charlotte's Web*); and Harry, Ron, and Hermione (from *Harry Potter* books) are only a few of the many possibilities that students name. Joan says, "Wait, Ron and Hermione don't always get along."

"Remember, now we're listening. Discussing and evaluating come later," I say.

As we practice this skill, the children are learning that all ideas are accepted as important during brainstorming. Children's minds are opened up.

Next we move to the social realm by practicing brainstorming fun class activities. "Which games could we play with our first grade buddies when we meet them on the playground this afternoon?" I might ask. Or "Let's celebrate our first month together by doing something special this afternoon. What could we do?"

Again, all ideas are treated as equally important. Once we have a long list of ideas, I congratulate the class on the variety they've generated.

NARROWING THE IDEAS

Once children are comfortable with brainstorming, I have them practice narrowing a long list of brainstormed ideas down to a few feasible ones.

For example, I have them look over the list of possible games we could play to celebrate our first month together and then ask them to consider our realities. Which ones do we have the supplies for? We have sets of checkers and chess. Four Corners; Red Light, Green Light; and Red Rover require no supplies. We don't have a Monopoly board game, so we cross that one off the list.

I tell the class that I've allowed thirty minutes on Friday afternoon for our games period. Which games will fit into that time frame? Labyrinth takes lots longer than thirty minutes, so we cross it off the list as a choice that's "not possible."

Of the games in the "possible" list, we determine which ones most students want to play.

Several children want to play a whole-group game such as Four Corners, which doesn't take that long. Others want to play small-group games such as checkers and chess. We don't have time to do both. Which shall we play?

This is where respectful listening comes in. I remind the children of the rules we've worked so hard to create. Matt says we're celebrating being together as a whole class, so we should play a whole-group game. Alexi says we can play a game like Four Corners anytime, and chess and checkers are more special. Ron says if we go outside to play a game like Fishy, Fishy in the Sea, we'll all be together and it will feel special. There are lots of smiles and nodding heads in response to Ron's statement.

I take a "straw vote." I tell the children that I want to check out what they're thinking about the games, so I'm going to ask them to raise their hand for their first choice. This isn't a binding vote; it's just to get a sense of what they're thinking. Every hand goes up for outdoor games such as Fishy, Fishy in the Sea. (If there hadn't been such an obvious consensus, I would have used the consensus process used for class meetings, explained in Chapter Five.)

On Friday afternoon, we spend a half hour outside playing Fishy, Fishy in the Sea; Red Light, Green Light; and Red Rover.

Practicing with hypothetical conflicts

The next step is for children to apply their skill to hypothetical conflicts. I choose ones that resemble the conflicts they're likely to encounter in everyday school life. Young children tend to do well with simple conflicts such as two students both wanting to use the same crayon. Older students might practice with scenarios such as two students continuously passing the ball to each other during recess football and not allowing other players to touch the ball.

As in the earlier practice, I challenge the class to come up with as many ideas as they can for solutions. They're engaged. They've all had plenty of experience in conflicts, and more emotion is involved here than when we talked about characters from literature or even games to play on a Friday afternoon. I chart all ideas and remark on how many the class has devised. I then guide them in narrowing the list down to the most feasible ones.

Using the skills in real conflicts

Now the children are ready to use these skills in real life. At this point I still haven't formally introduced the full conflict resolution protocol. But as students come to me with conflicts, I prompt them to brainstorm and choose mutually acceptable solutions as I coach them in resolving the problem.

Students need lots of opportunities to continue using their newly learned skills under their teacher's watchful guidance. Calming down, making nonthreatening I-statements, listening respectfully, paraphrasing, brainstorming, and narrowing solutions are challenging for many adults, let alone children. Ample practice will help ensure that children succeed when they eventually try to resolve conflicts on their own.

Clarifying which conflicts are for adults to handle

It's not enough that teachers are clear in their own mind which kinds of problems are suitable for students to handle independently and which require adult intervention. They also need to teach students to make the distinction. The results are potentially disastrous if students believe they should deal on their own with problems such as physical violence, unkind teasing, and bullying.

To teach children when they can handle conflicts themselves and when they should get adult help, I've gathered the class in a circle. "I've noticed that you're working to resolve your conflicts the way we've practiced. I've seen you listening and working to find a solution," I tell them.

"I want us to take a look at the different kinds of conflicts that have come up in this class," I say next. "Without naming names, let's hear some conflicts you've been involved in."

As the children name conflicts, I list them on a chart. I put the ordinary ones—arguments about sharing, how to pick teams, who gets to play with whom—on the left side of the chart. When conflicts such as physically hurting each other or intentionally hurting each other's feelings are named, I list them on the right side of the chart.

I tell the class that the conflicts on the left are ones they can solve on their own, but for the ones on the right, they need to get adult help. I label the left column "Conflicts that are OK to solve on your own." I label the right column "Conflicts adults need to know about." "It's the job of the adults in this school to make sure all the children are safe—in their bodies and in their feelings," I say. I make sure students understand that safe feelings matter as much as safe bodies, and that it's important for adults to know about anything that might make someone unsafe.

Gradual independence after ample coaching: Introducing the full conflict resolution protocol

After the whole-class lessons, it's time for coached practice. Younger children will need many months of this practice; older children, perhaps only a week or two. Once they've had sufficient coached practice, children will be ready to try the conflict resolution protocol independently.

I usually formally introduce third graders to independent conflict resolution during the winter. First graders often aren't ready until spring, whereas fifth graders are so ready for this process that they can often handle independent conflict resolution by November. An important factor that influences timing is whether the students have practiced independent conflict resolution in previous grades.

Each class of children is unique, so I suggest you watch your students carefully. When you notice that they're very comfortable with the process, needing little support from you, that's your cue that they're ready for independence.

Whole-class introduction to independent conflict resolution

I've gathered the children for a whole-class lesson to launch independent conflict resolution. If the class has been practicing well under my guidance, this should be a fairly smooth transition. Before the meeting, I've prepared a chart—our Peace Talk chart—listing the steps in a conflict resolution meeting. (See sample chart on page 128.) I've also prepared some large index cards for writing down Peace Talk ground rules that we'll compose as a class.

CREATING GROUND RULES

"You've been practicing Peace Talks as problems come up," I say. "I think you're ready to begin doing this on your own, without me. But we'll need a couple of ground rules first. What's the most important part of solving a problem with someone?"

Children immediately chime in, "To listen." They've had enough experience now to know that this is paramount. I write on an index card, "Listen respectfully," and announce that this is our first ground rule. This wording is easy to remember and, importantly, it's in the positive—stating what to do rather than what not to do. This positive framing emphasizes that rules are our community ideals rather than restrictions on our behavior.

"Why is it important to listen?" I ask.

Chloe raises her hand. "Because if you don't listen carefully, you don't know what the other person thinks and then you can't solve anything."

Her classmates nod.

"The other important thing to remember," I say, "is to work to solve the problem."

Again children nod in agreement. "Why is that so important?" I ask.

Manny says, "Because if one person isn't working to solve the problem, he only wants his own way and the problem never gets solved."

I write "Work to solve the problem" on the same index card. This and "Listen respectfully" will be our two ground rules.

In addition to these rules, some conflict resolution methods call for rules such as no interrupting, no put downs, look at the other person, and use respectful words and body language. Because our classroom rules include broad ideals such as "Be kind and friendly" and "Show respect," they already give us guidance in these specifics. I therefore prefer to keep Peace Talk ground rules to those that are most important and specific to this process.

I copy our two ground rules onto another index card so that each student in a Peace Talk can hold one card to refer to the rules. Kindergarten teachers who use this process sometimes add picture clues to the cards.

"FISH BOWL" DEMONSTRATION

Now I give the class a demonstration of the formal conflict resolution protocol using the "fish bowl" method. Two students act out a short scene, with classmates sitting in a circle around them, watching from outside the "fish bowl."

I ask a pair of children to reenact an actual conference they had or a fictional conference. I plan carefully who the actors will be and ask them ahead of time. This is an important moment in the life of our class, and we need actors who will take the roles seriously.

Janey and Silvia have agreed to do today's demonstration. They are revisiting a Peace Talk they actually had yesterday. With the conflict resolution steps posted for everyone to see, and with Janey and Silvia each holding one of the ground rules cards, Janey begins by doing the "Cool off" step, breathing deeply. After a few deep breaths, she says calmly, "Silvia, I'd like to have a Peace Talk with you."

Then she gives an I-statement: "I felt hurt when you walked off and left me on the playground because I thought we were going to jump rope together. What I want is to jump rope with you at recess."

"So, you're saying that you were counting on playing jump rope with me and instead I walked off and left you," Silvia paraphrases.

In this manner, the two actors complete each step of the protocol, agreeing at the end to jump rope together today at recess. They shake hands and say "Peace."

When they finish, I ask how each actor felt while listening to the other. Then I ask the audience to share what they noticed. This post-demonstration reflection helps children consolidate their learning.

ONGOING OBSERVATION

I post the Peace Talk steps on the back of our easel chart stand, a spot that's out of the mainstream of classroom traffic, and put the two ground rules cards in a basket nearby. I announce that the Peace Talk area is now open. This will be where children will go to resolve their conflicts.

Now I step back and watch as students try conflict resolution on their own. I observe without actively intervening, though I remain available for help as needed. I watch to see if there are skills that children still need help with, skills that I might reteach to the whole class.

Keys to Success with Conflict Resolution

The following guidelines can help you teach and coach conflict resolution effectively.

Be a helper, not an arbitrator

I spent many teaching years solving students' conflicts for them. Although it was time consuming and energy draining, it was also a familiar and oddly comfortable role. I was the all-powerful arbitrator and judge.

Shifting to the student-to-student conflict resolution approach required me to reframe my thinking, to back off from the familiar "solve it for them" mentality. I still wanted to know about children's conflicts, but not so that

I could fix everything. Rather, I wanted to be informed so I could provide assistance, if needed, as the children solved their own disputes.

One important way for teachers to maintain this role as helper, rather than arbitrator, is to avoid inadvertently advancing our own preferred solution as we observe or coach a conflict resolution session. If we appear to be taking a side, even by nudging ever so gently, children will slide back into their old way of seeing us as judge. Younger children will quickly come to expect that we'll fix everything for them. Older children may push their conflicts under the surface to avoid "tattling."

I know how easy it is to slip though. One day I was helping two students, Lenore and Tina, use student-to-student conflict resolution to handle a disagreement about who would get to play with a third student, Sarah. Lenore and Tina were brainstorming possible solutions when Lenore said, "We could take numbers like in the grocery store." Forgetting that in brainstorming, all ideas are accepted without judgment, I burst out, "Sarah's not a piece of meat!"

Following my model, Lenore and Tina began interjecting what they thought about each other's ideas, effectively ending the brainstorming. And they both gave up the hard work of solving the problem altogether, simply looking to me instead to decide who would play with Sarah. I learned a lesson and redoubled my efforts at keeping my opinions to myself.

Admittedly, there are times when the teacher needs to arbitrate. When children's entrenched conflicts are destroying the classroom's feeling of safety and community, the teacher needs to step in. For example, when Marlee said, "Yuck, I won't work with Camillo or any other boy," the simple statement, "In this class we work with everyone. I'll be watching to make sure you're working with Camillo in a friendly way" reaffirmed classroom rules and let Marlee know that her behavior was unacceptable.

Emphasize the process, not just the solution

In teaching conflict resolution, we're not only helping children solve the immediate dispute, but teaching skills that they will be able to use in the rest of their schooling and throughout their lives. That's why it's important to emphasize the entire conflict resolution process, not just the

Conflict Resolution among a Small Group

Once children are proficient at one-on-one conflict resolution, they can use this protocol for conflicts involving a group of three or four. (For groups larger than that, the process gets unwieldy. The class meeting structure described in Chapter Five might be more effective in those cases.)

For example, Daniel and Zoë wanted to build a Popsicle-stick plank house for their group's social studies project on Kwakiutl shelters. Andy and Mai wanted the group to create a poster. The children became polarized and set in their opinions.

As the foursome began debating, I prompted them to use the Peace Talk approach. I reminded them that it was important for everyone to have a chance to speak, using I-statements and simple statements of fact, and for listeners to paraphrase their understanding of what was said.

I then stood back and observed, ready to coach if needed. The children managed the steps independently, agreeing in the end to create a plank house *and* an explanatory poster.

Some years I coach the small-group variation of conflict resolution on the fly, as needed. Other years I teach it explicitly when I teach the Peace Talk protocol.

Before you suggest that a small group use this format, make sure the conflict concerns all those gathered around. Children love to be involved and will often want to join in because that's where the excitement is. Discern who is truly involved, and have only those students engage in the Peace Talk.

solution. Be sure to stick to all the steps when teaching and guiding children in using the protocol. At first, you may even find it helpful to follow a script for what to say about each step. (A script is provided on page 126.)

In our time-crunched school days, it's tempting to gloss over the whole-class lessons and the individual coachings described previously. But when we do this, we compromise the quality of our students' resolution of immediate conflicts as well as their lifelong learning.

Model effective language

As you go about classroom life, be sure to use the kind of respectful, nonthreatening language you want students to use in resolving conflicts. Your example, along with reminders as needed, is crucial in helping them grow into this new way of speaking.

If you slip, don't hesitate to "do it over." It shows children that everyone makes mistakes, and that mistakes can be fixed. When I said to Brian, "You always...," I caught myself and said, "Oops, rewind, Brian. I feel frustrated when I see your coat on the floor. I would like you to pick it up so our classroom is neat and safe." You can also direct children to "rewind" and restate their concerns if they forget to use I-statements.

Establish a time and place for conflict resolution

Early in the year, when you're introducing conflict resolution during teachable moments, these talks can take place anywhere you deem conducive to a focused conversation—on a playground bench, in a corner of the lunchroom, at the reading table in the classroom. The talks can take place in the moment as long as they don't disrupt a lesson or activity.

Once students are using the conflict resolution protocol on their own, however, it's important to establish a place and appropriate times for this activity. Some teachers have a special table with the conflict resolution steps posted nearby. In my classroom, there wasn't space for a special table. Instead, we used the spot behind my teaching easel chart stand, where students could sit on the floor and talk. We established that appropriate times would be during independent work or choice times, and an inappropriate time would be during a whole-class lesson.

Follow up after the conversation

It's one thing to agree on a plan and another to actually follow through. Early in the year, when I'm coaching children in conflict resolution, I make a point of briefly following up sometime in the next few days with a quick "How's that plan going?" Sometimes my follow-up is simply to take notice—whether the two who were arguing about spending time together at recess are playing smoothly now, whether the partners are taking turns as they agreed to do, whether the excluded child is being included.

As students begin to have independent Peace Talks, I encourage them to get together after a few days and see if the agreed-upon solution is working for both of them. This just takes a minute if things are going well.

Revisit the conversation if needed

If the solution isn't working, children may need to revisit the brainstorming stage to look for a new solution. Even with the best of intentions, things don't always work out the way we've planned. For example, Silvia meant to play with Janey as they had agreed, but her friend Maddie pulled Silvia away for a private "emergency" chat.

The next day Silvie and Janey met again, taking a realistic look at what Silvia might do if she'd promised to play with Janey but another friend needed a private emergency meeting. A new idea they brainstormed was for Silvia to say to Janey, "I'd really like to play with you today, but something's come up. Could we have lunch together instead?"

Janey was satisfied that her needs had been considered. Janey, Silvia, and Maddie played jump rope together the next day.

Foster sincerity in apologies

Often at the end of a Peace Talk, a child will blurt out a sincere "I'm sorry." Once children have seen things from another's point of view, they usually do feel sorry. Showing their partner their remorse can do a lot to soothe the hurt and heal the relationship. For this reason, many teachers put a lot of value in apologies.

But appreciating students' sincere apologies is different from telling them to apologize. Our goal is to teach children to be authentic, and telling a child to apologize can promote insincere apologies. "I'm sorry" can then become code for "Let's get this over with."

If we want to teach children to apologize sincerely, the most effective way is to model doing so ourselves. When we accidentally send the wrong child to the end of the line after a pushing match, we can offer a heartfelt apology, acknowledging our responsibility by saying something like, "I thought you were the one who pushed. I should have paid more careful attention."

This shows children what a sincere apology looks and sounds like. When we apologize for unintentionally calling on children out of turn order and then make a point of keeping a list of whose turn it is, we're showing children what it is to make amends. Children learn from what we do. They learn how to treat others from how we treat them.

Although it's important to teach children to give and accept sincere verbal apologies, sometimes amends are made not in words, but in actions. After Marissa had a Peace Talk with her cubby mate, she made an effort to hang her coat on the hook. Her cubby mate knew that Marissa had truly listened during their Peace Talk and responded in kind, asking Marissa's permission before moving her coat when it was in the way. Joanne and Emily had a Peace Talk; the next day they happily played together. In both cases, the participants "fixed" hurt feelings by carrying out the mutually agreed upon solution.

Occasionally, students will show they're sorry with a little gift. Emma teased her close friend, Maureen, about "liking" Russell. The next day I noticed Emma giving Maureen a beautiful portrait she'd drawn of Maureen, with an inscription at the bottom, "I know you don't really like him." Angela lost control and screamed at me when I told her to put away her project before going to recess. She returned to school the next morning, full of remorse, with a folded paper box that she'd created for me, a gift to help keep the reading table more organized.

The common thread through all of these apologies is that they were sincere. The student was not told to "say you're sorry," or to "show that you're sorry," but rather had seen things from another's point of view and thus was able to practice that rare art, the sincere apology.

Weaving Conflict Resolution Lessons into Academic Teaching

THESE CONFLICT RESOLUTION SKILLS...	CAN BE WOVEN INTO THIS ACADEMIC TEACHING...
Making I-statements	What a character in literature might say as an I-statement
Listening respectfully	How to listen to partners during writers' workshop
Paraphrasing	Paraphrasing a paragraph just read
	Paraphrasing the morning message (part of *Responsive Classroom* Morning Meeting)
Brainstorming	Brainstorming possible strategies to solve a math problem
	Brainstorming characters in literature who have an important friend

Questions from Teachers

Will I need to modify the conflict resolution format for my fifth and sixth grade students?

Fifth grade is actually an ideal age for learning conflict resolution. Ten-year-olds tend to be very concerned with issues of fairness. They also love to organize things and can follow step-by-step protocols easily. As tens grow into eleven-year-olds, however, they usually become quite concerned with saving face. This means you may need to find a private place for sixth graders and older fifth graders to work on conflict resolution.

Recognizing this growing independence and desire for privacy among children this age, my colleague Melanie Carroll allows her fifth graders to resolve their conflicts in the hall, right outside the classroom door. Ms. Carroll stands in the doorway so that she can supervise the class while providing coaching to the conflict resolvers from a respectful distance.

But although conflict resolution is age-appropriate for fifth and sixth graders, don't be surprised if they initially look on it with suspicion. They may think it's just a new way to "get someone in trouble."

My experience, and that of many colleagues, is that if we hold firm to the prescribed steps and to the language of conflict resolution when teaching this strategy, these students will soon see how effective it is. The fact is that peer-oriented ten- and eleven-year-olds, concerned with friendships and prone to forming cliques, often need this strategy even more than younger children.

Some modifications to how you introduce conflict resolution can further make the strategy appealing to older children. Try teaching the protocol outright, skipping the informal coaching stage. Have students act out hypothetical conflict resolution meetings for the class. Once they know the protocol, encourage them to use it, first with your supervision and later independently.

Do I really need to take months to coach conflict resolution before letting students do it on their own?

We adults sometimes expect that children can develop conflict resolution skills quickly. Especially on the playground, I often hear adults say "Go solve it yourself" when children tell them of a conflict, even though the children don't yet have the skills or experience for success.

Although our intention might be to nurture independence, this response, without careful instruction, leaves children trying to row their boat out of the storm without an oar. Sending children off to muddle through on their own before they're ready can encourage dangerous behaviors such as bullying. Our job is to teach and allow children to practice under our watchful eye until they can take over and solve their conflicts independently and successfully.

Besides the whole-class lessons on conflict resolution I have described, teaching conflict resolution is about offering in-the-minute coaching as problems come up and listening in as children begin to try out these skills with some independence. Taking time for this is necessary and worthwhile.

Teaching conflict resolution skills does not always have to take additional time in our day's schedule, however. I find there are ways to work it into academic blocks. (See the box "Weaving Conflict Resolution Lessons into Academic Teaching" on page 118.)

What if a student's behavior doesn't change after a conflict resolution meeting?

The resolution of a conflict does usually require one or both parties to make some kind of behavior change. But some children need more teacher support to do this than others. Susan's books and papers cascaded onto the floor and into her classmates' work space. She irritated tablemates with her many folded paper "friends," illustrated erasers, and other treasures. Her table had a Peace Talk. (See "I get mad when you take my things" on page 121.) Susan's belongings mostly stayed in her own area for the next couple of days. But then she was right back to spilling over into others' space.

The reason was that even though Susan wanted to change once she became aware of how her intrusions annoyed others, she didn't know how. So I coached her on organization, helping her remember where notebooks were stored in our classroom and finding a spot for her special "friends" to live. Because of my individual work with her, she developed the skills to actually change her behaviors.

If a student's behavior doesn't change after a conflict resolution meeting that apparently went well, think about whether the child is missing the skills needed for the behavior change. Then teach those skills to the child directly and individually.

My students would have Peace Talks all day if I let them. What should I do?

Sometimes students get engrossed in the "air time" afforded by conflict resolution. I remember a class of second graders who would have happily spent the entire day in Peace Talks if I had allowed it. And when I first taught this strategy to a class of fourth graders, it felt as if they were manufacturing conflicts to have the fun of intricate problem-solving among friends.

If you notice the conflict resolution process getting out of hand, set up a clear, limited time for it. Plan a daily independent work period and allow twenty minutes of it for conflict resolution. Have students sign up for slots during that time. Some students won't need their slot once it arrives—they'll have had time to cool off and let the disagreement dissipate. Those who want a Peace Talk for the excitement of it more than anything else will gradually lose interest once it's no longer available "on demand."

Examples of Conflict Resolution Meetings

EXAMPLE 1

"I get mad when you take my things": Conflict resolution among third grade tablemates

"I can never find my things!" exploded Susan. "The kids at my table take my stuff. They do it on purpose to make me mad."

I was surprised because there aren't a lot of "things" for students in my class to take. We share pencils, crayons, and other school supplies. "What do you mean?" I asked her.

"I can't find my writer's notebook. I can't find my personal spelling dictionary. I can't find the math problem I was working on."

Susan struggled with organization. My suspicion was that she was responsible for her lost work, but I remained neutral, careful not to reveal my thoughts. I didn't want to make Susan defensive by seeming to take sides. "Why don't you try a Peace Talk with your table?" I suggested.

This was late February, and by then the class had become proficient enough with Peace Talks that I felt confident letting these four hold one independently. But a group conference can be tricky. Observing from a distance, I was available to step in if needed.

The four students sat at their places at the table. Because this talk involved all four of them, their table seemed a more natural place than the spot behind the chart stand.

Susan began with an I-statement. "I get mad when you take my things because I need that stuff for school work. I want you to stop taking my things."

Donnie responded, "I hear you saying that we take your things, and that makes you mad." He glanced at Susan, who nodded. With this confirmation that he had understood Susan correctly, Donnie continued, "I don't mean to take your things, but they're spread all over our table. When it's time to clean up, you don't help, so I just try to figure out some place to put your things. I put them where I think they go." Although Donnie's words sounded somewhat inflammatory, he was actually stating a simple fact. Susan became so overwhelmed by cleanup tasks that she, in fact, did not help.

At that point Devon chimed in. "I hear you say that we take your things. Your things are in my work area. I already have trouble paying attention in school, and all of that stuff makes it even harder. When it's cleanup time, I put your things in the bin where they go." Devon, a student with an individual special education plan, often had trouble communicating his needs. I was excited to see him take an assertive role with the support of his tablemates.

Susan said, "I hear you both saying that my things get in your way, so you put them where you think they go." She looked at the two boys, who both nodded. "It's hard for me to keep my notebooks organized. I need more space," she added.

"I hear you say that it's hard for you to keep your things organized," said Farheen. "We need space to put our things, too."

Susan had relaxed a bit. The fact that her tablemates had listened to her seemed to have helped even though they hadn't agreed that they were maliciously stealing. Listening to them and summarizing their thoughts was also helping her see things from their point of view.

The group began to brainstorm possible solutions. "We could each keep our work in our own area," suggested Farheen.

"We could all clean up when it's cleanup time," added Devon, pointedly looking at Susan.

"We could ask each other where things go before we put other people's things away," said Susan, looking at Donnie.

Susan then realized that the next step was hers. "I'll try to keep my work in my area and clean up at cleanup time if you all agree not to put my things away without asking me."

"Let's try that for two days and see if it works," said Farheen, always the realist.

The four students shook hands all around and said, "Peace."

The next day I noticed that Susan's work was, for the most part, contained to her quadrant of the table. At cleanup time, the others were checking with Susan before they put her work away.

THINGS TO NOTE about this group Peace Talk

- *Respectful listening:* Susan, a student with behavioral and learning challenges, had really listened to her tablemates and taken their ideas seriously.

- *Equal participation:* All four students spoke up. All four remained fair and respectful. If anyone had stayed out of the conversation or dominated, or if Susan's three tablemates had ganged up meanly against her, I would have intervened immediately.

- *Adherence to the protocol:* In following the steps of the Peace Talk, the group learned new insights about a thorny problem. Summarizing each other's thoughts allowed them to begin seeing one another's point of view.

- *Group ownership:* Everyone contributed at least one potential solution, stretching the group's thinking and ensuring group ownership of the resolution.

- *Follow-up:* This experienced group planned on their own to reconvene in two days to see how things were going. If they hadn't, I would have checked in on them in a couple of days. If the solution wasn't working, I would have prompted them to choose a different one to try.

EXAMPLE 2

"You didn't pass the ball to me": A conversation between two fifth graders

The fifth graders piled into their classroom, full of conversation about the events of recess. Ms. Jones rang the chime, their class signal for silence, and told the students to gather with their reading partners.

Sammy, lower lip out and feet dragging, shuffled over to his partner, Micah. Micah sat down but Sammy remained standing. "Read by yourself today," Sammy announced to Micah in a belligerent tone. Micah glared at Sammy. He didn't look surprised but nonetheless replied, "Was' up?"

Sammy drew a deep breath and took a walk over to the I-statement poster on the classroom wall to calm down. When he returned, he said, "I was mad at you during the football game. You didn't pass the ball to me. You only pass the ball to Liam."

By this point in the year, early spring, the class had had plenty of practice in conflict resolution, and both Sammy and Micah were able to use the format without their teacher's involvement.

"You don't like it when I pass the ball to Liam instead of to you," responded Micah. "But Liam and I are on Travel All-Stars together. Liam's a better player than you are."

"So, you pass the ball to Liam because he's a better player than I am," stated Sammy. "I'll never get to be a better player if I never get the ball. I want to get the ball sometimes, too."

Micah thought about that for a minute. "You want to get the ball sometimes. You think more practice might make you a better player. Alright. Tomorrow I'll try to pass the ball to you sometimes, not just Liam."

"Okay," replied Sammy, and the two boys sat down with their two copies of *Rescuing Josh Maguire*. "We're on chapter seven, right?" asked Sammy. Sammy and Micah began to read.

THINGS TO NOTE about this conflict resolution conversation

- *Preparation:* The class had practiced conflict resolution carefully. Sammy and Micah were comfortable using the strategy independently.

- *A trusting relationship:* Sammy and Micah were reading partners. They had a history of working together and helping each other.

- *Listening:* Micah listened to Sammy and realized that he had a point, that Sammy would become a better player if he got the ball sometimes.

- *A quick resolution:* Once Micah understood Sammy's point of view, he quickly agreed to pass the ball to him sometimes. There was no need to brainstorm possible solutions before reaching agreement.

A SCRIPT FOR COACHING CONFLICT RESOLUTION

When you begin coaching children in conflict resolution, it may help to have the following script handy for quick reference.

Help the first child (aggrieved party) state the issue:

Say to first child: *Tell _____ (second child) what you told me. Make sure you look at her. _____ (second child), your job is to listen carefully.*

Help the second child listen and restate what she heard:

Say to second child: *First let _____ (first child) know that you understood her by telling her what you heard. You can start with "I heard you say that...."*

After second child speaks, say to her: *Now check with _____ (first child) to make sure you understood her accurately.*

Help the second child state her point of view:

Say to second child: *Now it's your turn to tell _____ (first child) your point of view about what happened. _____ (first child), you're going to listen carefully.*

Help the first child listen and restate what she heard:

Say to first child: *Now tell _____ (second child) what you heard her say. Later you'll get a chance to say whether or not you agree with her. Right now you're letting her know that you understood her, by just saying what you heard.*

After first child speaks, say to her: *Now check with _____ (second child) to make sure you understood her accurately.*

Continue the process until both children have been heard:

Say to first child: *Do you have anything to add?*
If the child says yes, repeat the process described above.

Then say to the second child: *Do you have anything to add?*
Again, if the child says yes, repeat the process described above.

Help the children reach a solution:

Say to first child: *Do you have any ideas for solving this problem?*
Say to second child: *Do you have any ideas for solving this problem?*

 **Making it work for you**

Posting the steps in a conflict resolution meeting, with key reminders under certain steps, helps children stick to the format. Here's how such a chart might look.

1. Cool off.

Walk around the classroom, take some "yoga breaths," or get a drink of water.

2. Think of an I-statement

"I feel/felt _____ when I see/saw (or hear/heard) _____ because _____. What I would like is _____."

Tell your partner "I have an I-statement for you." Use respectful body language.

Go to a special place to talk. Look over the ground rules.

3. Tell your partner your I-statement.

4. Your partner says her/his understanding of the I-statement.

"I heard you say _____" or "So, what you're saying is _____."

5. Your partner tells you her/his ideas (either an I-statement or a statement of facts).

6. Say your understanding of your partner's ideas.

"I heard you say _____" or "So, what you're saying is _____."

7. Keep going until both of you have said everything that you need to.

Remember to state what you understand your partner to have said each time.

8. Brainstorm for solutions.

"Maybe we could solve the problem by _____."

9. Choose one idea that you are both comfortable with.

10. Make a plan to try that idea. Shake hands and say "Peace."

CHAPTER FOUR

Role-Playing

The children in Ms. Smith's second grade class are getting ready for a fall nature walk. The class has learned about the appropriate use of hand lenses. Ms. Smith knows that problems may arise because there are only twelve hand lenses for twenty-four students. She also knows that with an active second grade science curriculum, the children will be sharing hand lenses frequently all year. She decides to call the children to the meeting area to address the potential problems proactively.

"When we go outside to observe plants, each pair of students will share one hand lens," she says to the class. "Let's pretend I'm in one of the pairs. I really want to use that hand lens as much as possible. I want to look at those plants up close. But I know my partner wants to use the lens, too. One of our rules says 'Be fair.' What can I do to be fair in this situation?"

Students contribute ideas. Bobby suggests that the partners take five-minute turns. Fallon suggests that each person look at one plant and then pass the hand lens to the partner. Miuke suggests that the partners hold the hand lens together and look at the same time. Ms. Smith lists all of the children's ideas on a chart.

Then she says, "We're going to do a short play about the hand lenses. Fallon, will you be my partner?" Ms. Smith chooses one of the listed ideas to dramatize. "Fallon, I'll look at a plant and then pass the hand lens to you." She acts out using the hand lens to examine a plant and then passes the lens to Fallon. Fallon acts out examining another plant and then passes the lens back to Ms. Smith.

"Cut," Ms. Smith says. The play is over and the class discusses what they noticed.

The class continues to try out ideas from the chart in short role-plays. After each round, they discuss the effectiveness of the idea.

The entire exercise takes about fifteen minutes. When the children go out to explore in the field, Ms. Smith sees that partners are respectfully sharing the hand lenses, using the ideas from their short role-plays and discussions.

Purpose: Preparing Children to Deal with Social Dilemmas

Role-plays like the one just described teach children skills for handling everyday school problems—problems they're likely to encounter or problems that have already come up and seem likely to become chronic. Situations suitable for role-playing spring from the real life of the classroom and range from how to share supplies to how to tell someone she's hurt your feelings.

The purpose is to help students develop a repertoire of positive responses before the problems occur or reoccur. Then, when the problems do come up, the children are more likely to handle them well—in ways that are caring of the individuals involved and of the classroom community as a whole.

Role-playing is one way to bring classroom rules and expectations to life. The dramatic element of role-plays helps children think concretely about how to apply global rules and expectations to specific situations. They're challenged to use reason and ethical thinking, to look at situations from many points of view, and to communicate with assertion and kindness. By helping children develop verbal and nonverbal skills for negotiating complex situations, role-plays teach them to be empathetic, fair, and creative problem-solvers.

When to Do Role-Plays

Teachers can introduce role-playing shortly after the class agrees on its rules. One year one of our rules was "Be kind." We dramatized various ways we could be kind during lunch toward people we didn't know very well. Role-plays continued all year long about issues such as how to apply our rules "Be honest" and "Be kind" when giving partners feedback on their work, and how to honor our rule "Take care of each other" when picking teams for recess games.

The goal, however, is not to role-play everything. This strategy is meant for the following types of situations. (See the box "Typical Situations to Role-Play" for specific examples.)

Dilemmas with more than one right solution

There is not one right way to include everyone, not one right way to build on each other's ideas in a discussion, not one right way to express hurt feelings. Role-plays, because they encourage children to consider many possible ways to navigate through interactions with others, are meant for these kinds of complex situations.

In this way, role-playing differs from modeling. Modeling teaches children one prescribed behavior. If we want to teach children one right way to do something—for example, how to use certain equipment safely, how to give a friendly handshake, or how to go to their seat if they come to class late—we use modeling, not role-playing. (For a brief description of modeling, see Appendix B.)

Common and challenging situations

Teachers use role-plays to address dilemmas that come up frequently, dilemmas they know from prior experience may be challenging to students. For example, during the first week of school, first graders may need

Typical Situations to Role-Play

We can't, and wouldn't want to, dramatize every classroom situation. None of us has time for that. Nor would students stay interested if we engaged them in incessant role-playing. Within the broad guidelines provided in this chapter, it's up to each teacher to decide which situations to enact, depending on students' needs and experiences. Here are some typical situations to role-play.

Beginning of the year

Social situations

- Inviting someone eating alone at lunch to sit with you

- Starting a conversation with your lunch partner

- Asking if you may join an activity at recess

- Inviting someone to join an activity at recess

- Choosing a good spot in the Morning Meeting circle

Academic situations

- Sharing limited materials

- Working independently while the teacher is working with other students

- Deciding what to do if you forgot your homework

- Sharing a book during buddy reading

- Telling your partner about the book you're reading

- Building on others' ideas during literature circles

- Solving a math problem with a small group

- Making kind and honest comments about classmates' work

Later in the year

Social situations

- Including a new class member at lunch or recess

- Taking action if you see someone making fun of another student

- Choosing teams fairly

- Being a good sport if you're losing (or winning) a game

Academic situations

- Working on a collaborative project: listening to group members, asserting your own ideas, figuring out what to do if you each want something different

- Explaining your work to a parent at a school "open house" or work exhibition

help figuring out how to share school supplies with tablemates. Sixth graders may need ideas for how to include everyone at lunch. Children in all grades could benefit from role-plays on respectfully telling someone to stop a bothersome behavior or pointing out someone's mistake in a friendly way.

Situations that have not yet occurred

Role-playing works best when children are calm and able to rationally imagine a range of solutions. This is therefore not a strategy to use in the middle of an active conflict, but rather before a predictable conflict flares up.

For example, when children are getting ready to work together to design and build models for a social studies project, a teacher might initiate a role-play about how to decide who's going to take the final project home, thereby averting a conflict she knows is otherwise likely.

Often it's useful to role-play situations that led students into a conflict and that are likely to come up again. In those cases, however, it's important to wait until tempers have calmed.

For example, a group of students had a heated argument on the playground about sharing the basketball. Their teacher waited until the next day before leading a role-play about how to decide who gets to use the basketball first and how to make sure everyone gets a turn. Role-playing would not have been a good strategy for handling the argument in the moment.

To help students in the middle of a conflict, consider using conflict resolution (see Chapter Three).

Steps in a Role-Play

A role-play consists of these steps:

1. Describe a specific situation.

2. Name the positive goal.

3. Record children's ideas.

4. Act out one idea, with the teacher taking the "tricky role."

5. Ask children what they noticed.

6. Act out another idea, with a student taking the "tricky role."

7. Ask children what they noticed.

8. Continue acting out the other ideas listed.

9. Sum up lessons learned.

10. Follow up.

The sample role-play that follows illustrates these steps. It's a role-play I did with a third grade class one September. The students were getting to know each other. Within our room and under my watchful eye, they were treating each other kindly and fairly.

I knew, however, that it was more challenging for them to be friendly to everyone at recess, where there was less supervision. I wanted to underscore the fact that our classroom rules about kindness and friendliness still applied at recess, even though the children physically stepped out of the room.

I decided a role-play would be a good way to do this. We would dramatize a scene in which a student was standing around with no one to play with. I allotted twenty minutes for this role-play. If I had been teaching younger children, say kindergartners or first graders, I would have broken the role-play up over two days and allotted ten minutes for each session.

I gathered the children in a circle and introduced the role-play by telling them we were going to do some short plays about recess. They were excited. They loved drama. Once they were settled, I went through each of the ten steps. It's important to do each step because each one is critical to the overall success of the role-play.

Step 1. Describe a specific situation

Using an "I" voice to draw the children in and put them right into the action, I said, "Let's pretend it's time for recess, and I'm so excited to see all of my friends after the summer. I can hardly wait to see Shadia from Ms. DiStasio's class. I haven't seen her since June. I love to play with Shadia."

Then, referring to our classroom rules, I continue, "But wait, there's a new girl in our class. She might not have anyone to play with. Our rules follow us wherever we go. One rule says 'Be kind and friendly,' and it's not kind to leave people alone on the playground unless they want to be alone."

I was careful to include and acknowledge the difficulty of the situation. We're all happy to see old friends and sometimes forget others around us as a result. Acknowledging these feelings makes the role-play real.

I might have enhanced my description with some simple acting, perhaps making the motions of starting to play with a friend and then looking over at another student who's nearby. It's perfectly fine to add such actions if it will help students picture the scene.

Either way, I stop the description at the point where I must decide how to behave—in this case, what to do about the fact that I want to play with Shadia yet have a responsibility to be kind and friendly to the classmate standing around alone. I don't name possible behaviors. That step is for the students.

Step 2. Name the positive goal

In this step, I tell the students what positive goal to achieve as they brainstorm for solutions to the dilemma. Continuing in the "I" voice, I asked, "How can I be friendly to students I don't know very well? What can I do that takes care of myself and Shadia and the other students, too, especially ones who don't have friends to play with?"

Step 3. Record children's ideas

This is a collaborative strategy. After I state the issue, the children begin contributing ideas.

Nicky raised his hand. "You could ask someone who doesn't have anyone to play with to join you in shooting hoops." Nicky loved to play basketball on the blacktop with a couple of good friends.

"What would that look like and sound like?" I asked.

"You could say, 'Would you like to shoot hoops?'" Nicky answered.

I wrote his idea on the chart.

Rayanne raised her hand next. "You could ask someone new to our school to play jump rope. You might say, 'Do you like to jump rope? Some of us are going to jump over by the swings. Come and join us.'"

I added Rayanne's idea to the chart.

In similar fashion I wrote down other ideas the children offered. If someone had suggested something that didn't honor our rules, I would have redirected the brainstorming by referring to the rules. "I'm concerned that that might not feel kind and friendly," I might have said.

Soon we had a list of various ways to ask someone to play:

Would you like to shoot hoops?

Do you like to jump rope? … Come and join us.

We're going to walk around the yard. Would you like to join us?

Would you like to play Four Square with us?

In this role-play we brainstormed four ideas. At the beginning of the year, it's usually best to enact all brainstormed solutions so all children who suggested solutions will feel their ideas are being honored. That means taking two to four ideas, about what children's attention span and our classroom schedules will allow.

Later in the year, when the community is stronger, it's fine to brainstorm more ideas than will be dramatized. The process of choosing some ideas to enact naturally weeds out ones that are less comfortable for the children. As the year goes on, children no longer take it personally if their idea isn't chosen.

Step 4. Act out one idea, with the teacher taking the "tricky role"

I told the children that I was going to choose one of the ideas—the "Do you like to jump rope?" idea—for us to try in a short play. I asked a student, Clarissa, if she would be in the play with me. I told the class that Clarissa would play the child who was new in the school, and I would play the "tricky role," the student who would act out the idea.

I also told the children that the audience had an important job. They were to watch carefully and think about how they might feel if they were my character and if they were Clarissa's character. And they were to notice how we were both being kind and friendly.

With this particular class, we started the play by all saying, "Lights, camera, action," complete with gestures. This step is not necessary, but some classes enjoy it.

Clarissa stood at the edge of the circle, alone. I looked at the chart, then walked over to Clarissa and, with a smile and a friendly voice, said, "Do you like to jump rope? We're playing over by the swings. Would you like to come and join us?"

Clarissa smiled and said, "I'd love to."

"Cut," I said. It's important for the teacher—who always retains the role of director even if she's playing a character—to stop the play as soon as the positive behavior is acted out. This keeps the scene short and the children's attention focused on the positive behavior.

Step 5. Ask children what they noticed

I asked the audience, "What did you notice during our play?"

Amy said, "You were friendly. You looked at her and smiled. I would have been happy if I was Clarissa."

Jimmy said, "She looked lonely when she was standing by herself. When you asked her, she smiled like she was hoping to make a friend."

Julius said, "What if Clarissa didn't like to jump rope? What would've happened then?"

I turned to Clarissa and asked, "What might you have done?"

Clarissa thought for a minute and said, "I could've said, 'I'd like to come and watch.'"

Turning to the class, I said, "What I did in this play is something you might try doing to be friendly to students whom you don't know very well."

Step 6. Act out another idea, with a student taking the "tricky role"

I asked Clarissa if she'd like to play the "tricky role" this time. I knew that she would play it with a genuinely kind and friendly demeanor. I wanted the students to have a mental image of kindness and friendliness, so it was important to avoid any possibility of a student's playing the opposite or playing a parody of these qualities.

I asked Lalo if he'd take the role of a student who didn't have anyone to play with. He eagerly agreed. Like most children, he loved to dramatize and wanted to participate.

I told Clarissa to pick one of the ideas from our chart. She picked shooting hoops. If I had been teaching much younger children, say kindergartners, I would have picked an idea for the actor to dramatize.

"Lights, camera, action!" the class said.

Lalo stood at the edge of the circle, looking lonely. He was into the part. Clarissa walked over to him. "Would you like to shoot hoops?" she asked. "Sure," Lalo answered, and they walked across the circle together.

"Cut," I said.

Step 7. Ask children what they noticed

I asked for observations, and again the children noted friendly expressions and friendly voices. They noticed how lonely Lalo looked, standing by himself. Alex said that if he'd been Lalo, he would have been "so glad" that someone had asked him to play.

Maeve said, "It sounded funny to just go up to someone and ask if they wanted to shoot hoops. It sounded like Clarissa needed to say something else first, like 'Hi.'"

"Shall I add that to our chart?" I asked. The class agreed, and I wrote "Hi" in front of "Would you like to shoot hoops?"

Step 8. Continue acting out the other ideas listed

We continued to act out all the ideas on the list. In each round I picked the actors, paying attention to choosing pairs that would work seriously together. Each time, the actor playing the "tricky role" picked a new idea from our brainstormed list to dramatize.

Just before our twenty minutes were up, I stopped the activity to do a brief closure.

Step 9. Sum up lessons learned

Summing up the role-play, I said to the class, "So, here are the ideas that we've generated and dramatized for including classmates we don't know very well:

Hi. Would you like to shoot hoops?
Do you like to jump rope? … Come and join us.
We're going to walk around the yard. Would you like to join us?
Would you like to play Four Square with us?

We're going to try these ideas this week."

Then I left the children with a summing-up reflection question: "How will these ideas help you be friendly to each other at recess?" It was almost time for PE, so rather than holding a whole-class discussion, I had the children think quietly for a minute and then share their thoughts with a neighbor. They were lively and engaged, thinking about how they'd be friendly to students they didn't know very well.

Step 10. Follow up

In the days and weeks after a role-play, it's critical to follow up on the lessons learned. For example, before children go into potentially rocky situations, the teacher might remind them of the positive behaviors they role-played for such situations. Afterward, she lets the children know that she noticed them using the behaviors.

Following up might also mean creating opportunities for the children to do some self-noticing and self-reflection on their use of the behaviors. Following up helps children consolidate their learning and shows that their teacher is serious in expecting them to adopt the role-played behaviors.

I found several opportunities during the week to do quick follow-ups of our role-play on friendly playground behavior. As the students lined up for recess the next day, I reminded them about our ideas for including everyone. After recess, when they were all lined up in the hall for a quick bathroom break, I asked them to put their thumbs up if they had tried "Would you like to shoot hoops?" and then thumbs up if they had tried each of the other ideas.

Later in the week I asked a question on the written message we use for

Morning Meeting about whether they, personally, were feeling included at recess.

If needed, I could also have easily folded a follow-up into a writers' workshop, asking the children to do a quick-write on how included they felt at recess that day or what they did to include someone else.

Keys to Success in Role-Playing

The following can help you get the most out of role-playing.

Plan how to describe the dilemma and the goal

Careful teacher planning makes for more effective role-plays. An important part of this planning is thinking about how to describe the dilemma to be role-played and the positive goal children should aim for when brainstorming solutions. Here are some tips.

Acknowledge children's real feelings

When framing the dilemma, include enough detail and realism so children will be engaged. To come up with these realistic details, I try to empathize with the children.

For the recess role-play described above, I thought about why it might be hard for children to be friendly to everyone on the playground. I knew that many students are excited to see their friends after the summer. They probably just aren't thinking about a student who might not have friends yet. I planned to acknowledge these understandable feelings as part of my initial description of the problem.

On the day of the role-play, my words, "I'm so excited to see all of my friends after the summer. I can hardly wait to see Shadia from Ms. DiStasio's class. I haven't seen her since June. I love to play with Shadia" showed students that I understood where they were coming from. Such acknowledgement of students' difficulties leads them to take the role-play seriously. This is especially true with older students.

Refer to classroom rules

In stating the dilemma and the goal that children are to aim for, refer to the classroom rules the class created. Early in my teaching career, my class would agree on our rules the first day of school, I would put them up on the wall, and we would never discuss them again.

Over the years, I've learned that I can keep the rules alive by constantly referring to them. These references subtly remind students that they agreed to be kind and friendly—or respectful, or safe, or whatever were their stated ideals. Referring to the rules during a role-play also increases students' interest because they're invested in the rules. After all, they had worked hard to create those rules.

For the recess role-play, I planned to underscore our classroom rule "Be kind and friendly." I worked it into the description of the dilemma by saying, "One rule says 'Be kind and friendly,' and it's not kind to leave people alone on the playground unless they want to be alone."

And when naming the behavior goal I referred to the rule by saying, "How can I be friendly to students I don't know very well? What can I do that takes care of myself and Shadia and the other students, too, especially ones who don't have friends to play with?"

Clarify the behavior goal to yourself

To be able to name for children a positive goal to aim for as they brainstorm solutions, we need to first clarify the goal to ourselves. For the recess role-play, I articulated to myself that I wanted the children to take care of themselves, their friends, and their classmates who don't have friends to play with, which is an application of the class's "Be kind and friendly" rule.

From there it was easy to come up with the goal "take care of myself and Shadia and the other students, too, especially ones who don't have friends to play with."

Name how you want children to behave

In naming the behavior goal, it's important to say what behavior is desired rather than what is not desired. This helps children envision and practice positive behavior.

In the goal I stated in the recess role-play, the words "take care of …" get children to picture positive actions. Words such as "safe," "helpful," and "kind" and phrases such as "fun for everyone" and "so that everyone can learn" all frame children's thinking, guiding them to form a positive vision of how school can be.

Think ahead about who should play the roles

In a role-play, the tone is set by the first players. That's why in the first round, the teacher always takes the "tricky role," the character who must decide how to respond to the dilemma. The teacher can then model how to play the part with positive and caring affect.

But other players set the tone as well, so think about which children would take the activity seriously. Sometimes I also think about whether a certain student's empathy might be stretched or self-confidence boosted from playing certain roles.

For the recess role-play I decided to ask Clarissa to play the child who needed a friend because I knew she would take the dramatization seriously. In addition, I thought that as someone with many friends, she might, through playing this role, develop greater empathy for those who didn't have friends.

For subsequent rounds in a role-play, think about assigning the "non-tricky role" to children who have difficulty with the skill you want to teach. Putting them in the role-play, but on the receiving end of the positive behaviors being dramatized, can raise their consciousness about the desired behaviors without the risk that they'll play their roles inappropriately.

Be careful, however, to avoid having two such children play opposite each other in the same round, or the role-play may end up illustrating negative behaviors. For example, I asked Raub and Lee, both children who preferred to play exclusively with their good friends, to be in a role-play about inviting an unfamiliar person to play. Raub was to be the inviter and Lee the invited.

When Raub asked Lee to play, his voice sounded more annoyed than friendly, and he looked away. His verbal language and body language conveyed that he'd rather do just about anything than play with Lee. Lee, in turn, didn't even look at Raub but scraped his foot on the ground and mumbled unintelligibly. This performance most emphatically did not meet the goals I'd had in mind when I'd planned the role-play.

Plan when and where the role-play will take place

I set aside twenty minutes each week for role-playing and other social skills lessons. With young students, kindergartners and first graders, I break up this time into two ten-minute sessions. For the third grade recess role-play, I decided we would meet in the early afternoon, during the twenty minutes between Quiet Time and music class. I knew the students would be attentive right after Quiet Time.

The children would sit in a circle on the meeting rug to encourage face-to-face conversation. I would sit in the circle next to a chart stand so that I could record their ideas. With fifth or sixth graders, two students can come up to the chart to do the recording, which encourages student ownership and investment. But these third graders would be able to focus better without that added responsibility.

Dramatize only the positive behavior

Just as it's important to name only the desired behavior when stating the behavior goal, it's also important to dramatize only the positive behavior. That way, the ideal, the way we want things to be, is what is firmly cemented in students' minds.

When I first began teaching, my classes often dramatized the "right" way and the "wrong" way to handle a situation. I can still remember one role-play that my student teacher and I did, in which we acted out not listening to each other, complete with every rude flourish. Of course we acted out respectful listening as a contrast, but I have no lasting mental image of that. What did it look like and sound like? I have no idea. The high drama of the negative model is what sticks in my mind. Children, likewise, are more prone to remembering the negative model than the positive.

Even when acting out the situation in the initial setup for the role-play, I try to stay away from dramatizing negative behaviors. For example, I might have a student dramatize being alone on the playground in setting up a role-play about inclusion, but I would avoid having a student grab a toy away from another as a setup for a role-play about sharing.

Honor children's perceptions

Be open to students' ideas when discussing possible ways to handle the dilemma. If children, especially older children, think there's only one acceptable answer—the teacher's—they'll become disengaged and sometimes silly.

When the class discusses what they noticed in the role-plays, again be open to students' observations. Use your words and tone to show your intention. The simple words "What did you notice?" powerfully honor children's perceptions. If children suggest ways to fine-tune what was role-played, as when Maeve suggested saying "Hi" before asking a classmate to shoot hoops, take the suggestions seriously as long as they're made with sincerity and respect.

As the class gains experience with role-playing and builds trust in their community, you can ask questions beyond "What did you notice?" You might ask "When is it hard to do this? When is it easy?" This lets children know that you want and expect them to be honest with themselves and the group.

Keep it fast paced

A role-play often takes between fifteen and twenty minutes, sometimes less. Keep it moving. Dramatize two to four scenarios. Allow time for children to discuss and reflect, but don't belabor anything. Children will be more attentive and engaged if things move right along.

Model the naming of positive behaviors

After each round of acting, teachers ask children to name what they noticed and to put it in positive terms—to say what the actors did, such as "Clarissa used a friendly voice" or "Lalo looked at him and smiled," not what the actors didn't do. Sticking to the positive like this reinforces the positive behaviors.

This can be a challenge for children, though. Often their first impulse is to say what negative behaviors their peers didn't use—for example, "He didn't say 'gimme.'"

The most effective way to prepare students to name the positive behaviors they saw is to do the same ourselves in everyday classroom life. We are powerful role models for our students. Practice saying "I noticed … " or "I saw … " when students take care of each other and follow the rules. For example, "I noticed you asked for that book in a friendly voice" or "I saw that you got your folders calmly and quietly."

Be careful not to use this positive naming as a way to manipulate other children into copying the wanted behavior. For example, if Julie came to the meeting circle quickly and quietly, let her know in private that you noticed, rather than announcing to the class, "Julie came to the circle nicely" in hopes of cajoling or shaming the other children into doing the same. If you want to reinforce a behavior that the entire group is showing, name the positive behavior to the class in a matter-of-fact voice. "You all got ready for lunch quickly and safely."

Children can tell manipulation from direct, honest acknowledging. It's the acknowledging that we want them to receive and learn to give.

Questions from Teachers

What if the actors or audience members get silly?

Remember that the teacher is the director. You can stop the action at any time. Simply saying, "We'll stop now and come back to this later," is your prerogative as the leader of the classroom community. As you reflect on what might have caused the silliness to begin with, you might think about the following questions.

Are you honestly open to all sincere and respectful ideas that your students may contribute? Children can get silly if they don't think this strategy is really about their ideas.

What about choice of actors? Have you chosen two actors who have a different agenda from the one you planned? This is what happened in a role-play on inclusiveness in my classroom one year, when two students acted out playing exclusively with each other, perhaps to show the others what good friends they were—not what I envisioned when I planned the role-play. Or have you chosen two actors who are painfully shy and uncomfortable in the role?

Once things get off track, children, perhaps feeling uncomfortable, can get silly and out of control. Try again with a slightly different cast.

When things go awry and I think it's because of the way I structured things, I find that it's best to simply restructure things in the future rather than discussing the off-track behavior with my students. Revisiting mistakes that were more mine than theirs doesn't help them. If the silliness continues another day, then it's time for a discussion of the purpose and importance of role-play.

What if we role-play a skill, but the children don't use it in real life?

Are you reminding the children about the role-play right before they encounter a potentially tricky situation? For example, a simple "Remember, friendly and kind" said right before recess can help children remember the behaviors they dramatized yesterday.

Sometimes children need more than a role-play. If you've role-played including everyone on the playground and you remind children of the role-play before they head out to recess, and they still aren't being inclusive, perhaps you need a class meeting (see Chapter Five). These meetings allow children to explore their thoughts and feelings about the issue and often give teachers new information about what's going on with their students.

I remember a year when one student, Sonia, seemed to be off by herself during nearly every recess. The class role-played including everyone, but it didn't help. Then we had a class meeting on this topic. We'd agreed at the beginning of the meeting that no one would name any names, and the children abided by that agreement. But comments such as "Some kids say that you shouldn't play with some other kids" made it clear to me that a couple of socially powerful girls were purposely excluding Sonia. The class came up with strategies to make sure that everyone had someone to play with, and I dealt with the two excluders privately.

My sixth graders are very self-conscious. What would help them be comfortable revealing honest thoughts and feelings in role-plays?

My colleague Melanie Carroll addresses this issue by having her classes role-play situations drawn from literature. This way, she keeps the problem one step removed from the classroom, which enables children to be a bit more dispassionate and objective than they might otherwise be.

So many young adult novels and sophisticated picture books explore social situations that are common in our classrooms. For example, in Eleanor Estes' still timely 1944 novel *The Hundred Dresses*, Peggy begins to "have fun with"—in other words cruelly tease—an immigrant girl. Her best friend, Maddie, feels uncomfortable about the teasing but is afraid that if she objects, she could be the next object of Peggy's "fun."

The first three short chapters develop the story of how the teasing began and gained a life of its own. At the beginning of the fourth chapter, Maddie expresses her fears that she could be teased next and says, "If only Peggy would decide to stop of her own accord."

This is the spot at which to stop and ask students questions that put them there, in the story. "How do you think Peggy is feeling right now? What might be hard for Peggy?" and "What might be hard for Maddie?" We can then draw students' attention to their own feelings and behavior by asking "Have you ever felt the way Maddie is feeling? Have you ever found yourself acting like Peggy? Like Maddie?"

Once the students have discussed these questions, you might state the positive goal: "If Maddie were in our class, with our rule to 'be kind,' what might she do next to live by that rule?" Students can then brainstorm ideas and try them out as short role-plays.

Here are just some of the many other children's books that offer situations for role-plays.

Young adult novels

Blubber (by Judy Blume)—Linda is teased by classmates about her weight. Caroline and Wendy start to harass Linda in the girls' room. They tell Jill to pull off Linda's Halloween costume. What should Linda do? Later on the kids throw Linda's lunch around the cafeteria and Linda gets blamed because her food is on the floor. The girls make a list of things they don't like about Linda. What would you do if you were there? Like *The Hundred Dresses*, this book provides a springboard for looking at the role of the bystander and ways to support classmates.

Flying Solo (by Ralph Fletcher)—How can we respond to mean teasing? A sixth grade class spends the day without their teacher. Christopher sings a silly song about Sean's name (in the chapter "8:12 AM, First Bell"). Bastian teases Vicki about her size (in the chapter "9:00 AM, Kids Rule"). How might Sean and Vicki respond? How might their classmates respond?

Follow My Leader (by James B. Garfield)—How do you reconcile with a friend who's hurt you? Jimmy loses his eyesight when Mike throws a firecracker on the baseball field. Jimmy gets a seeing-eye dog, and Mike teases Jimmy's dog, leading the dog to bite Mike. In Chapter Sixteen, Jimmy decides to reconcile with Mike. What might Jimmy say? What might Mike say?

In the Year of the Boar and Jackie Robinson (by Bette Bao Lord)—Shirley is a recent immigrant. She doesn't know American customs and is having trouble making friends. In Chapter Five, Mabel invites Shirley to play stickball. The other kids don't want Shirley to join. What might Mabel say? What might Shirley say? When Shirley doesn't understand the game, what might her teammates do to teach her?

The Real Me (by Betty Miles)—What might you do if you disagree with a school policy? On the first day of middle school, Barbara discovers that the only PE choices for girls are slimnastics and field hockey. She'd rather play tennis, but that's for boys only. What might Barbara do?

Emma-Jean Lazarus Fell Out of a Tree (by Lauren Tarshis)—Emma-Jean has limited social skills. She "helps" some of her seventh grade classmates with their social dilemmas with varying success. Kaitlin, Colleen's best friend, has shifted her allegiance to Laura. Emma-Jean's solution backfires. What might Colleen do to take care of the problem herself?

Sophisticated picture books

A Day's Work (by Eve Bunting)—An immigrant day laborer and his grandson pull up the newly planted seedlings and leave the weeds. What might they do to fix their mistake?

The Brand New Kid (by Katie Couric)—Lazlo is the new boy in school. The other children tease him. Katie realizes how unhappy he is. What might she do to be kind to Lazlo?

Odd Velvet (by Mary Whitcomb)—Odd Velvet is different from the other children. Everyone is polite to her but no one wants to pick her for a partner. What might Velvet do to be true to herself and make friends? Little by little her classmates get to know Velvet. They are intrigued. What might they do to make friends with Velvet?

Weslandia (by Paul Fleischman)—Wesley, very much an individual, is tormented by the other boys. Later, Wesley creates his own civilization. The other boys are intrigued. How might Wesley reach out to the other boys while remaining true to himself?

Wings (by Christopher Myers)—Ikarus Jackson has wings that help him fly above the earth. Kids tease him. What might he do? Ikarus starts to hide his wings. But when one student supports him, Ikarus lets his spirit soar. This is another book that provides a springboard for a role-play on being true to oneself.

Smoky Night (by Eve Bunting)—Set during the Los Angeles riots, this book provides a way to look at reaching out across racial divisions. An African American family and a Korean American family keep their distance. When rioting breaks out in the street, their building catches on fire. Later on the firemen arrive in the shelter with Daniel's cat and Mrs. Kim's cat, saved from the fire. What might Daniel say to Mrs. Kim?

The Other Side (by Jacqueline Woodson)—Clover and Annie, an African American girl and a Caucasian girl, live next door to each other. The setting is 1950s United States, and they're expected to avoid each other. The two girls watch each other. How might they make friends?

Examples of Role-Plays

EXAMPLE 1

Kindergartners: Learning to share crayons

It was the third week of school. The children in Ms. Stark's kindergarten had developed classroom rules and were now learning how to follow them. Ms. Stark knew that sharing materials is typically challenging for kindergartners. Kindergarten is the first school experience for many children, and even children who've been in preschool typically need review about sharing materials.

Ms. Stark gathered the kindergartners in a circle and introduced the role-play by telling them simply, "We're going to do some short plays."

Describing a specific situation

"Yesterday we learned about our new crayons and began to use them," said Ms. Stark.

"Let's pretend that I'm drawing a picture of my mom and our cat. I love drawing my picture. My mom's going to have a blue dress. I need that blue crayon to draw her blue dress. Micah is using the only blue crayon at our table. He's drawing the sky, which needs to be blue. Our rules say to be kind."

Notice that Ms. Stark acknowledged a reason that a five-year-old might feel she needs the crayon: "to draw her blue dress." This made the dilemma feel real to the children.

Naming the positive goal

"How can I get Micah to give me that blue crayon and still follow our rule to be kind?" Ms. Stark asked.

Recording children's ideas

"There's more than one way to ask for a crayon kindly," said Ms. Stark. "Who has an idea about how I might ask Micah for the blue crayon in a way that's kind?"

Ms. Stark was explicit about the fact that there are many ways to ask kindly. She wanted the children to know they weren't searching for one right answer that the teacher knows, but rather finding answers together as a class.

Mina's hand popped up. "We could say, 'Could I use the crayon next?'" Ms. Stark recorded "Could I use the crayon next?" on the chart.

Pete raised his hand. "Say, 'I want that crayon. Give it to me now.'"

Ms. Stark wasn't comfortable with Pete's idea. Using a respectful voice, she said, "'Give it to me now' is something that kids sometimes say, but it doesn't go with our rule to be kind." Ms. Stark didn't want to discourage Pete from contributing, so she was careful to keep her tone positive and acknowledge that students sometimes use those words, but she didn't include his idea on the chart.

"We could say 'Please,' like 'Please give me the crayon.'" Phong said.

Ms. Stark recorded Phong's idea.

The class had generated two ideas. Ms. Stark said, "Now we're going to put on short puppet shows about these ideas." The use of puppets helps kindergartners, with their still-tenuous grasp of pretend versus real, remember that the role-play is pretend. Ms. Stark also used puppets because she knew they would engage the kindergartners. The children listened attentively. They were excited about puppet shows.

Acting out one idea, with teachers playing roles

Because this was the class's first role-play, Ms. Stark and her teaching assistant would play both roles in the first round. She wanted to make sure the children understood exactly what was expected, and she knew that five-year-olds would benefit from seeing a role-play before they took the acting roles.

Ms. Stark said, "Hmm, I think I'll try Mina's idea. Ms. Stephen, would you be in the play with me?" Then she told the class, "Now I'm going to start the play. I'm going to say 'Action,' and then it begins."

"Action."

With the bear puppet on her hand, she turned to Ms. Stephen, who had the rabbit puppet on her hand, and said, "Rabbit, could I use the blue crayon next?"

Rabbit/Ms. Stephen replied, "I'm using it right now, but you can use it when I'm finished."

"Stop," said Ms. Stark.

Asking children what they noticed

Ms. Stark turned to the students sitting in the circle. "What did you notice about the way Bear asked?"

"Bear used a kind voice," said Ben.

"Bear didn't grab," said Ava.

Later in the year, Ms. Stark might have asked Ava, "What *did* Bear do if she didn't grab?" But for the first role-play of the year, she let this go.

"How was Bear following our rule, 'Be kind'?" asked Ms. Stark.

"She asked kindly and didn't, like, say, 'Gimme,'" said Ming.

Acting out a second idea, with students playing roles

In the second round, Ms. Stark played the "tricky role" herself again, but asked a student to play the other role. She invited a child who sometimes had trouble asking for things kindly.

"Kim," said Ms. Stark, "would you like to play the part of Rabbit in our next play?"

Notice that Ms. Stark asked. If Kim hadn't wanted to play the part of Rabbit, that would have been okay. Kim, however, was excited and put the rabbit puppet on her hand. "Hmm," said Ms. Stark, "this time I think I'll try Phong's idea. When I say 'Action,' we'll start."

"Action."

"Please give me the blue crayon," said Bear/Ms. Stark.

Rabbit/Kim responded, "Okay, when I finish my sky."

"Stop," Ms. Stark said.

Asking children what they noticed

"What did you notice about the way Bear asked for the blue crayon?" Ms. Stark asked the class.

"'Please' is a polite word," contributed Greta.

"I noticed that Rabbit looked like she didn't want to give the crayon to Bear, but when Bear said 'please,' she said, 'When I finish my sky,'" added Paul. "She thought she could finish first."

This was the kindergartners' first experience with role-playing, so Ms. Stark decided to end it right there. The next day the class would role-play again, focusing on how to answer when someone asks for a crayon.

Summing up lessons learned

"How might these ideas help us ask for crayons or other supplies when we need them?" Ms. Stark asked the class.

Paul, always the summarizer, replied, "We need to ask, not tell."

Phong, remembering the idea that he shared, said, "We need to say 'Please.'"

Following up

The next day, as the children were beginning their drawings of their families, Ms. Stark said, "Remember our plays yesterday. Ask for crayons with a kind voice."

THINGS TO NOTE about this kindergarten role-play

- *A realistic scenario:* Ms. Stark described a situation that comes up often and feels real to the kindergartners.

- *Reference to classroom rules:* Ms. Stark asked, "How can I get Micah to give me that blue crayon and still follow our rule to be kind?"

- *Honoring children's suggestions:* Ms. Stark made it clear that there was more than one right way to meet the challenge.

- *Modifications for kindergartners:* The use of puppets, for example, made the role-play extra engaging for these children. The puppets also helped the kindergartners, who might have confused pretend with real, understand that this role-play was pretend. In addition, Ms. Stark asked her assistant to role-play with her initially because she knew the children were not ready to play roles right away.

- *Ruling out inappropriate ideas:* Ms. Stark directly but respectfully let a student know his suggestion did not honor the classroom rules.

- *Positive teacher language:* Phrases such as "be kind" and "in a way that's kind" peppered Ms. Stark's questions and comments, reinforcing the positive goal the class was working toward. Language such as "What did you notice?" showed the children that their reflections were valued.

EXAMPLE 2

Fourth graders: Giving kind and helpful feedback on a classmate's writing

It was January. Since the fall I'd been teaching this fourth grade class how to participate in writers' workshop. Writers' workshop is central in the curriculum for all my classes because it offers rich opportunities for children to deepen their academic and social skills. As children help each other improve their writing, they learn the art of giving respectful, helpful comments while getting to know each other as writers and human beings.

But I knew from past experience that giving helpful and respectful feedback is hard for children. My job is to protect the community from hurtful comments while encouraging feedback of sufficient honesty and substance to deepen academic learning. To that end, I had structured daily writing blocks that consisted of a mini-lesson, a quiet writing time, and a whole-class sharing time when children commented on each other's work.

I had carefully modeled giving helpful and respectful feedback during the sharing portion, and the students were doing a reasonably good job following my example in this whole-group setting, under my watchful guidance.

For the second half of the year, however, I planned to assign children writing partners. Partners would work with each other privately without my close supervision. Students would therefore need to offer respectful, helpful feedback on their own. I gathered the class for a role-play to teach this important skill. I shortened the mini-lesson and the quiet writing time so that we could have an extended sharing time, which we would use for the role-playing.

I told the children that to celebrate the new year, I would be assigning them writing partners. "Your job is to help your partner with her or his writing, to help your partner express her or his ideas. Today, for sharing time, we will do some short plays about how to respond to classmates' writing."

Describing a specific situation

"Let's pretend I'm meeting with Julia to listen to the story that she's working on," I began. "We're all describing our settings today. Julia reads her description of her setting to me. It doesn't give me a picture in my mind. In fact, it's sort of confusing."

"Carmen, will you play the part of my writing partner, Julia, and act this out with me?" I asked. I chose Carmen because I believed that as a strong writer and a self-confident child, she would be comfortable playing the part of a student who needed a little help. Carmen agreed to play the part.

Carmen began to read. She was getting into the role. She looked at me with trust, ready for kind and helpful feedback. I listened attentively, playing the part of a writing partner who's a bit puzzled, a confused look on my face.

"Stop," I said. "Let's pretend I didn't understand Julia's description. Our class rules say 'Be kind' and 'Help each other learn.' What am I going to do? I want to be kind, but I also want to help Julia describe her setting well."

Naming the positive goal

"When I give Julia feedback about her setting, how can I be kind and help her learn?" I asked the class. This goal of taking people's feelings into consideration while being honest is of paramount importance: An atmosphere of emotional safety must be in place if we are to learn at our best. Yet accomplishing this is a challenge for everyone—children and adults. I was truly anxious to hear these students' ideas.

Recording children's ideas

Megumi raised her hand and said, "You could notice what Julia did well first and then tell her where it's confusing, like, 'I could really imagine the tree when you told about the leaves, but then I wondered where the tree was. Is your setting the woods, a park, or a backyard?" Megumi was describing a strategy that I'd used frequently in adding my comments during writers' sharings. On the chart, I wrote, "Notice what the person did well and then say what you're wondering about."

J.T. raised his hand. "You could say, 'I wish I knew more about the setting. I was wondering if it was the woods, a yard, or a park." This was another strategy that I'd used and the children had imitated during writers' sharings. I wrote, "I wish...I wonder," on the chart.

The children offered two more suggestions, which I added to the list. One was "I can't quite see it in my mind. Could you add some more details?" The other was "I want to understand the setting better." The class generated some terrific ideas. Now we would see them acted out.

Acting out one idea, with the teacher taking the "tricky role"

"Carmen, now I'm going to pick one of these ideas and try it. I think I'll try J.T.'s idea," I said.

Carmen held her notebook in her lap, waiting for my feedback. I said, "Hmm, I wish I knew more about the setting. Is it in the woods, a park, or a backyard?" My comment delivered, I stopped the action by saying "Cut."

Asking children what they noticed

Before asking the class what they noticed about the role-play, I decided to ask Carmen to reflect for a moment on how she felt hearing my feedback. This is a strategy I sometimes use if I judge that the class is ready for it, as this class clearly was. It was January, and our community was solid. The students were adept at role-playing, having used it in other grades and practiced it frequently in this class during the past few months. I myself was secure with the strategy. I was confident that I could probe Carmen's feelings in a way that was kind and controlled enough that no one would become silly or uncomfortable.

I turned to Carmen and asked, "How did you feel when I gave you feedback on your writing?" I referred to our positive goal by adding, "Did my feedback feel kind and helpful?"

"I liked it when you told me what you wished," Carmen replied. "It made me feel like you wanted to know where my story took place, and it reminded me that I hadn't put that in."

"I felt comfortable, too," I said. "I felt like I was helping you in a kind way."

Then, turning to the class, I continued by taking their observations. "What did the rest of you notice about ways that I was both kind and helpful?"

"You leaned in toward Carmen as you gave your comment," said Mim. "It made it look like you really cared."

"Your voice was kind and you looked right at Carmen," said Kevin.

"So, this is a strategy that you might use when you have writing conferences," I stated.

Acting out a second idea, with a student playing the "tricky role"

"Jon, would you like to go next? You can try another idea from our chart, an idea about how to be kind and helpful while commenting on your partner's writing. Kay, would you like to be Jon's partner?" Jon and Kay both agreed.

I knew that Jon would use a kind voice as he commented on Kay's writing, so I trusted him with the "tricky role." Kay, on the other hand, could be abrupt when she helped classmates. Assigning her the role of the receiver, the less active partner, could heighten her awareness of helpful feedback-giving language while avoiding the risk that she would behave inappropriately in the role-play.

Jon looked at the chart and said, "I'm going to try Megumi's idea." After Kay pretended to read her passage, he turned to her and said, "I could really imagine the tree when you told about the leaves, but then I wondered where the tree was. Is your setting the woods, a park, or a backyard?"

"Cut," I said.

Asking children what they noticed

Again, I began by asking the actors how they felt during the role-play. "Kay, how did you feel when Jon asked you about your setting? Did his feedback feel both kind and helpful?"

"I felt good," responded Kay. "I felt like he was interested in my story and wanted to know where it took place. He smiled at me and looked at me while he asked me about the setting."

"How did you feel, Jon, while you asked Kay about the setting?" I asked.

"I felt interested in her story. She looked at me, and I thought she cared about my ideas."

"What did the rest of you notice?" I asked.

"I noticed that Jon used a kind tone when he asked Kay about her setting. He didn't just tell her what was wrong. He asked if the setting was the woods, the park, or a backyard," contributed Carl.

Continuing to act out the other ideas listed

We acted out one more item on the list with another pair of students, skipping the last idea because we had used up the twenty minutes I had allowed for this activity. Because it was January and these students were familiar and comfortable with role-playing, no one's feelings would be hurt if his or her idea wasn't enacted. Also, the two ideas that we did enact had given the children some concrete ideas about how to offer feedback that was both kind and honest. The children had a place to start.

Summing up lessons learned

"Tomorrow I'll assign writing partners, and you'll get a chance to try some of these ideas," I said. "Remember to speak kindly, to look at your partner, and to show that you're interested in your partner's ideas. Be kind and helpful."

Following up

The next day, after our quiet writing time, I announced the writing partners. The children took their writer's notebooks and sat beside their new partners. I said, "Remember, your job is to be kind and helpful to your partner. Here are some ideas about how to do that." I pulled out our chart from the day before and posted it on the chart stand, calling on volunteers to read aloud the ideas on the chart. With this reminder, the children were ready to begin.

For the next several weeks, I posted the chart during every writers' workshop sharing time. I often noticed children glancing at the chart before they offered feedback to their partners. When children made kind, helpful comments, I reinforced the behavior by briefly, privately, and matter-of-factly letting the children know I'd heard them.

THINGS TO NOTE about this fourth grade role-play

- *The children's interest:* The children were enjoying writers' workshop and wanted to do their best. Now familiar with the workshop routine, they were also ready to learn about a more challenging piece of it.

- *The children's readiness:* I had demonstrated making positive and helpful comments about students' writing over the past few months. Those demonstrations had given the students some idea of helpful feedback and made for a smooth transition to role-playing.

- *Careful selection of actors:* I considered which students would feel self-confident, were likely to demonstrate kind feedback, and could benefit from the practice provided by playing the various roles.

- *Careful consideration before asking actors how they felt:* I made sure that our classroom community was strong, the children trusted each other, and I felt confident in my ability to keep the atmosphere safe.

- *Supportive teacher language:* Language such as "What did you notice?" and "How did you feel?" invited children to participate. Words such as "be kind *and* help Julia learn," and "I felt like I was helping you in a kind way" helped children envision the goal.

- *Reinforcement of the goal in the wrap-up:* At the end of the role-play, the children were reminded again of the goal: "Remember to speak kindly, to look at your partner, to show that you're interested in your partner's ideas. Be kind and helpful."

- *Visual reminder of skills learned:* After the role-play, the children could look at a chart to remind themselves of ways to give kind, helpful comments. The chart was up long enough for students to solidify their learning but not so long as to become part of the classroom "wallpaper."

EXAMPLE 3

Sixth graders: Expressing feelings honestly

For eleven-year-old girls, life can be a constant musical chairs of who's "in" and who's "out." For example, best friends Ruby and Rachel are suddenly "in a fight," and Ruby has allied with Annie and Sonia, telling stories about Rachel to the other girls.

According to developmental psychologists Lyn Mikel Brown and Carol Gilligan, eleven-year-old girls' relationships are governed by the "tyranny of nice and kind." With cultural stereotypes expecting them to act polite, forgiving, and submissive—simply put, "nice"—girls this age often push their real feelings of anger or resentment underground rather than finding honest and respectful ways to express them (Brown & Gilligan, 1992).

Researcher Rachel Simmons (2002) further found that girls often corral support from others, forming groups to express hostile feelings they're uncomfortable expressing alone.

One way to protect girls from forming these destructive cliques is to teach them to express their feelings directly. To this end, sixth grade teacher Ms. Olsen planned a role-play for the girls in the class. Although boys could benefit from such a topic as well, Ms. Olsen knew the girls would be more honest without the boys around.

It was November when the girls did this role-play. By then the class had developed a sense of trust, and they knew that Ms. Olsen valued their ideas. They'd used role-playing to explore some lower-risk situations such as making fair teams for softball and being a helpful math partner. Ms. Olsen felt they were now ready for this riskier topic.

"Join us at lunchtime today to practice kind ways to tell friends how you feel," the note placed in each girl's mailbox read. After recess the girls arrived, intrigued and a little excited about a girls-only lunch.

Ms. Olsen introduced the topic by referring to the class's rules, what they called their "constitution." "Our constitution says we'll be kind to everyone, but sometimes that's not so easy to do," she said. "I remember when I was a girl, my friends and I would get together and do mean things to classmates. I've noticed that sometimes that happens in this class, too. Sometimes the best way to be kind is to tell friends right away when they make us mad, so it doesn't turn into something bigger."

Many of the girls looked skeptical. Expressing h2urt feelings honestly was a nice ideal, but they couldn't see doing it in real life.

Describing a specific situation

"Let's say Sarah hangs out with Robin just about every day at recess," Ms. Olsen said. "Robin loves to tell Sarah what to do. She tells Sarah what to wear and whom to have for friends. Yesterday Sarah got tired of the way Robin treats her and ignored Robin on the recess field. Instead, Sarah walked around the field with Susan, whom Robin doesn't like. I'm going to pretend I'm Robin. I'm so angry that Sarah ignored me. That is harsh. She should spend time at recess with me. She's my best friend!"

Ms. Olsen used fictional names and a fictional scenario to keep the situation removed from the actual classroom dynamics.

Naming the positive goal

"Our class constitution says to be kind," continued Ms. Olsen. "How can I tell Sarah how I feel in a way that's honest and kind? I want to keep her as a friend."

Recording children's ideas

The girls shared ideas as two students recorded them on the easel chart. Though they couldn't quite see themselves speaking so directly to their friends about hurt feelings, the girls were able to name some ideas in a hypothetical role-play.

Natalie spoke first. "Robin could speak to Sarah privately and say, 'I feel hurt that you hung out with Susan yesterday, even though you know I don't like her. I want you to stay away from Susan.'" Natalie was using the I-statements that the class had learned through practicing conflict resolution. (To learn about conflict resolution, see Chapter Three.)

Ms. Olsen accepted Natalie's idea even though it didn't respect Sarah's needs. With eleven-year-olds, it's so important to keep it real. Further in the role-play she would help the girls reflect on the effectiveness of Natalie's words.

"She could ask Sarah if she wants to spend recess together today," suggested Maura.

Aileen said, "She could tell Sarah privately, 'My feelings are hurt that you spent yesterday's recess with Susan,' and leave it at that."

Acting out one idea, with the teacher taking the "tricky role"

"Let's try some of these ideas," said Ms. Olsen. "I'll go first, playing the part of Robin. Vanessa, will you play the part of Sarah?"

"I'm going to try Aileen's idea," said Ms. Olsen. "Robin and Sarah are sitting together on the bus on their way to school."

Turning to Vanessa, Ms. Olsen said, "Sarah, my feelings are hurt that you spent yesterday's recess with Susan. I thought you were my best friend."

Vanessa responded, "I'm really sorry that you feel bad. I needed a break yesterday. I'm tired of the way you tell me what to do."

"Stop," Ms. Olsen said.

Asking children what they noticed

Ms. Olsen began by asking Vanessa how it felt to play Sarah. "Vanessa, how did you feel when I told you my feelings were hurt?" Ms. Olsen was experienced enough at conducting role-plays to know how to keep the tone kind, even if Vanessa were to express some strong feelings. So she felt safe asking this question.

Vanessa's response surprised some of her classmates. "I felt sort of relieved. I wasn't sure how to tell Robin I was tired of the way she bosses me around, and it sort of just came out."

"I felt surprised," said Ms. Olsen. "I didn't realize you were angry about the way I tell you what to do. I'm going to have to think about that one."

"What did the rest of you notice?" asked Ms. Olsen.

"Your tone of voice was serious but friendly when you told Sarah your feelings were hurt," pointed out Natalie.

"You said your feelings, and it was okay," said Molly. "When Robin told her feelings honestly, Sarah told her feelings honestly, too," added Maura.

Acting out a second idea, with a student playing the "tricky role"

For the second round, Ms. Olsen invited Bridgette and Laurie to take the roles. She chose these two girls because they were friendly but not friends. This kept the role-play hypothetical.

Bridgette looked at the list and began. She chose Natalie's idea, the problematic one that Ms. Olsen had nonetheless accepted. "I feel hurt that you hung out with Susan yesterday, even though you know I don't like her. I want you to stay away from Susan," Bridgette said.

Laurie bristled, "But I want to spend time with Susan. I like her. She's fun."

"Stop," said Ms. Olsen.

Asking children what they noticed

Here was Ms. Olsen's chance to have the group reflect on this idea that didn't respect Sarah's desires. "Laurie, how did you feel when Robin told you how she felt?"

"I was okay with her telling me she was hurt, but it made me mad when she told me not to spend time with Susan. What right did she have to tell me not to spend time with her?"

"Bridgette, how did you feel?" asked Ms. Olsen.

"I felt like I'd made a mistake. I just made her angry. If this play kept going it wouldn't turn out so well."

"What did the rest of you notice?" asked Ms. Olsen.

Tatyana chimed in, "When Robin just told Sarah her feelings were hurt, it was okay, but when Robin told Sarah not to spend time with Susan, it wasn't okay at all. It just made them angrier at each other."

Continuing to act out the other ideas listed

The group dramatized the third idea: Robin asking Sarah to spend time with her at recess today. The girls agreed that this was a friendly solution but that Robin wasn't telling Susan her honest feelings.

Summing up lessons learned

"Who can summarize what we learned from our role-plays?" Ms. Olsen asked.

Natalie offered, "We learned that if you're mad at someone, you can give them an I-statement, and that will help you understand each other."

Following up

Ms. Olsen asked the girls if they'd like to meet at lunchtime in two weeks. She suggested that next time they could look at the same scenario from Sarah's point of view: how to tell a friend in a way that's both honest and kind that she's being bossy. The girls were enthusiastic about a second meeting.

At Morning Meeting the next day, Ms. Olsen reinforced the skills practiced. On the morning message, she wrote a question to everyone: "When have you used I-statements in sixth grade?" Although only half of the class had participated in the role-play the day before, it was an appropriate question for the entire class because the entire class had been learning how to make I-statements.

Later in the week, for a ten-minute quick-write as part of writers' workshop, Ms. Olsen gave the prompt, "How have I-statements helped you understand a friend?"

THINGS TO NOTE about this sixth-grade girls' role-play

- *An atmosphere of trust:* Going into the role-play, the girls knew their teacher would honor all reasonable ideas and the discussion would be "real."

- *Comfort with role-playing:* Ms. Olsen waited until the class was familiar with role-playing and had done role-plays on lower-risk topics before doing this one.

- *Thoughtful framing of the topic:* Ms. Olsen named the class rules, her own experiences as a young girl, and the girls' desire to be "nice" despite inevitable conflicts between friends.

- *Fictional scenario:* The conflict role-played was between two fictional girls, which prevented individuals from feeling defensive.

- *Teacher playing the "tricky role" first:* This set a tone of honesty and friendliness.

- *Open-ended questions that elicited rich discussion:* Simple questions such as "How did you feel?" brought forth new insights from the girls. Ms. Olsen felt comfortable asking this question because she was experienced with role-playing, and the girls had built a sense of community.

■ *Students recording ideas:* Having two students write the group's suggestions on the chart helped these sixth graders take responsibility for the process.

■ *Positive teacher language:* Language such as "in a way that's honest and kind," "tell friends right away when they make us mad," and "so it doesn't turn into something bigger" reinforced the goal of being both honest and kind. Language such as "What did you notice?" and "How did you feel?" encouraged participation and honored the girls' thoughts and feelings.

ROLE-PLAY PLANNING SHEET

Careful planning helps make role-plays successful. You may find this sheet useful in your planning.

Introducing the situation briefly to the children

What do you plan to say?

Describing a specific situation

What do you plan to say? *(Remember to use an "I" voice, describe the situation from a child's point of view, refer to classroom rules, and stop the description at the point where you must decide how to behave.)*

Identifying the positive goal: What we want the children to do

How will you word the goal?

Asking children to generate ideas for how to meet this goal

How will you word this question?

If a child suggests an inappropriate idea, what will you say to redirect the child while referring to the general goal?

How many ideas will you take? How many will the class dramatize?

Choosing actors

Which student will play opposite you in the first round? Why this student?

Which students will be actors in subsequent rounds? Why these students?

Dramatizing the situation

Where will you stop the action so that the drama stays positive?

Summing up lessons learned

How will you sum up the lessons learned?

Following up

How and when will you follow up on this role-play?

CHAPTER FIVE

Class Meetings

The fifth graders efficiently gather their chairs into a circle. Using a matter-of-fact but serious tone, Mr. Sawyer says, "I called this class meeting to discuss a problem we need to solve as a group. Yesterday I was out to attend an important meeting on how to teach our new science curriculum. Ms. Cossi agreed to be our guest teacher. One of our rules says to respect everyone. I hear that this room was not a respectful place yesterday. What happened? We'll go around the circle. You may share what you noticed about what you did or how it felt, or you may say 'Pass.'"

The children's day with Ms. Cossi had been a disaster. Mr. Sawyer had heard all about it this morning in the teachers' room. He wants to avoid lecturing the class, yet he wants to be clear that he knows they hadn't treated Ms. Cossi respectfully and that he expects appropriate behavior the next time they have a substitute, or "guest teacher."

This class has been practicing the use of such class problem-solving meetings for six months and is familiar with the protocol. The children begin going around the circle. Sean says, "She just sat there and didn't do anything, so we got sort of out of control."

Miwa says, "Some kids raced around the library and threw books off the shelves. I didn't do anything to stop them, and I started screaming to Yvette across the library."

Many children comment that Ms. Cossi didn't read the "Dear Guest Teacher" book, the handbook they had worked hard to create and that explains their classroom rules and routines.

Once all the students have had an opportunity to say what they had noticed about the problem, they go around the circle again, this time suggesting solutions. Ideas range from "We could make helping the guest teacher a classroom job" to "Pretend she's your mom and think about how you'd feel if the kids were treating your mom that way."

With all ideas listed on a chart, Mr. Sawyer reads the list. Students put thumbs up for ideas they favored, thumbs in the middle for ideas they could live with, and thumbs down for ideas that they couldn't live with.

Two ideas, "make helping the guest teacher a classroom job" and "go across the hall to get Ms. Lanvin if things start to get out of hand," have the greatest number of thumbs up and no thumbs down. The class agrees that they'll try both of these ideas.

A week later, Mr. Sawyer was out sick. Mike, the "host" for the week, helped the guest teacher read the "Dear Guest Teacher" book. Students behaved respectfully and treated Ms. Jones like a guest in their classroom.

Mr. Sawyer's work with the children after their bad day with Ms. Cossi took about thirty minutes and is an example of a class meeting for resolving a problem that involves all members of a group, such as a whole class, all the children on a particular school bus, or all the children who play softball at fifth grade recess.

Children in all elementary grades can benefit from exposure to at least parts of the class meeting protocol. Because of the challenges involved in group decision-making, I recommend that you try a full class meeting only if you teach grades two through six. Children in kindergarten and first grade can share what they've noticed about a problem and suggest solutions, getting a sense of empowerment in the process. But once it's time to make a decision, it works best if their teacher takes the lead in choosing which solution to try. (See "Modified Class Meetings in Kindergarten and First Grade" on page 184.)

The term "class meeting" refers to different types of gatherings in different classrooms and schools. In this chapter, the term refers to a meeting for the purpose of solving a group problem. Secondarily, a class meeting can be a format for group event planning or decision making, such as choosing a class name or mascot. I describe this secondary type of class meeting as a step toward a problem-solving class meeting, a way for children to learn the meeting protocol and practice the prerequisite skills.

Purpose: Solving Whole-Group Problems Respectfully and Collaboratively

The purpose of class meetings is to enable a group to solve a problem while keeping the classroom rules front and center, sharing information, and using reasoned thinking.

Class meetings teach children to work together, respect everyone's needs, and compromise to reach agreement. When everyone's opinion is heeded, everyone is more likely to help make sure the agreed-upon solution is implemented.

For this reason, I describe in this chapter decision-making by consensus. I define consensus as collaboratively reaching a decision that is acceptable to everyone.

Reaching consensus requires listening to each other and making compromises. The eventual solution reached may not be anyone's first choice, but it is a choice that everyone can live with. Unlike voting, which often leaves children feeling like either winners or losers, consensus promotes a feeling that we are a caring community that worked together to solve a problem.

I recognize that leading a class to reach consensus may be a daunting proposition. Kindergarten and first grade children generally are too young for this sophisticated process, and students of any grade who haven't had much experience with whole-group problem-solving may find consensus a challenging stretch. I have found myself having multiple class meetings on one issue, working with the group toward consensus.

If you feel that reaching consensus is more than you and your students are ready for right now, keep in mind that you can work toward it gradually. There are interim steps that set the stage for students to use consensus later. (For ideas, see "Modified Class Meetings in Kindergarten and First Grade" on page 184 and "Questions from Teachers" on page 206.)

When to Use Class Meetings

Class meetings are intended for the following types of situations.

When agreed-upon rules aren't working

Class meetings are for the daily problems of group life. The class has agreed upon its rules, yet sometimes the whole group slides into not following them. The group behaves disrespectfully to a substitute teacher. Some children aren't included in the lunchroom, and no one does anything about it. Teams are chosen unfairly at recess. Homework incompletion is a chronic, class-wide problem. Class meetings can be a forum for solving these kinds of problems and restoring kindness and respect to group functioning.

Note that class meetings are not intended for teaching or practicing new skills. They're not meant for teaching students ways to include a lone classmate at lunch, for example, or for practicing strategies for choosing teams fairly. Role-playing, discussed in Chapter Four, is a method for doing that. If, after the rules, skills, and strategies have been taught and children stumble in applying them, then class meetings may be an appropriate forum for figuring out what to do.

When a problem involves *all* group members

Class meetings are for problems that involve or affect all members of a class or some other large group. When a problem is between two children or a few children, it's not appropriate to engage the entire class in resolving it. Conflict resolution (described in Chapter Three) is a more appropriate strategy for these because it allows the players to reach a solution with some privacy and with control over their own relationships.

When a problem involves a single child, a teacher-student problem-solving conference (described in Chapter Two) or an individual written agreement (described in Chapter Six) are appropriate strategies.

Sometimes it can be hard to decide whether a problem affects just a few students or the whole class. For example, when one particular student is consistently being excluded in the social life of the classroom, is that an individual problem or a group problem?

Each teacher has to sort through the issues carefully. I suggest that when in doubt, first try treating it as an individual problem. If, while working with one child you hear lots of references to classmates' role in the problem and sense that group input is key to its resolution, then hold a class meeting.

When you want student input

Use class meetings only when you want student input. In some cases the teacher alone should resolve an issue, even if it's one that affects the whole class. For example, if a student suggests changing a longstanding procedure such as the one for leaving the room to use the restroom, it's sometimes best to simply state the policy and move on. Otherwise we might find ourselves endlessly negotiating with students about issues that shouldn't be up for negotiation.

Steps in a Class Meeting

Class meetings follow a specific, preset protocol designed to give all group members an opportunity to describe their understanding of the problem and an equal say in how to solve it. The protocol encourages listening, compromise, and respect for everyone's needs and desires. The following example, from a third grade class I taught, illustrates this process.

It was April. The class had made an effort all year to include everyone during the unstructured times of day, such as lunch and recess. The children socialized smoothly in the lunchroom irrespective of gender, nationality, or race. This was no small achievement, given that—as observant teachers know and authorities have noted—the lunchroom is the most racially and gender segregated part of American public schools. (To learn more about this, see "Mix It Up" from Teaching Tolerance, www.tolerance.org/teens.)

We'd begun the year with preplanned "lunch dates" that had children inviting a different classmate to eat with them each day. We'd progressed to class-planned lunch tables, which gave students a chance to eat with a different group of classmates each week. With the coming of spring, the students had progressed to free choice seating at lunch, with the understanding that the whole group would take responsibility for making sure everyone had a friend to sit with.

One Friday I arrived in the lunchroom to pick up the students and noticed that Laila was sitting by herself at an unoccupied table. Later in the afternoon, I mentioned to Laila, privately, that I'd noticed her sitting alone. Laila blushed and looked uncomfortable. I didn't want to embarrass her further, so I dropped the subject.

On Monday, as I made copies in the staff room, I asked Ms. Convers, one of the lunchroom supervisors, about what I'd noticed. She said that she'd seen the same thing recently, that sometimes individuals from my class sat and ate their lunches alone.

I decided this was a problem that needed attention.

Teacher Planning

My first step, before involving the class, was to do some planning alone. I needed to think about three things:

Should we have a class meeting about this?

For the type of class meeting described in this chapter, it's always the teacher who makes the final call on whether to hold a meeting and what the topic will be. Although students may suggest topics, the teacher either approves them or decides to resolve them through other strategies. This is because the teacher is in the best position to discern whether a problem is a whole-group issue, a small-group issue, or an individual issue.

In this case involving possible exclusion problems at lunch, I concluded that because including everyone was a responsibility that the entire class had agreed to, and because it seemed to be the class as a whole that was falling down on this responsibility, we should have a class meeting about it.

How should I state the problem during the meeting?

The teacher sets a collaborative tone for the meeting by the way she states the problem. For this meeting, I knew it was important to use positive language that would remind students of their agreement to include everyone.

One way to do this would be to refer to our classroom rules, which the class had created together. None of our rules explicitly stated "include everyone," but the rule "be kind and helpful" certainly was broad enough to cover inclusion. I decided to refer to it.

Another way to set a collaborative tone would be to recall relevant past decisions or events in the life of the class. When this class instituted open seating at lunch, it was with the important caveat that we would still make sure everyone had some company. I would talk about this decision as well.

I wrote down what I planned to say, being careful to keep it brief. Children stop listening when we go on and on.

When should we meet?

I looked for a slot in our schedule about half an hour long, not long enough for academic subjects. There was such a period the next morning, after PE and before recess. I reserved that time for the class meeting.

Although I use the *Responsive Classroom* strategy of Morning Meeting, I purposely did not fold this class meeting into that time. Morning Meeting is intended as an opportunity for students to build community and warm up for the day by greeting each other, sharing news, doing an activity together, and reading the morning message I've written for them. Class meeting is for solving a problem. Each is important, and each needs its own time.

The Meeting Itself

The class meeting itself consists of the following steps:

1. The group reviews its ground rules for class meetings.

2. The teacher states the reason for the meeting—that is, the problem that needs solving. (Later in the year, when children are experienced with class meetings, a student may state the problem.)

3. Students each state what they've noticed about the problem or how it makes them feel, or say "Pass."

4. Each student suggests a solution or says "Pass." The teacher, or in older grades a pair of students, records these ideas.

5. Students comment on the solutions suggested.

6. The group reaches agreement on a solution to try, using "thumbs up, middle, or down" to indicate how they feel about each solution.

7. The teacher sums up and compliments the group on their collaboration skills.

8. The teacher follows up with reminders and check-ins.

When the class came back from PE, I gathered them into a circle so that everyone could see everyone else, face to face. This setup promotes clear communication and gives the message that everyone's voice is important.

Step 1. The group reviews its ground rules for class meetings

I told the class that we were gathered for a class meeting about a problem that I'd noticed involving the whole class. Before stating the problem, I got out a chart listing our ground rules for class meetings and posted it near the circle. These were rules that the group had generated in the fall when they were first learning about class meetings. (See "Teaching How to Hold a Class Meeting" on page 188 to learn about that step.) The rules were:

- We will listen to each other.

- We will work to find a solution.

I asked two students to read the ground rules aloud in turn, one rule each.

Step 2. The teacher states the reason for the meeting

"We decided together, when we went to open seating at lunch, that each person would take responsibility for making sure everyone had someone to sit with," I said as I had planned. "That's a way of taking care of our rule to be kind and helpful. Recently I've noticed that sometimes students are sitting by themselves."

The children were listening seriously, nodding, showing that perhaps they, too, had noticed this development.

Step 3. Students each state what they've noticed about the problem or how it makes them feel, or say "Pass"

In this step, the children go around the circle to share their observations about the problem. The key word here is "observations"—just descriptions of the problem or how the problem made them feel, not ideas for solving it. Solutions come later. By allowing only observations and feelings in this early step, we ensure that everyone has a clear understanding of what the problem is before jumping to solve it.

"What have you noticed?" I asked the class to solicit their observations. "We'll go around the circle, sharing what you've noticed or how you're feeling." I added, "Today we won't mention names as we share." I didn't think specific names were relevant to this problem; furthermore, children might feel more comfortable if their names weren't mentioned. (See "Set up ground rules for class meetings" on page 193 for more about naming names.)

Katie, immediately to my right, began. "Some kids want to sit alone because they want to sit near friends in other classes." So, that explained why Laila was sitting alone, I surmised. She wanted to visit with her friend Kaylene in Ms. Carey's class.

Paul said, "Some of us are so busy with our friends that we haven't noticed kids who might be by themselves." Many heads nodded. It was understandable that after a busy morning, children would be engaged in socializing rather than noticing who might be alone.

The next four children passed. They hadn't paid attention to who was alone either.

When Noah's turn came, he said, "Some people are alone at lunchtime. I know because one of them is me." Noah usually chose to eat lunch with

Kamran, but Kamran was often absent from school with asthma. "Maybe we should go back to lunch partners," Noah added.

"Remember, we're just sharing what we noticed. Solutions come later," I interjected. If this format is to work, the teacher has to keep students on track, insisting that they follow the protocol precisely.

By the time we completed the circle, it was clear that a sizeable minority of the class felt they sometimes were forced to sit alone. We also learned that most children were so busy at lunch that they hadn't noticed that some classmates might be lonely. For them, just having their awareness raised was invaluable.

If there had been any disagreement in children's description or understanding of the problem, I might have stopped the meeting and asked everyone to observe the lunchroom for a few days to gather more information about the problem. In this situation, even though a group of children had been so busy enjoying their friends that they hadn't noticed some classmates being isolated, they had listened during the meeting and now understood the problem. Further information gathering therefore was unnecessary.

Step 4. Each student suggests a solution or says "Pass"

"This time when we go around the circle, we'll suggest solutions," I said.

"We should keep free seating but be careful to notice who's alone," suggested Katie. I wrote Katie's idea on the chart. With older classes, two students would be in charge of charting the proposed solutions.

"We should look around the tables," added Paul.

"That idea sounds a lot like Katie's to me," I said. "Is it okay if I put a check next to Katie's idea?" Paul nodded. Asking Paul for his okay was a deliberate move on my part. I was taking the first step toward narrowing down the suggestions and showing the children ways their ideas were similar. But if Paul had objected and said his idea was different, I would have respected his preference and written his idea down, too.

When Lenny's turn came, he said, "I think we should sit with whoever we want. Kids who are alone can take care of themselves. Lunchtime is our free time."

I responded to this idea right away, saying, "We agreed to take care of each other at lunchtime. That's a way of taking care of our rule to be kind. Our rules apply in the lunchroom as well as the classroom." I didn't record his idea. It's the teacher's job to rule out any clearly unacceptable suggestions.

Mara suggested that we resume planning lunch partners each morning so that all children would know whom they were going to eat with.

Other children either passed or agreed with one of the two predominant ideas:

- Keep free seating but be careful to notice who's alone.

- Go back to planning lunch partners each morning.

I didn't add an idea in this meeting. Class meeting is a strategy for group decision-making, and the teacher, as part of the group, can suggest a solution. But I am careful about adding my ideas because I don't want the children to come to rely on the teacher supplying the "right" idea. On the other hand, if I have an idea that I think will solve the problem and it hasn't been suggested yet, I go ahead and say it, adding to the collection of potential solutions.

Step 5. Students comment on the solutions suggested

This third time around the circle, I invited the children to say what they thought of the various solutions suggested. "Remember, we're looking for a solution that's good for everyone," I reminded them.

Commenting on the suggested solutions is a step I sometimes omit if I'm teaching seven-year-olds, who tend to be sensitive and who may not be ready to hear classmates' perspectives on their ideas. Even with older children, this is the step I teach last because it takes well-developed logical thinking to evaluate others' ideas and considerable tact to express the evaluations in a kind way.

As this third grade class went around, Laila said, "I think we should keep having free seating because some kids like to sit near friends in other classes."

Paul said, "It's more fun to sit where you want. That's why I think we should have free seating."

Mia said, "I think we should have free seating because we can be careful to make sure that no one's alone. We just needed a reminder."

When it was his turn, Noah protested, "But kids forget and some of us are nervous asking if we can sit with somebody. I think we need to go back to assigned seats."

Each child had to speak in turn. This prevented the children from arguing about one idea and instead kept the focus on a multiplicity of viewpoints. If time allows, and if the children seem consumed with the urgency of their ideas, I sometimes give them an additional turn around the circle to make further comments.

Step 6. The group reaches agreement on a solution to try, using "thumbs up, middle, or down"

Now that students have heard classmates' thoughts about the various solutions suggested, it was time to indicate, by a show of thumbs, where they stood on each idea. Thumb up means "I want this solution." Thumb in the middle, held parallel to the floor, means "I can live with it." Thumb down means "I can't live with it."

Although it seems simple, this method requires fairly sophisticated thinking and a genuine spirit of compromise in the children. For this system to work, students have to resist the urge to put their thumb down for every solution that isn't their first choice, but to exercise that third option—thumb in the middle. It takes careful teaching and lots of practice to get children to this level of thoughtful evaluation. But once they get there, the method becomes a powerful tool for asserting themselves while respecting others.

This being April, and the class having practiced the thumbs method all year, these children were ready to use it effectively.

I read the first proposal, that we keep free seating, with everyone being careful that no one's alone. Most students put their thumbs up; they liked the self-sufficiency of free seating. Mara and several others put their thumbs in the middle. Noah put his thumb down. He was feeling stressed by free seating.

Next I read proposal two, that we resume preplanned lunch partners. Several thumbs went up immediately. It was clear that some children preferred the security of knowing in advance whom they'd be eating with. Laila and Lenny put their thumbs down. Laila wanted to sit near Kaylene in Ms. Carey's class, and Lenny felt grown up choosing where to sit each day. The rest of the thumbs were in the middle, in the "I can live with it" zone.

In the consensus approach that I'd taught this class and that they'd been practicing for months, only the solutions getting a thumb up or thumb in the middle from everyone are acceptable. So everyone understood that we wouldn't make a decision Noah couldn't live with. It was clear that this was important to him. He'd told us that he'd been feeling lonely at lunch sometimes, and he liked the security of assigned seating.

We also couldn't make a decision that Laila and Lenny couldn't live with. Laila seemed to need to sit near Kaylene, and Lenny really wanted to be able to choose his own seat each day.

Neither solution was going to fly at this point.

I might have stopped the meeting there, saying that as the teacher, I would make a decision until the group could reach consensus. This is a strategy that I use when the group seems stuck or when one child is digging in her heels, unwilling to listen to or negotiate with the group, apparently because of simply wanting to have her way. In this case, however, I felt that the children were trying to meet a variety of real needs.

Therefore, we continued to negotiate, searching for a solution that would be acceptable to all. I was confident that, because this was April, the children would be ready to think about each other's needs and work toward a compromise. We all knew Noah well, and I believed that his classmates understood his concerns. Such understanding and care is crucial to the consensus process. It must be in place for consensus to work.

"Does anyone have an idea about how we can help Noah feel safe while Laila and Lenny still get to have the freedom they're asking for?" I asked.

Bobby told Noah that he'd eat lunch with him any time Kamran was absent. Julia told Laila that she'd love to sit with her at lunch and that Julia could still play with Kaylene during recess. "We could get to be better friends if we ate lunch together sometimes," said Julia.

I read the proposals again. This time there were no thumbs down and more thumbs up for proposal one: continuing free seating with the understanding that all class members would help make sure everyone had a lunch partner. This became the solution we would adopt.

Step 7. The teacher sums up and compliments the group on their collaboration skills

"We've agreed to continue free seating, as long as everyone's included," I said. "You'll all take responsibility for checking to make sure that everyone has a lunch partner. You did some real compromising here, finding a solution that everyone could live with."

Notice the language I used. I offered a compliment that was specific and genuine. The children had compromised; some students had given up something they wanted for the needs of the group. I avoid general praise such as "Good job," which doesn't tell children what it is that they did well. Naming the specific behavior—in this case compromising—lets them know what behavior was helpful and what to keep doing in the future.

This class meeting lasted about thirty-five minutes. I try to keep class meetings to between twenty to thirty-five minutes, depending on the problem to be solved and the age of the children. If the problem needs more time, I try to break the meeting up into two sessions on two different days.

Step 8. The teacher follows up with reminders and check-ins

Before the children went off to lunch the next day, I said, "Remember, make sure no one's lonely at lunch." A one-sentence or one-phrase reminder has more impact than a long lecture.

A few days later, I wrote this question on the morning message, part of the Morning Meeting that launches each school day: "How are things going in the lunchroom?" This led to a brief discussion in Morning Meeting about how our open seating solution was working. It seemed to be working fine.

The next time Kamran was absent, I checked with Noah after lunch to make sure he'd had a lunch partner. Yes, he had, he said. It was Bobby.

Sometimes for the follow-up I schedule a second class meeting. But often these types of short check-ins, a conversation with an individual student or a quick chat as part of Morning Meeting, are sufficient.

Modified Class Meetings in Kindergarten and First Grade

Although the full class meeting format described in this chapter is too developmentally advanced for most kindergartners and first graders, these young children can benefit from getting a taste of it by doing the first steps: making observations about the problem and suggesting solutions. By telling what they've noticed about a problem, they sharpen their powers of observation. By brainstorming possible solutions, they develop logical thinking.

Making observations about the problem and suggesting solutions

Kindergarten and first grade teachers can begin their class meetings by stating the problem, tying it to classroom rules the group has generated. Children can share what they've noticed about the problem or how it makes them feel.

The group can then brainstorm ideas for how to solve the problem as the teacher records their ideas on a chart stand. The teacher writes every idea down. So far the process is the same as for older grades.

The rest of the process, however, is greatly simplified for these younger children.

Choosing an idea to try

Typically, the next step in a kindergarten class meeting is for the teacher to choose an idea to try. Looking at the list, the teacher picks an idea that seems workable and says, "We'll try this one for a few days." Later, the group comes together to discuss how that solution is working.

With first grade classes, some teachers add a step of narrowing down the list of possible solutions with their students before choosing one to try. My colleague Lisa Garsh goes down the list with her first graders and says, "Which idea could we try that would work?" For each potential solution, she asks the students, "Is this solution realistic? Could we actually do it?"

She crosses off the solutions that she or the children recognize as unrealistic. She then thinks about the students' comments throughout the discussion. Sometimes the children are passionate about one of the ideas. On the basis of the students' responses and her own sense of which solution might help, she chooses one idea, saying, "We're going to try this one."

A few days later, the group comes together again to evaluate the success of that solution.

Timing

Keep it short. Fifteen or twenty minutes is about how long five- and six-year-olds can sit and attend to a class meeting. That's another reason for abbreviating the meeting format for younger children.

Some kindergarten and first grade teachers conserve time by asking for volunteers to share their observations and solutions rather than going around the circle. Although that works in many classrooms, a risk is that the more confident or talkative children will dominate, squeezing out their quieter or more reserved classmates.

As you plan your class meeting, think about your students, their ability to sit and participate, and what will allow all voices to be heard.

Too many "presents": A kindergarten modified class meeting

My colleague Suzy Stark's kindergartners loved to draw pictures for each other during choice time, giving each other "presents," as the students called it. This trend began slowly, but before long the children had present fever. They would tape pictures to each other's bodies, front and back, and put pictures in each other's mailboxes.

The problem was some children ended the day festooned with presents while others had none. Some children's mailboxes were stuffed while others' were empty. Ms. Stark saw value in nurturing the students' generosity and creativity but was concerned about the unevenness of the gift giving. She decided it was time for a class meeting.

The meeting took place one day in December, right after an activity time, when, after being physical, students would be ready to sit and listen thoughtfully. Ms. Stark gathered the children in a circle on the floor.

The group reviews ground rules

First the class reviewed their class meeting ground rules. "We will listen to each other," said Manuel. "We will do our best to solve the problem," said Laura.

The teacher states the reason for the meeting

"I've noticed," Ms. Stark said, "that some children are getting lots of presents while others are getting none. Our rules say that we'll take care of each other. I'm wondering how we can make and give presents so that everyone is taken care of."

Students each state what they've noticed about the problem or how it makes them feel, or say "Pass"

"We're going to start by going around the circle," said Ms. Stark. "You may tell what you've noticed about the presents and your classmates' feelings or say 'Pass.'"

The children had plenty to say. Ms. Stark and her teaching assistant had taught the children to say "I feel sad when …" or "I feel mad when … " as part of conflict resolution, and the children were using that wording.

"I feel sad when lots of kids get presents and I don't," said Ray.

"I feel angry when other kids have presents taped all over them, and I don't have even one," Sophie contributed.

"You can have some of my presents," offered Nate when it was his turn.

"My mom says I can't have a birthday party," added Faye. Not every kindergartner got what the meeting was all about. Faye understood that it had something to do with presents, so she figured talking about her birthday was appropriate. Knowing that this kind of literal misunderstanding is typical of five-year-olds, Ms. Stark let it pass. Some of the kindergartners were more ready for this type of problem-solving than others.

Each student suggests a solution or says "Pass"

"This time, when we go around the circle, you may offer suggestions for what we can do about the presents so that everyone feels good, or you may say 'Pass,'" said Ms. Stark.

Matt, who hadn't received any presents, said, "I think we should stop the presents. No more presents."

Joy said, "I think that every time someone makes a present, they should make a present for every single person in our class."

Paul said, "We could put presents in mailboxes. If someone's mailbox doesn't have a present, we could make a present for that person."

Everyone had an opportunity to share thoughts, and nearly everyone did share. The children were transfixed, listening attentively to each other's ideas. They were able to listen and participate longer for class meeting than for anything else during their day.

The teacher sums up and compliments the group on their collaboration skills

Ms. Stark didn't expect kindergartners to make a decision together. Her goal was to raise the children's awareness of the problem. So she ended the meeting here by telling the children that she hoped they would all notice who didn't have presents and make sure everyone got one. "I'll watch the mailboxes," she said, "to make sure they all contain presents."

Ms. Stark added that she noticed their careful listening and thoughtful ideas during the meeting. "We are all learning how to take care of each other," she said. The meeting took about twenty minutes.

The teacher follows up with reminders and check-ins

In the days following the class meeting, Ms. Stark and her teaching assistant noticed that more children indeed received presents. Children like Matt who hadn't gotten any before had them in their mailboxes sometimes now. Ms. Stark quietly and privately let children know when she noticed them giving presents to a wider range of friends. Before free choice work periods, she would say, "Remember, take care of your classmates when you give presents."

Teaching How to Hold a Class Meeting

It takes careful teaching and plenty of practice before children will be able to use the full class meeting protocol effectively. The third grade class meeting on lunchroom seating described previously, for example, was conducted in April. The children had had many class meetings by then and were comfortable with the format, tone, and expectations. They had learned to work together, to listen to each other, to express their ideas honestly, and to make compromises to enable the group to reach agreement. Here's how I help children reach this level of skill.

Teaching the fundamental skills

I find many opportunities in the regular course of our school days to teach the following fundamental skills. I concentrate on them especially during the first weeks of school but reinforce these crucial life skills all year long.

Listening carefully

Class meetings require children to listen carefully to each other. Otherwise, class meetings can become simply a new way for people to say and campaign for what they think without taking in and seriously considering other people's points of view.

One way I teach and have children practice listening is through our daily Morning Meetings. Children listen to and learn each other's names as they greet each other. They listen as classmates share information or news about themselves. They're held accountable for remembering what they heard as we play games that require them to recall who likes to skateboard after school or what Joey's and Maria's favorite book is. We play games that necessitate careful listening, such as guessing the category the leader has in mind when she says "Aunt Minerva likes Alaska but she doesn't like Florida. She likes Popsicles but she doesn't like soup."

Another way I teach listening is through "life boxes." Beginning in the first week of school, children collect three to five small objects that tell something about themselves, put them in a small box, and bring the box in to share with the class. I head off the dreaded "Bring and Brag" by modeling first with my own life box, sharing such simple objects as a pencil to show that I like to write.

Before the speaker begins, I remind the children to listen carefully because we're going to play a game afterwards using the information they learn about the sharers. The games are riddles about classmates, such as "Who loves baseball?" and "Who has four sisters?" and "Who moved here from another country?" At first we play these games right after the three or four life boxes for the day are shared. Later I increase the challenge by including the riddles in the next day's Morning Meeting message.

There are many other opportunities for children to practice careful listening in the course of their school days. For example, after children partner-chat about books they're reading or ways they solved math problems, I ask them to tell the whole class what their partner said. As children learn that they're expected to paraphrase their partner's thoughts, they listen more acutely, eager to get to share in whole-class discussions what they heard their partner say.

(See Chapter Three, "Student-to-Student Conflict Resolution," for more on teaching listening.)

Seeing things from another's perspective

Seeing things from someone else's perspective is a stretch even for adults. Yet children will need to be able to do this if class meetings are to be successful. We can help children begin on this journey by helping them get to know each other well.

We can provide a variety of structures for doing this. In Morning Meeting, for example, for the sharing component we can have children take turns sharing on the topic "something I'm good at" or, a little into the year, say by October, when they feel more secure with their classmates, "something that's hard for me."

As they get to know each other, children start to see things from each other's points of view. When children hear that it's hard for Jenine to share with her five sisters, they begin to understand why sharing in school is sometimes hard for her. When they learn about how much Paul enjoys shooting hoops after school, they understand why it's so important to him to get a turn with the basketball at recess.

Responding honestly and kindly to classmates' thoughts

Unless students express their honest thoughts and feelings, it'll be hard to have a meaningful discussion. Unless they respond to each other's thoughts with kindness, the atmosphere of safety will be compromised and students won't feel comfortable expressing themselves honestly. Students can practice these skills throughout the day as they discuss their reading, writing, and other academic work.

For example, a group of fourth and fifth graders are getting ready for student-led literature groups, when they'll be responding to each other's ideas about the book. First we collect ideas about how we might respond with honesty and kindness when we disagree with someone.

"You could say, 'I hear what you're saying, but I had a different thought,'" suggests Sean.

Mel suggests "That's an interesting idea. When I read that chapter I noticed something else."

After role-playing some of these ideas (see Chapter Four for more on role-playing), the students gather in groups of four. Two students discuss, trying to be both honest and kind. The other two watch, tallying times they noticed honesty, times they noticed kindness. Then the partners switch roles—the observers discuss and the discussers observe.

Compromising in everyday interactions

Children love to write stories together, to solve math problems together, to partner-read their independent reading books, and to do science experiments in a small group. All of these activities call for compromise. *What shall we say next in our story? Which math strategy shall we try first? Which book shall we read, and who gets to turn the pages? Who will do which step of the science experiment?*

Whenever we guide children through these decisions, we have an opportunity to send a message that give-and-take is expected in this class and to give a mini-lesson on how to do it.

As first graders begin to partner-read, a few minutes of discussion about how to choose a book with their partner can go a long way. Modeling what holding the book together looks like, and how to agree on whether the partners will take turns reading or choral read, will set children up for success in working together.

As fifth graders begin their collaborative social studies research about ancient Egypt, role-playing how to include each group member's ideas can help students begin to compromise.

My colleague Melanie Carroll begins by stating the goal, "to include each group member's ideas." With a student volunteer, she shows the class what it might look like to combine two ideas about which artifact to create. The student has suggested they create a large papier-mache mummy. Ms. Carroll, in the role of the other student, has suggested a small painted sarcophagus. The third idea, a compromise, is to make something large and painted, a large painted sarcophagus.

Ms. Carroll asks students what they noticed about how she and her partner came up with the third solution. Then she has another pair of students demonstrate another possible way to combine two ideas and again asks students what they noticed.

With all of this explicit learning under their belts, the students go off to practice compromising as they begin their group projects.

Starting with an easier type of meeting

While continuing to reinforce these foundational skills, I begin teaching the class meeting format. I find it helpful to start with a class meeting to plan a group event or to make a group decision. These use a format similar to that of problem-solving class meetings, but the topics tend to be much less emotionally charged.

For example, early each year, often around the sixth week of school, I gather the children for a class meeting to choose a class name—the Intrepids or the Learning Leopards or some such. In contrast to calling ourselves "Ms. Crowe's class," which implies that I'm the most significant figure in the group, choosing a name together develops our sense that all group members are important.

This relatively straightforward task affords a good opportunity for children to learn the class meeting protocol. Later, they can transfer the skills they learned to more charged issues such as what to do about classroom cliques or how to include everyone on the playground.

Here's what this class name-choosing meeting looked like in one fourth grade class.

Preparation before the meeting

To pave the path for the initial class meeting, for a week I used our daily Morning Meetings to get the children thinking about potential class names. Each day I included a question in the morning message that allowed them to express their thoughts in this area. One day I asked, "Which animal is like our class?" Another day I asked, "Which adjective describes our class?" Children wrote their answers on the message chart and explained their reasons.

Stating the reason for our meeting

On the day of our first meeting, I gathered the children and began by telling them we were going to work together to choose a name for our class. They were excited. This sounded important to them.

I explained that many other classes had chosen an animal name coupled with an adjective. They knew what I meant: Many of these children had seen the sign at this classroom door in previous years and knew that the class members inside were known as the Helpful Pandas or the Caring Lions.

"We're becoming a community," I reminded the children. "It's important for us to choose a class name that everyone in our community feels comfortable with because names are important."

Set up ground rules for class meetings

Even though my students and I always create classroom rules and refer to them frequently, I, like many teachers, find it helpful to create some specific rules for class meetings.

"So we can choose a name that everyone feels comfortable with, what might be important for us to do as we all share our thoughts?" I asked.

Sandy raised her hand. "We'll need to listen to each other's ideas," she said. Children who had experienced any kind of classroom discussion nodded their heads vigorously. They knew what it felt like to share their ideas when no one was truly listening.

I wrote Sandy's idea on the chart and referred to our newly created classroom rules, one of which was "We will listen carefully to classmates and teachers." I said that even though we already had this as one of our class rules, having it also as a meeting rule would be a helpful reminder before we started our meetings.

"The reasons we have class meetings are to plan events, make decisions, or solve problems," I added. "We'll have one more rule for all of our class meetings: 'Work to solve the problem.' Why might that rule be important?"

I simply supplied this rule because I thought it was a key to successful class meetings, and I didn't think the students would come up with it on their own.

"You just said that's what class meetings are for, to solve problems," said Jake. "If we're going to solve problems, we're all going to need to work at it."

Thus we arrived at our two class meeting rules:

- We will listen to each other.

- We will work to solve the problem.

Another common class meeting rule is "Avoid blaming. State your own role in the problem."

Some teachers add "Avoid using names." This is a tricky one. If the problem is that Joey, Rick, and Jay all want to be on the same team at recess and everyone knows it, it can be awkward to keep saying, "Some kids only want to play on the same team together." On the other hand, lots of naming of names can degenerate into blaming. I usually tell the children at the beginning of the meeting, "No naming names today" or "If it helps to describe the problem, you may mention a name," depending on what the issue is.

Gathering ideas by going around the circle

The children went around the circle, each contributing his or her suggestion for a class name and including the reason for it.

- Dave wanted us to be the Brave Eagles because we were courageous and strong.

- Amy wanted the Bookmunchers because we loved to read.

- Stephanie suggested the Helpful Kittens because we were fun and funny.

- Zach wanted us to be the Community of Elephants because we were "one awesome community," loyal like elephants.

- Kevin suggested the Caring Crows, since my name is Ms. Crowe and we cared about each other.

- Some children who'd had siblings in my class in previous years suggested the names their siblings had chosen.

I wrote all of the names on a chart.

Some children looked to me to see how I was responding, but I was careful to remain neutral, even passing when my turn came around the circle. As a member of the group I certainly could have suggested a name, but I wanted to be judicious about sharing my opinions. If we had been problem-solving, and I saw a clear solution that no student was naming, I would have named it. But in this situation of brainstorming for class names, putting my suggestion in the mix could have derailed the focus on student opinions.

Inviting children to respond to the ideas suggested

I reminded the children of two more of our newly created classroom rules, "Be kind" and "Be honest." Then we went around the circle again, this time with each student expressing thoughts about the suggested names.

Dave said, "Girls like kittens. I want something more exciting, like the Brave Eagles." As children took their turns, it was clear that many of them liked the idea of being eagles because eagles are strong.

Other children spoke for the Caring Crows because it was based on my name and it sounded good.

Even though I frequently withhold my opinion so as to avoid swaying the class, in this case I thought it was worth weighing in because it's important that our class name not focus on me. So when it was my turn, I said that I didn't think we should be Crows. "Calling ourselves Crows makes it sound like the most important thing about our class is me, not the whole community," I explained.

Amy, noticing that Brave Eagles had such a following, suggested that we might be the Bookmunching Eagles because we all loved to read.

May said elephants were big and looked clumsy. She didn't want to be something big and clumsy, so she had a problem with the Community of Elephants.

Dan, ever the politician, said, "What if we were the Community of Bookmunching Eagles?"

Teaching children to reach consensus

Once every student had a say, I explained to the children that we were going to choose a name that everyone felt comfortable with. I would read each name out loud, and after each name they would put their thumb up if the name was their first choice and their thumb in the middle if it wasn't their first choice but they could live with it. If they felt really uncomfortable with a certain name, they could put their thumb down.

But first, I discussed with them what "can't live with it" really means. Sometimes children think that achieving consensus is just like voting and want to put their thumb down for every choice except their favorite. When this happens, decision-making becomes a competition rather than a collaboration, and the process grinds to a halt.

To help them understand the thumb-down option, I said, "When choosing a class name, think to yourself, 'Would I be embarrassed or upset to be called this name?' You only put your thumb down if you dislike a name that much. And if you put your thumb down, you should be prepared to explain why honestly."

I told them that some examples of names that children have put their thumbs down for in past years are the Fluffy Kittens (because it was too sweet), the Fierce Tigers (too scary) and the Crazy Monkeys (we're trying to be less reckless, and monkeys are reckless).

I continued, "If a name is not your favorite, but you wouldn't be embarrassed or upset to be called it, then you put your thumb in the middle. This is your way of saying 'This choice is not my favorite, but I can see why others like it, so I can live with it.'"

With this explanation, we showed thumb positions.

- Stephanie and Julia put their thumbs up for the Helpful Kittens. All of the boys had their thumbs down for that one.

- No one put a thumb up for Caring Crows—the children had taken my thoughts to heart.

- The Community of Elephants had no thumb up—the class had considered May's objections.

- Dave put his thumb up for his suggestion, the Brave Eagles, but no one else did.

- The Community of Bookmunching Eagles, the compromise class name, had seventeen thumbs up and one thumb down—Dave's.

Even with the teacher's careful explanation of what thumb down means, when children are just beginning to learn this process someone inevitably gets stuck in thumb-down mode, unable to see things from classmates' point of view. That's what happened to Dave. He had put his thumb down for nearly all suggestions except his own. As a result, there was no name that had no thumb down.

When this happens, it usually helps to engage the class in a further round of discussion, in which children tell more about what they think and why. First I reminded the class about our ground rule, "Work to find a solution," and then we began the round.

Among the reactions surfaced this time were Dave's feeling that eagles who munched on books didn't seem very brave or cool. Dan responded that eagles were always brave, so just saying "Eagles" felt brave. He also thought "bookmunching" made the eagles seem smart, and being smart was cool.

When we went around the circle to show thumbs again, Dave put his thumb in the middle for the Community of Bookmunching Eagles. That became our class name.

If the second round of showing thumbs had not broken the impasse, I would have closed the discussion and resumed it at a subsequent meeting. Often, after having more time to reflect and build trust in each other, children become more open to their peers' points of view.

The challenges of reaching consensus are one of the major reasons for practicing the class meeting format by choosing a class name, planning an event, or making some other non-emotionally laden decision. Problem-solving class meetings come later, when children have a firmer understanding of the process and deeper trust in each other.

Teaching negotiation

Children can easily get stuck in a thumb-up or thumb-down position, as Dave did in the preceding example. As we begin to hold class meetings, I model some strategies for getting unstuck. Children learn from my example and soon use the strategies themselves.

The key here is for children to listen to classmates, figure out what they want, and think of compromises that will meet everyone's needs. My language helps to remind students that we're trying to take care of all members of the community, moving the group to a compromise. Questions such as "How can we take care of Dave's need to have a name that feels exciting while we take care of everyone else's needs to have a name that they like?" can point children in a direction of compromise.

Probing children's reasons is another strategy for helping them negotiate. In the example above, we asked Dave why he couldn't live with the Community of Bookmunching Eagles. Once he explained that eagles munching on books didn't sound cool or brave, Dan was able to respond to those concerns and break the impasse.

Summing up the decision and complimenting the group on collaboration skills

I announced that our class name would be the Community of Bookmunching Eagles and asked for a volunteer to make a beautiful class door sign.

The children had worked hard. Reflecting their specific constructive behaviors back to them would help their learning. "I noticed that you made respectful comments about the suggested names. You listened to each other and compromised. That's not always easy to do. When so many of you liked the name Eagles, you figured out a way to choose a name that incorporated eagles, community, and your love of books."

This meeting took about forty minutes. The children had been engaged throughout and thus I had made the decision to push through and keep going despite how long they'd been at it. I might have stopped the process after about twenty minutes and resumed the meeting the next day if I'd felt that the students weren't ready for such a long block of work.

In the weeks ahead, we continued to practice the class meeting format, using it to plan events that were less emotionally laden than our later problem-solving experiences would be. Class meetings to plan a Halloween party and to decide on a way to celebrate diligent preparation for parent-teacher conferences are good choices for such practice. These issues are important to children but not too threatening.

Keys to Success in Class Meetings

The following go a long way toward making class meetings effective.

Build a trusting and respectful classroom community

Class meetings will be most successful if the classroom atmosphere is one of trust and respect. If children feel safe, they will express their thoughts and feelings honestly. If they respect each other, they will listen and be willing to compromise. Such an atmosphere is built slowly.

For teachers using the *Responsive Classroom* approach, Morning Meeting is a daily opportunity to build trust and respect. After students share about themselves, teachers can model asking a respectful question or making a caring comment and then guide students in offering their own questions and comments. As children participate in greetings and group activities, teachers can model and have students practice safe and careful ways to tap a partner's hand or give a gentle "high five." (To learn about Morning Meeting, see Appendix A.)

Our positive teacher language also promotes an atmosphere of respect. As we call students by name, use a respectful tone of voice, and avoid belittling students or using hurtful sarcasm, students imitate our language and behavior, treating each other with consideration.

When we expect that students will treat each other respectfully and hold them to that standard, they rise to the occasion. When we stop the group discussion as students begin to interrupt each other, we show students that listening is important. When we expect students to restate a belittling comment to a classmate in a positive way, we show students that respectful conversation is valued.

In some cases, part of the class meeting itself can be used to build a sense of community and trust. When I began using class meetings, I started each meeting with a compliment session to set a friendly tone.

There are many ways of doing this. Children can draw names and tell one helpful trait they see in the person whose name they drew or describe one helpful thing the person did that week. For example, a student might say, "I noticed that Devon helped Tomey figure out a good ending for his story." Alternatively, all community members might compliment one child at each meeting, with children taking turns being the complimented one. Or each child can simply choose a classmate to compliment.

After I fully integrated the *Responsive Classroom* approach with its community-building strategies into my teaching, I stopped including compliments as part of our class meetings because we gave and received compliments regularly as part of our Morning Meeting and closing circle activities. I recommend, however, that you do include this step if your students don't have many other opportunities to give and receive compliments.

Emphasize classroom and meeting rules

In my classes, our classroom rules are always front and center. We spend considerable time creating them in September and refer to them frequently throughout the day, the week, and the year. As discussed previously, we also create specific ground rules for class meetings.

At the beginning of each class meeting, I have the class review our class meeting ground rules. The combination of ongoing reference to classroom rules and specific review of class meeting rules helps keep children's interactions positive and respectful in the often emotionally laden discussions of a class meeting.

If a student begins to show disrespect during the meeting, I sometimes simply say "Remember, meeting rules," just as I often say "Remember, classroom rules" when students begin to misbehave at other times of the day. Frequently I find that a brief reminder like this is enough to bring students back on track.

Allow student suggestions for meeting topics, but make the final decision yourself

Most times in the life of a classroom it's the teacher who realizes the class has a problem that needs solving; sometimes it's the students who do. Collaborating with students means considering their ideas and sharing control of the meetings with them. The question is where that fine balance lies between too little and too much student control.

When I first started trying class meetings, I opened up the agenda to everyone with a "Class Meeting Agenda" sheet prominently displayed on the bulletin board.

I soon found that children were posting such problems as "Sal picks on me" and "Let's not have homework this week" that, for various reasons, were not suitable for whole-class discussion. Even worse, children started using the sign-up sheet for revenge. I started hearing angry statements like "I'm going to put you on the agenda."

I took down the sign-up sheet and installed a closed box for meeting agenda suggestions. This allowed me to evaluate the items as they came in, and it kept the agenda from being so public and a potential object of classroom strife. But it meant that I ended up discussing each item with the student who submitted it. I now plan the agenda myself.

Of course, even if we plan the agenda ourselves, it's still crucial to incorporate students' desires and needs. The most important way to do this is to notice them. How are things going? I make it clear to students that I want to hear their concerns, and then I listen carefully.

When a student complains about exclusion in the lunchroom, frustrations with distribution of classroom recess materials, or another issue that affects the whole class, I consider whether it's an appropriate class meeting topic, whether it needs a conflict resolution talk, or whether it's something I alone should solve. This approach keeps me in the role of leader of the meeting while giving students ownership.

Some teachers use part of each class meeting to generate agenda items for future meetings. Once the topic at hand is resolved, they ask, "Who has an item for a future meeting?" With this approach, they're allowing plenty of room for students to suggest items within the structure of the teacher's leadership.

In deciding whether to bring a problem to a class meeting, consider the following.

Is this an issue you want student input on?

Such suggestions as "Let's not have homework this week" are unsuitable for whole-class decision-making. Homework is governed by school and district policies. Also, it's the teacher's job to make sure students have adequate practice with academic skills.

Is this an issue that the students, at their stage of development, can handle?

For example, a group of literal-minded five-year-olds wouldn't be ready for a class meeting about how to lessen the school's environmental impact. But this is a topic that fifth graders can discuss productively, find solutions to, and act on.

Is the issue already taken care of by class or school rules?

I don't have the class decide whether exclusive "clubs," for example, are okay because in our school there's already an expectation, in fact an explicit rule, about including everybody.

Is this a whole-group problem?

Sometimes it can be tricky to figure this one out. When I first started using class meetings, I had a student who annoyed everyone at recess. In his desperate need to connect with others, Mike pulled off classmates' caps, snatched the ball away from games, and even threw rocks at others. The other students asked for a class meeting to discuss Mike's behavior. "Well," I thought, "Mike's behavior is affecting everyone. Let's try a class meeting."

What a mistake. Mike already knew he irritated other children, so he didn't learn anything new at the meeting. The other students weren't in a position to teach Mike more positive social skills. The meeting served to further alienate Mike from his classmates rather than bring him into the fold.

In retrospect, a private problem-solving conference with Mike or an individual written agreement would have helped him more. (See Chapter Two and Chapter Six to learn about these strategies.)

In contrast to this example, sometimes an issue seems like an individual problem, yet it's a productive one to discuss as a class. An example might be a child who is excluded from play during recess. Seeing this as a matter of inclusion would reveal it as a whole class issue. The group might have a productive class meeting about how to make sure everyone in the class has someone to play with at recess. All class members would learn compassion and responsibility for others as they plan how to include everyone.

Plan carefully how to state the reason for the meeting

If children are to care about finding a solution that's comfortable for everyone, the teacher needs to state the reason for the meeting with thought and precision. After many years of conducting class meetings, I still think about what I'm going to say ahead of time and write down a sentence or two in my lesson plan book.

Here are some things to think about in crafting the problem statement.

What, specifically, is the problem?

"Recess is chaotic" is imprecise and likely to confuse the children. But "students are being excluded at recess" or "the football game is rough" is specific and understandable. Sometimes before I craft the problem statement, I need to do some focused observation to hone my own thinking. I watch at recess. What's making it feel so chaotic? What are children doing and not doing?

How does the problem relate to the classroom rules?

In my classrooms, the students and I create the rules together, so the students feel significant ownership of them. Relating the problem to the rules therefore not only keeps the rules foremost in our minds but also makes the problem feel important and relevant.

I might begin by saying, "We all agreed to be safe, but recess isn't too safe right now. Yesterday, four students went to the nurse during recess." (Notice that I took care to be precise: "Four students went to the nurse" is specific enough so that children can understand exactly what the problem is.)

What positive language can I use?

Even though we're talking about a problem, it's important to use positive language that helps students envision how things might be better in the future. This promotes their investment in reaching a positive solution. Phrases such as "so that we can all be safe" and "so that everyone can be a part of our community" describe a positive ideal. "Safe," "careful," "friendly," "kind," and "caring" are all words that might be part of this ideal.

I might add to my statement about recess so that it becomes "We all agreed to be safe, but recess isn't too safe right now. Yesterday, four students went to the nurse during recess. During this meeting, let's figure out together how to make recess safe and friendly for everyone."

What previous event can I call up?

Sometimes there's a previous event in the life of the class that relates to the current problem. It might be a performance the children saw about an interpersonal issue, a story they shared as a read-aloud, or a previous decision they made.

"Remember when we decided we can't say 'You can't play'? How might that help us decide how to create fair teams for soccer games?" I might ask. Or "Remember when we read the story *The Other Side*? How did the girls make friends? How might that help us figure out how to be friendly on the playground?" Such references can help children understand the problem.

If the class meeting topic is one that a student suggested, think about whether to have her state the problem during the meeting. This often gives the discussion added power. Not every student is ready to take this risk, however. If a student is ready, I work with her to plan how she'll state the problem, going through the same planning questions that I go through myself. (For a sample meeting initiated by a student, see "The boys are making fun of me" on page 213.)

Rule out solutions that go against classroom or school rules

The teacher, as group leader, is responsible for maintaining a respectful tone and keeping the process on track. Part of this role is to remind children of classroom rules when an individual suggests a solution that doesn't honor those rules.

For example, in the class meeting about inclusion in the lunchroom early in this chapter, I ruled out Lenny's idea that "Kids who are alone can take care of themselves" because that approach would go against our rule to "be kind" and against our previous agreement to make sure everyone had company at lunch.

Stick to the protocol yourself

As leader of the group, the teacher makes sure children stick to the steps of the meeting. The children each get a say going around the circle. Interrupting or speaking out of turn is not allowed. When someone disagrees with a classmate's suggested solution, he must wait until the commenting step, when the group goes around the circle to say what they think about ideas shared so far.

To protect the integrity of this process, it's important that the teacher stick to these steps, too. When Kevin suggested that we name our class the Caring Crows and then, even worse, when lots of students seemed to like that name, I was so tempted to say right away, "No, no, that's not what this is about. We're looking for an alternative to being 'Ms. Crowe's class.'" Instead I waited until the point in the meeting when we were making comments about the ideas suggested.

If I set an example of following the steps, children are more likely to follow the steps. If I break out of the format, I'm giving them permission to do the same.

Hold class meetings regularly

As students participate in regularly scheduled class meetings, the format becomes second nature to them. Many teachers schedule a weekly class meeting. Others start there and then move to bi-weekly meetings once the children are very familiar with the steps.

Such regularly scheduled meetings might be used to plan events—*What shall we do with our first grade buddies next week?* They might be used as check-ins on decisions made in the past—*How are things going in the lunchroom? Is everyone feeling included?* Of course, they will also be used for solving problems as needed—*How can we take better care of our classroom library?*

Because I use the *Responsive Classroom* approach, my students have lots of regular practice sharing ideas, listening to each other, and reaching compromises. For this reason, once the group is comfortable with the class meeting format (usually by January), I move to using class meetings only as needed. Depending on the group and its needs, this translates to a meeting about every two to four weeks.

Questions from Teachers

What's the difference between class meetings and Morning Meetings?

Morning Meetings are held every day for the purpose of building community and warming up for a day of learning. Unlike class meetings, Morning Meetings are not used for solving problems or making group decisions such as choosing a class name. Instead, the children use the time to greet each other, share personal news, do a lively group activity, and read a motivating message from their teacher about the day ahead.

When classes hold both Morning Meetings and class meetings, however, the social skills, the habit of collaboration, and the trust they build through Morning Meetings often lead to more successful class meetings.

(To learn more about Morning Meetings, see Appendix A.)

My students go off on tangents in class meetings and soon aren't even discussing the initial problem anymore. How can I keep them focused?

This is why the format is so important. Are you holding the group tightly to all of the steps? Even though the teacher is a member of the group and takes turns with everyone else, she's also the group leader. The teacher stops the group as soon as they begin to veer off. I remember my colleague Chip Wood conducting a class meeting with fifth graders about their tendency during work periods to chat about things unrelated to the lesson. Predictably, the students chatted off-topic during the class meeting, too. Chip kept saying to them, "Isn't this hard? This meeting only works if we follow the rules." Somehow, it felt like it was the rules themselves, rather than Chip, that was keeping the group on topic.

I want to help my students use consensus, but I'm overwhelmed. Are there ways to introduce consensus incrementally?

Remember how my colleague Lisa Garsh teaches her first graders to come to consensus? You might try her method with older children, too, if reaching a decision collaboratively is new to them or if they need an interim step for any other reason. After the class has brainstormed a list of possible solutions and combined very similar ones, go down the list with the class. For each idea, ask "Is this realistic? Is this respectful?"

With a narrowed-down list after eliminating the unfeasible solutions, you, the teacher, can pick one idea and say, "We're going to try this one for a week. Then we'll come back together and discuss how it worked."

This would be an appropriate moment to say, "Today I chose which idea to try by considering the needs and feelings you expressed. But I hope that soon our class will be ready to find a solution everyone in the class can agree to."

With that comment, you've set the stage for working up to making decisions by consensus. At the next meeting, the class might be ready to choose, via consensus, among solutions that the group has deemed respectful and realistic.

In a recent meeting, several students kept putting thumbs down for every idea but their favorite. How can I prevent that in future meetings?

You're not alone. Many teachers report having this problem even after the class has had a second round of commenting on the suggestions.

Sometimes students need further help realizing that reaching consensus is different from voting. I would suggest having a class discussion about the purpose of class meetings. Make sure all students understand that the purpose is to find a solution that's comfortable for everyone, not to push for what they themselves want most.

This also might be a good time to refocus on building your classroom community. Try having students play games that require working with everyone. Also try assigning random partners for academic work so that students can get to know and trust all of their classmates.

That said, at times a student has a good reason to put her thumb down for all but one choice. We shouldn't underestimate the power of one. The student who holds out for a particular decision may be the one person who's seeing things most clearly. If you think the lone holdout may have a good point, you might have her explain her thinking. Then go around the circle again with everyone responding to what she said.

Remember Noah in the class meeting about lunchtime seating? He was holding out, putting his thumb down because he had important needs that weren't being met and wouldn't be met with the solutions the other children wanted. Once the group came up with a solution that also met Noah's needs, he moved out of thumb-down mode.

Examples of Class Meetings

EXAMPLE 1

Lots of people forgetting homework: A second grade class meeting

In my school district, homework begins in second grade. Homework is a new experience for all the second graders and something of a shock for many. I myself remember, more than fifty years ago, hiding my second grade homework in the bushes on the way home from school, hoping it would just go away.

My colleague Mr. Parrish had carefully taught homework routines to his second graders. The children had chosen a place to do homework at home and practiced doing "homework" at school while Mr. Parrish observed. After students started doing homework at home, the student in charge of "pass out and collect" put homework sheets into student mailboxes before the end of each day so that everyone would take the work home. Mr. Parrish knew that six- and seven-year-olds tend to be industrious workers, so he believed that the children wanted to and were capable of doing the simple homework he assigned.

Nonetheless, many students were showing up at school in the mornings without their assignments. Some days only a few students remembered. Not a single student remembered consistently. One Tuesday, no one returned completed homework. This was a whole-class issue, and Mr. Parrish decided to address it with a class meeting.

Mr. Parrish gave himself some time to think before acting. He didn't want to meet with the students while he was feeling frustrated. On Friday morning the class gathered in a circle, right after math and before art. They played a brisk round of Head, Shoulders, Knees, and Toes and then sat down comfortably in a circle on the floor.

The group reviews ground rules for class meetings

The expectation for class meeting, "Work to solve the problem," was posted on the chart stand. Mr. Parrish asked Mike, the helper of the day, to read the expectation aloud. Then he asked the children which of their classroom rules might help them have a successful class meeting.

Kenji raised his hand and said, "Take care of each other."

"How will we do that?" asked Mr. Parrish.

Students chimed in, "We'll listen" and "We'll try to help each other."

The teacher states the reason for the meeting

"Lots of people are forgetting their homework," said Mr. Parrish. "On Tuesday, not one single student brought homework back," he continued. "One of our rules says to 'Do your best.' What can we do so that we all do our best at homework?"

Students each state what they've noticed about the problem or say "Pass"

"We'll go around the circle," said Mr. Parrish. "You may say what you've noticed about your part in the homework problem, or you may say 'Pass.' Who would like to begin?"

Albert raised his hand. "I have too much to do," he explained. "I have soccer, cub scouts, and religious ed after school. I don't have time for homework, too."

Mr. Parrish was thinking, "What's most important, school or after-school activities?" But he remained silent and calm, making an effort to remain open to all of the children's observations.

Kim, sitting next to Albert, went next. "I do my homework every night, but I forget it. I leave it on the kitchen table."

Lisa, sitting next to Kim, said, "My mom checks my homework when she gets home from work. She gets home after I'm asleep. Then I forget to put it back in my bag in the morning. I'm in a hurry then."

"It's noisy at my house, and I can't pay attention to my homework," said Melissa. Melissa and her large family lived in a small space.

"Sometimes my homework is too hard. We learned how to do those math problems in school, but I forgot by the time I got home," said Joe.

The children continued around the circle. Everyone contributed something. This was a topic of intense interest. Some children were too busy, others too tired. Some needed to play outside, others to watch TV.

When it was Mr. Parrish's turn, he thought about how he might have contributed to the problem. "Maybe I'm giving assignments that are too hard for second graders to do at home," he said. He knew that six-year-olds sometimes get overwhelmed by work that seems daunting and seven-year-olds take comfort in doing tasks they can manage easily. He was reevaluating whether his students could, without teacher support, do some of the tasks he'd been assigning.

Each student suggests a solution or says "Pass"

"We'll go around the circle again and collect ideas for how to solve our homework problem," said Mr. Parrish. Mr. Parrish recorded the children's ideas on a chart as they spoke.

"I think we should have homework two nights a week, not every night," said Albert, who was so busy.

"Mr. Parrish could write a letter to our parents and tell them how important it is to bring homework back to school," said Kim, the one who often left her homework on the kitchen table.

"We could all write letters to our parents and ask them to help us remember to bring our homework to school," added Lisa, whose mother checked her homework after Lisa went to sleep.

"Maybe we could have homework choices, so that kids could choose homework they can do," suggested Joe. Mr. Parrish gave students choices in math and spelling work in school, so choice at home made sense to Joe.

Some children passed this time. They had no idea how to resolve the issues of noisy homes and not enough playtime.

Because each student had raised a suggestion fitting his or her own problems with homework completion, there was no need for the class to comment on each other's suggestion. Mr. Parrish therefore skipped that step. Furthermore, Mr. Parrish thought that some of the students, tense and sensitive as is typical of seven-year-olds, would have trouble giving each other meaningful feedback.

The group reaches agreement on a solution to try, using "thumbs up, middle, or down"

Mr. Parrish could have stopped the meeting here. He could have complimented the children on their hard work and then made some decisions himself about how to handle the problem on the basis of the information he'd gathered from the children.

The class, however, had practiced reaching consensus, and he decided to try that strategy today. He told the children that he had to give them homework four nights a week. "I have to follow certain rules. One of them is that second graders do homework four nights a week," he told the students. Then he read aloud the list of suggested solutions that were allowable under the rules he had to follow:

- Mr. Parrish writes to parents about homework.

- Students write to parents about homework.

- Mr. Parrish gives homework choices.

Because the children were just learning how to reach consensus, Mr. Parrish told them they could put their thumbs up for one choice, their first choice. Later in the year he might let them put thumbs up for any choice they liked, but for now it would be more straightforward to make only one thumb-up choice. He told them they could put their thumbs in the middle for any choice that seemed okay to them, any choice they could live with. He told them to put their thumbs down for any choice they "couldn't live with," one that seemed too hard.

Many children put their thumbs up for "Mr. Parrish writes to our parents." They were feeling the need for a little more support at home.

A few put thumbs up for "Kids write to parents about homework," though several put their thumbs down because writing to parents felt too hard for them.

"Mr. Parrish gives homework choices" had the largest number of thumbs up and no thumb down. Many children knew they'd be more successful if the homework allowed them to practice skills they were very comfortable with rather than more recently learned skills. They trusted Mr. Parrish to give such choices.

The teacher sums up and compliments the group on their collaboration skills

Mr. Parrish complimented the class by saying, "I noticed careful thinking today. You told about your problems with homework honestly and you came up with many ideas that we might try. Starting next week, I'll offer homework choices every night. Then we'll talk again next Friday about how things are going."

The entire meeting lasted about twenty minutes. Now it was time to get in line for art.

The teacher follows up with reminders and check-ins

During the intervening week, many, but not all, students completed and brought back their homework. It was clear to Mr. Parrish that with choices in assignments, the students for whom homework had been too hard were now able to do their homework. The students who had reported lack of support at home, however, hadn't improved.

On Friday, Mr. Parrish announced that homework had improved. The class applauded themselves. He then told the children that he planned to write to their parents, asking them to find a quiet place for homework and to help their children return completed assignments each day. This subsequent step led to further improvement.

THINGS TO NOTE in this second grade "forgetting homework" meeting

- *Appropriate topic:* All students were having difficulty turning in their homework, so this was a whole-group problem. The topic was also of interest to all the children.

- *Teacher's calm attitude:* Mr. Parrish waited until he was calm and open to children's ideas before holding the meeting.

- *Circle seating:* The group sat in a circle where everyone could see and be seen by each other.

- *Reminder about rules:* Mr. Parrish took a minute to remind the group of their meeting expectations and general classroom rules.

- *Clear problem statement:* Mr. Parrish explained the problem briefly and clearly, connecting it to the classroom rules.

- *Democratic process:* All children had the opportunity to speak.

- *Teacher learning:* Mr. Parrish came to understand the problem better as a result of the children's contributions.

- *Foundational skills:* The children had had previous practice reaching consensus.

- *Follow-up:* When the solution "Mr. Parrish gives homework choices" produced change but not enough change, Mr. Parrish decided to try the group's second-choice solution as well.

EXAMPLE 2

"The boys are making fun of me": A fourth grade small-group meeting using the class meeting structure

Sometimes the class meeting structure is an equitable way to reach understanding about a problem that affects a subgroup of the class, such as those in the class who ride bus number 3 or all those who play Four Square together. In this example, the meeting was of all the boys in a fourth grade class I taught.

One day P.J. spoke with me privately. "The boys are teasing me at lunch," he said. P.J. was having a recurrence of Tourette Syndrome and often twitched his head uncontrollably.

"Have you talked with them about your head shaking?" I asked.

"No. I don't know what to say," P.J. responded.

"Would you like me to help you?"

"Yeah, okay."

I thought about which strategy to use to address this problem. I ruled out conflict resolution (see Chapter Three) because although the boys were teasing P.J., it really wasn't a conflict—I suspected that the boys didn't know what was going on with P.J., and he hadn't felt confident enough to tell them. I guessed that it was all about misinformation. Also, the group, all the boys in our class, was too large to comfortably have a conflict resolution meeting.

Thus, I thought the class meeting format would be a good venue for allowing P.J. to explain his head shaking to the other boys in a safe environment. Using this format could help him to assert himself, the other boys to express their thoughts, and everyone to be more empathetic.

I announced that there would be a "boys' meeting" during lunch. All of the boys arrived at lunchtime with their lunches and sat in a circle on the floor.

The group reviews ground rules for class meetings

Kai, the "teacher's helper" for the week, read the class meeting rules: "Work to find a solution" and "Listen to each other."

The student states the reason for the class meeting

Before the meeting, I had discussed with P.J. whether he would like to state the problem during the meeting. When the problem is one that a student has identified, I like to let the student introduce it if possible. This helps the student feel competent and allows the rest of the group to see that student as a strong, take-charge person. Also, children often are more engaged in problems brought forth by a peer than by their teacher.

In this instance, P.J. agreed to state the problem. He and I practiced what he would say. On the day of the meeting, he was ready.

"My head twitches. I can't help it," P.J. began. "I don't like it when kids tease me about it. Our rules say to be kind, and that doesn't feel kind to me." His voice and body language were confident and assertive. His classmates listened attentively. The problem was half solved already.

Students each state what they've noticed about the problem or say "Pass"

The boys went around the circle, telling what they had noticed about the problem.

"I thought you were doing it on purpose to be funny," said Jamal.

"I thought you were having fun with us, so I was having fun with you," said Kai.

Some boys passed, but many made similar comments, saying they'd thought P.J. had initiated a silly game.

Each student suggests a solution or says "Pass"

Then the boys went around the circle again, seeking solutions.

"Now that I know you can't stop your head from shaking, I won't tease you about it," said Jamal.

"I'm glad you told us. Now we won't make fun of you," said Will.

There was no need to brainstorm and evaluate solutions in this meeting. Once everyone understood that P.J. couldn't control his head movements, a clear consensus, "Now we won't make fun of you," naturally emerged.

The teacher sums up and compliments the group on their collaboration skills

"You all listened to P.J. when he explained about his head twitching," I said. "You were able to reach a solution that will be kinder to your classmate."

The meeting lasted about fifteen minutes. After it was over, the boys relaxed on the rug, eating their lunches and talking about upcoming weekend events.

The teacher follows up with check-ins

A few days later, I checked in with P.J. "How's it going with the boys at lunch?" I asked.

"They don't tease me anymore," he replied.

> **THINGS TO NOTE** in "the boys are making fun of me" meeting

- *Student taking charge:* P.J. himself stated the problem to the group. His classmates understood that he was the one who had the concern, and they saw him in a strong, assertive role.

- *Rehearsal:* P.J. and I practiced how he would state the problem. He rehearsed telling the group a fact they didn't know, referring to class rules, and sharing his own feelings.

- *Support for the student:* P.J. was able to share delicate but important information with the group because he had teacher support in planning how to state the issue as well as the support of the class meeting structure.

- *Fidelity to the protocol:* The group stuck to the format, going around the circle, each child taking a turn telling his understanding of the problem and then each stating a solution.

- *Follow-up:* I checked in later to make sure the group was abiding by their solution.

Making it work for you

Meeting steps:

1. Teacher guides class in reviewing ground rules for class meetings.

2. Teacher states the reason for the meeting.

3. Each student suggests an idea or says "Pass." (Or teacher asks for student volunteers.)

4. Students comment on the ideas suggested.

5. Teacher picks an idea for the class to try.

6. Teacher explains that at their next meeting, the class will discuss how this idea is working. Teacher compliments the group on collaboration skills.

7. Teacher follows up, if appropriate, with reminders and check-ins.

CLASS MEETING PLANNING SHEET

For Event Planning or Decision Making in K–1

What is the event to plan or the decision to make? Be specific.

Are there restrictions the children need to know up front? (For example, "We have thirty minutes for our party.")

What positive language can you use to describe the event or decision? Write down two sentences.

How will you record students' suggestions?

When and where will you hold the meeting?

 Making it work for you

Meeting steps:

For Problem-Solving in **K–1**

1. Teacher guides children in reviewing ground rules for class meetings.

2. Teacher states the reason for the meeting.

3. Students each state what they've noticed about the problem or how it makes them feel, or say "Pass." (Or teacher asks for student volunteers.)

4. Each student suggests a solution or says "Pass." (Or teacher asks for student volunteers.)

5. Teacher picks one solution for the class to try.

6. Teacher explains that at their next meeting, the class will discuss how the solution is working. Teacher compliments the group on collaboration skills.

7. Teacher follows up with reminders and check-ins.

What is the problem? Be specific.

How does the problem relate to classroom rules?

Are there any previous events in the life of the class, such as past decisions, that relate to this problem?

What positive language can you use to describe the problem? Write down two sentences.

How will you record students' suggested solutions?

When and where will you hold the meeting?

Following the meeting, at what times in the day might you remind the children of the decisions they made?

What language will you use to give these reminders?

What language might you use to reinforce children's behavior when you see them following the decisions made at the meeting?

Making it work for you

Meeting steps:

For Event Planning or Decision Making in Grades 2—6

1. Teacher guides class in reviewing ground rules for class meetings.

2. Teacher (or a student) states the reason for the meeting.

3. Each student suggests an idea or says "Pass."

4. Students comment on the ideas suggested.

5. Class reaches agreement on a solution to try by using "thumbs up, middle, or down."

6. Teacher sums up the decision and compliments the group on collaboration skills.

7. Teacher follows up, if appropriate, with reminders and check-ins.

What is the event to plan or the decision to make? Be specific.

Are there restrictions the children need to know up front? (For example, "We have thirty minutes for our party.")

What positive language can you use to describe the event or decision? Write down two sentences.

Who will record students' suggestions? (This job usually rests with the teacher in grades 1–4 and a pair of students in grades 5–6.)

When and where will you hold the meeting?

Making it work for you

Meeting steps:

For Problem-Solving in Grades **2–6**

1. Teacher guides class in reviewing ground rules for class meetings.

2. Teacher (or a student) states the reason for the meeting.

What is the problem? Be specific.

3. Students each state what they've noticed about the problem or how it makes them feel, or say "Pass."

4. Each student suggests a solution or says "Pass."

How does the problem relate to classroom rules?

5. Students comment on the solutions suggested.

6. Class reaches agreement on a solution to try by using "thumbs up, middle, or down."

Are there any previous events in the life of the class, such as past decisions, that relate to this problem?

7. Teacher sums up the decision and compliments the group on collaboration skills.

8. Teacher follows up with reminders and check-ins.

What positive language can you use to describe the problem? Write down two sentences.

Who will record students' suggested solutions? (This job usually rests with the teacher in grades 1–4 and a pair of students in grades 5–6.)

When and where will you hold the meeting?

Following the meeting, what times in the day might you remind the children of the decisions they made?

What language will you use to give these reminders?

What language might you use to reinforce children's behavior when you see them following the decisions made at the meeting?

CHAPTER SIX

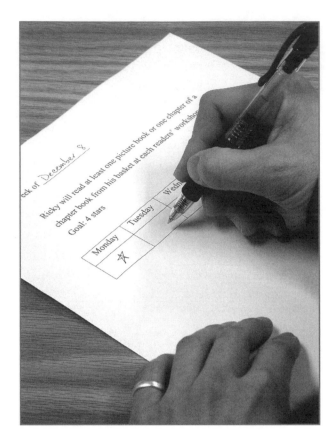

Individual Written Agreements

"I don't *want* to, I won't *do* it," Angela announced when I told her it was time to leave the computer and take part in our science lesson.

Earlier that day she had crawled under a table and refused to come out when I asked her to join us at reading group.

Such confrontations with Angela were a daily event in our classroom. A fourth grader with a history of defying teachers, Angela wanted to do what she wanted when she wanted.

The class had created and practiced classroom rules. I used firm, respectful language to remind and redirect her. I used logical consequences when she broke rules. She and I had met for problem-solving conferences (see Chapter Two to learn about this strategy) in which we'd created plans for me to give her reminders before she got into potentially challenging situations. We'd created plans for Angela to talk to herself about why it was important to follow directions, and for Angela to look around and see how her classmates were following directions. None of these things worked.

Andrew, the third grader I introduced in Chapter Two who threw tantrums when it was time to write, finally made progress after several problem-solving conferences. For about two months he wrote a passable amount, thanks to a plan we crafted that had him arriving before the other students in the morning and writing then, when his energy was high. But when I asked him to increase the amount of writing, his old resistance came back. Not only did he refuse to write more, he refused to write at all. It was clear to me that another problem-solving conference would not help.

Children like Angela and Andrew are not uncommon in our classrooms. These are children whose misbehaviors are ingrained, who are stuck in a rut or who've gotten unstuck briefly, only to return to being stuck again. Their teachers try all the classroom climate-building and problem-solving strategies discussed so far in this book, but nothing seems to work, or something works, but only for a short while.

For children in such situations, an individual written agreement may help. Such an agreement is a highly structured system of providing incentives for children to change course. It's a strategy that a classroom teacher can use, often with support from parents, behavior specialists, psychologists, and other adults who are part of the child's life. The basic structure can be adapted for successful use with children as young as kindergarten. When a child is struggling to change a behavior, an individual written agreement can provide extra motivation.

For example, Angela didn't seem to have sufficient motivation to follow any of the plans we came up with during our problem-solving conferences. I decided it was time to try an individual written agreement.

One day I asked her to meet with me to discuss her behaviors. I reminded her that it was important to do what teachers told her to without arguing. If she disagreed, she could discuss it with the teacher later on. So far, this was all information she'd heard from me before.

Then I suggested something different—that it might help Angela do what teachers told her to if we kept a record of her improvements and if she worked for a reward. The idea of a reward got her attention and excited her. Together we brainstormed rewards she might enjoy earning. We thought of extra computer time, extra time in the art area, and helping the art or music teacher or the school secretaries. Angela, who loved to organize things, chose to help the school secretaries.

I created a chart with Angela's goal written at the top: *Angela will do what teachers tell her to without arguing. If she disagrees, she may discuss it with the teacher later.* Throughout the day Angela had opportunities to earn stars for meeting her goal. I gave her frequent reminders and encouragement.

At the end of the week Angela had met the agreed-upon target of earning sixteen out of twenty possible stars for the week. On Monday morning she helped the school secretaries send out a parent mailing.

The following weeks saw similar improvement. Most days Angela earned at least four stars. The confrontations didn't vanish—earning four stars meant she still had at least one problematic time that day—but the change was notable. Angela spent more time working, less time arguing; I had more time and energy for teaching; and Angela's classmates began to see her as a more cooperative class member.

Andrew's behavior improved, too, after I established an individual written agreement for him, and it stayed improved for a good long while this time. We set a goal of writing at least four sentences and agreed that he would get to help the kindergartners with their writing if he met this goal in four of the five writing periods during the week. This was the external incentive he needed to re-rally the energy to write.

After a while, he even seemed not to need the reward every day. One day he wrote a whole page and then announced, "I'm learning to like writing; I don't need that agreement anymore."

Purpose: Giving Highly Structured Intensive Support

The purpose of individual written agreements is to give students who need it highly structured intensive support to change a behavior that is getting in the way of their learning or the functioning of the group. Over and over, I have seen this strategy bring about a positive change in behavior.

This success then begins to affect the way the child sees herself, nudging her self-perception from that of rule breaker toward that of rule respecter, from work avoider toward competent worker, from group disrupter toward group contributor.

Of course, our ultimate goal for these children, as for all children, is that they develop internal motivation to conduct themselves as hard workers and cooperative group members. We therefore wean them from external incentives as they're ready. Used well, individual written agreements lead the child to gradually value the satisfaction of a job well done over the receipt of a reward.

When to Use an Individual Written Agreement

Individual written agreements are intended for selective use. I recommend reserving them for the following situations.

When other strategies haven't worked

I consider using an individual written agreement after trying other strategies. I make sure the classroom climate is supportive and academic assignments are appropriate for the child. I try logical consequences. Then I try problem-solving conferences. I think about an individual written agreement if these strategies haven't modified the child's behavior.

Think carefully before you use this strategy. Researchers have found that external rewards can lower intrinsic motivation (Deci & Flaste, 1995). Working for a reward may modify the child's behavior in the short run. But because the child will be working for the reward at least initially, there is the risk that his development of intrinsic motivation will be impeded. It's possible that Angela will learn to think of herself as a reward earner rather than a rule respecter. She may continue on in school asking teachers, "What will you give me if I follow directions without arguing?"

I therefore reserve this strategy for behaviors that are highly detrimental to the child's learning or the classroom's functioning. Ricky refused to read and bothered classmates who were reading. Vanessa crawled under the table and chewed on other children's feet during quiet work times. Donnie was so rough with his classmates that they were afraid of him. I used individual written agreements with these children after other strategies proved ineffective.

When you're prepared to give frequent feedback

Before setting up an individual written agreement, also consider whether you're prepared to give the child frequent reminders and encouragement, because such feedback is the most crucial component of this strategy.

Children with ingrained behavior problems are often discouraged children, children whose months or years of academic or social difficulties have led them to feel helpless or incompetent. Or they are children who have come to believe they can achieve a sense of belonging or significance only through disruptive behavior. If such children are to become encouraged and to choose positive paths to satisfying their emotional needs, we must give them frequent reminders about how to behave and, when they do behave that way, show them that we noticed by offering positive feedback.

I have found that many children benefit as much or more from receiving hourly feedback from me as from the reward. Sometimes just seeing a chart that documents their success in meeting their goal for the day or the week is enough to encourage continued effort. The reward itself then becomes unnecessary. For this reason, if we set up an individual written agreement, it's vital to keep up the encouragement. If we begin giving feedback and then let it slide, we're sending the message, "This isn't that important."

As classroom teachers, our days are full of myriad responsibilities. One way to do a reality check about whether we can take on this additional task is to think to ourselves as we go through our day, "Could I give a quiet personal reminder right now? Could I give a quick star here?"

An individual written agreement can be just the thing to help a particular student. If, however, you decide to try this strategy, go in with your eyes wide open. Giving constant feedback can be overwhelming. This strategy will work only if you implement it with complete consistency.

If you're not ready for this, redouble your efforts in using logical consequences consistently, think about new ways to modify the child's school work, consult with specialists in your school about how to help the child learn, or consider another problem-solving conference (see Chapter Two).

Steps in an Individual Written Agreement

Effective use of an individual written agreement involves careful teacher preparation, introducing the contract to the student and parents, and faithful follow-through. Following are the steps in this process, illustrated with the story of Ricky, a third grader.

Ricky was the youngest of four children, all raised by their grandmother. Throughout his eight years he'd learned to avoid tasks he didn't want to do, both at home and at school. He'd found that busy adults eventually stopped trying to get him to make his bed, start his homework, or complete his assignments. Ricky was a bright child, but he had missed learning crucial math concepts, and lack of reading practice meant that he hadn't grown as a reader. He chose thick books to "read" and spent reading time alternately pretending to read and wandering around the classroom, bothering other children who were trying to read.

Ricky seemed caught in a vicious cycle: His lack of math and reading skills made him reluctant to engage in assignments, and his reluctance to engage made him fall further and further behind in his skills. By third grade his self-confidence was low. He didn't see himself as a learner.

I was both frustrated and deeply worried that Ricky was headed toward permanent school failure if something didn't change now. I knew that children who, by third grade, have already constructed a self-image as non-learners may very well become more and more set in that view as time goes on. It would only get harder for teachers to help Ricky change his self-image as he got older. This was the time to act.

Preparing for the Agreement

To prepare for the agreement:

- Make sure you're in a collaborative frame of mind.

- Think about possible reasons for the student's behavior.

- Make sure the student is getting needed academic and social supports.

- Try other problem-solving strategies first.

- Decide on the specific behavior you want the child to adopt.

- Think about acceptable choices for rewards.

- Contact the student's family.

Make sure you're in a collaborative frame of mind

Like all the problem-solving strategies in this book, the use of an individual written agreement is a collaborative strategy. The teacher gets on the same side as the student to help her grow. Often we are enticing the child to behave in a certain way by offering a reward; nonetheless, we must always keep a mindset of collaboration. For an individual written agreement to be effective, you and the child must feel that you're in this together, setting goals, evaluating progress, and determining next steps.

I will be the first to acknowledge that it can be very hard to get into this mindset with children who need individual written agreements. Let's face it—these are the children who have defied us, disrupted learning, or destroyed scarce classroom resources. They're the children for whom we've tried multiple strategies unsuccessfully.

I remember how annoyed I was with Ricky for wandering the room, disrupting others' learning. To be honest, my annoyance came partly from the fact that Ricky's behavior had made me doubt my own competence. If I couldn't keep Ricky from disrupting other students' learning, was I really a good teacher?

I knew that I wouldn't be able to help Ricky without first getting on his side. As I took my daily walk, I thought about him and tried to see things from his point of view. It was only after I spoke to our music teacher, whose son played with Ricky after school, and learned some details about Ricky's home life that I began to feel more empathetic. I was also able to set aside worries about my own competence and focus instead on Ricky—what made him tick, what school might feel like for him, what he needed to become an engaged learner. Then I felt ready to meet with Ricky again.

If you're not feeling so collaborative—and we've all been there—try taking a walk-and-think, have a go at writing about your feelings, or chat with a trusted colleague.

Then there are those moments when things aren't going well with a student and we're tempted to threaten, "If you don't stop right now, you'll have to have another agreement."

If you feel the urge to use an individual written agreement as a threat or a punishment, first take care of the immediate behavior. Use positive time-out either for the student or for yourself. I find that going to the "Take a Break" area myself and taking a couple of deep breaths can be amazingly restorative. Then take some steps to regroup emotionally. Find a time to reflect, go for a walk, talk to a colleague. Plan your strategy once you're calm and have reached a place of empathy with the student.

Think about possible reasons for the student's behavior

Thinking about possible reasons for children's behavior helps us develop empathy for them and tailor our responses. I thought about Ricky's basic human need for competence. I thought about his lack of engagement with any kind of reading. I wondered if Ricky had given up. Had his years of low achievement in school led him to feel helpless and unable? I find that it's the most discouraged readers who cling to those big fat books, saving face by pretending to read.

I resolved to encourage in Ricky any positive steps toward school success, no matter how incremental. He needed to feel successful. Whatever problem-solving strategy I engaged in with him, a key would be to set one or two specific, achievable goals at a time.

Make sure the student is getting needed academic and social supports

So often, students act out because they're struggling academically or socially. Before launching an individual written agreement, ask yourself whether you've used other supports that might mitigate the need for this strategy.

Are your academic expectations reasonable for this child? Is the child getting the academic support he needs? Have you modeled and provided guided practice for the behaviors that are challenging for this child? Do you refer to the community-generated rules throughout the day? Are you using encouraging and empowering language to help the child envision a better way of being in the classroom? Are you using your words and actions to show children how to live together with kindness and care?

My answer to all these questions in the case of Ricky was yes. I next thought about logical consequences. Had I used logical consequences to help him modify his behavior?

I had told Ricky that reading was an important part of third grade. If he didn't read during reading time, I had said, he would read during quiet time after lunch. The result was that Ricky didn't get his daily ten minutes of quiet puppet or blocks play, ten minutes that he very much anticipated and needed. But he still wouldn't read.

I thought a bit more about the academic supports. For his math difficulties, I had arranged for Ricky to receive some "catch up" help from a fifth grader. Ricky loved the attention from the older boy and learned quickly from him. With cautious optimism, I decided to continue that arrangement as long as it worked rather than jump to an individual written agreement for math improvement.

Reading was a different story. When I gave Ricky reading assessments, I noticed that he used picture clues to aid his reading comprehension. I met with the reading specialist and she suggested that I monitor his reading, giving him richly illustrated books we both gauged he could read. Nonetheless, he gazed at the books passively and put them down as soon as I left his side.

Because none of the academic and social supports given to Ricky were helping him with his reading difficulty, I realized that more intensive problem-solving was needed.

Try other problem-solving strategies first

With Ricky, I tried a problem-solving conference first (see Chapter Two to learn about that strategy). When we met, we looked at his nearly empty reading log together. I showed him the results of reading assessments he'd taken, drawing his attention to the assessments he'd done well on, assessments at his level with rich picture clues. I explained that we all become better readers when we read material we can comprehend. I said I wanted to help him find books at his just-right reading level so he'd be a better reader and asked if he'd like to work together with me on that.

Ricky showed no interest, no willingness to collaborate or even to consider whether his reading was a problem. His only response was to insist that he could read *Harry Potter*, a book that was clearly too hard for him. He maintained that he liked that book and wanted to keep reading it.

I decided it was time to try an individual written agreement.

Decide on the specific behavior you want the child to adopt

Once you're ready to try an individual written agreement, think carefully about specific and easy-to-measure goals for this child. What are the behaviors that, if changed, will make things different? Choose one or, at the most, two specific behaviors.

Think about how you'll state these behaviors. How can you state them in the positive so that the child can picture a new way of being? Rather than "don't hit," for example, you might state the behavior you want to see as "be gentle with classmates."

With Ricky, I thought about what incremental step he could, with encouragement, manage right now, a step that would take him closer to being a successful reader. Choosing or letting me choose for him a just-right book and really reading it during reading time seemed to fit the bill. I decided that would be the stated goal in his contract.

Think about acceptable choices for rewards

Children are often more motivated to follow through if they have some choice in the reward. This is something that many teachers know from experience and that researchers have documented (Dyer & Dunlap, 1990; Cosden, Gannon, & Haring, 1995). I therefore allow students to choose their reward whenever possible. I ask the child for ideas for possible rewards, but I also prepare by thinking of appropriate ones for them to choose from.

With Ricky, I thought about rewards that would build his badly needed sense of competence and be fun. An opportunity to build a positive relationship with an adult would help here, I thought. I knew that Ricky already had a good relationship with the PE teacher. What if one of Ricky's possible rewards was helping Mr. Stakel set up the gym for PE class? Mr. Stakel would be able to provide the support that would allow Ricky to be successful with the setup.

I talked to Mr. Stakel, who readily agreed to have Ricky help him on Monday mornings, if Ricky liked this idea.

Contact the student's family

The earlier and the more completely families know about the strategies we're using to improve their child's behavior, the more able they are to collaborate and offer helpful insights. Even if the parents have shown minimal involvement in the child's school life up to now, I let them know about my decision to use an individual written agreement.

Ricky's grandmother hadn't attended Back-to-School Night or the scheduled fall parent–teacher conference and had not completed the parent/guardian questionnaire I'd sent home in September. I had contacted her regularly, trying to build an alliance to help Ricky with his homework. But she remained hands off. Nonetheless, calling her was important. I knew that her support could help to ensure success with the contract, whereas her lack of support could undercut it.

I shared concrete information with her about how things were going with Ricky's math and reading. In a nonjudgmental, matter-of-fact way I shared specific details. Ricky's math was improving. He could now tell time and count coins. He still was not actually reading in school, preferring to flip through the pages of *Harry Potter* or wander around the classroom during reading time. I told her I was thinking of trying an individual written agreement and asked what she thought about it. She was enthusiastic, hoping that it would help Ricky. She even mentioned that she might try a written agreement at home if one was successful at school.

Families are usually enthusiastic about the idea of an individual written agreement. For the most part, when I have reached the point of considering such an agreement with a child, the family also sees the child's challenges and is eagerly looking for a solution. Family members, however, might have useful information that I don't have, such as "We tried that, and it only made things worse." In that case, I listen and continue talking with them and the child's adult team at school to search for alternative strategies.

Introducing the Agreement to the Student

With all the preparations done, I was ready to introduce the agreement to Ricky. Over the years, I've found that the following sequence of steps work best for gaining students' understanding and cooperation in using individual written agreements:

1. Invite the student to a private meeting.

2. State the problem and describe the plan.

3. Set a goal, write it down, and sign it.

4. Agree on the reward.

5. Talk about which other adults need to know about the agreement and when to revisit it.

Step 1. Invite the student to a private meeting

An individual written agreement will be most successful if the student feels that her desire for privacy is respected. Some students don't mind if classmates know about their agreement, but many prefer to keep it between themselves and the teacher. I always make sure that the first meeting to discuss the agreement is in a private spot.

As the children were arriving in the morning, I drew Ricky aside and quietly invited him to have lunch with me. I told him that I had an idea that might help him with his reading and I wanted to share it with him privately. At lunchtime he arrived in the classroom with his hot lunch, and we sat down together at the reading table.

Step 2. State the problem and describe the plan

As you would when doing any problem-solving with students, keep your tone matter of fact when introducing an individual written agreement. This conveys that the student's behavior is a problem to address rather than a crime to punish. Your calm tone will help the child be calm. Honest reflection and discussion will more likely follow.

I began by noting positives to enlist Ricky's cooperation. We looked at his reading assessments together, and I observed that he could read well when he read pieces with a few words and many pictures on each page. I noted that when reading such pieces, Ricky did what good readers do— used picture clues to help him understand what he was reading.

Then, in a nonjudgmental voice, I stated the problem, using concrete examples so that we would understand the exact problem we were addressing. We looked at his nearly empty reader's log. "I've noticed that you haven't finished any books this year," I said. "I've noticed that you still haven't tried *Would You Rather?*"

"But that's a baby book," insisted Ricky.

"I know that you look at *Harry Potter* every day, but to really read, we all need to choose books that are right for us." I said.

"No," Ricky argued, "I love that book."

I didn't want to make Ricky feel shamed or blamed, but we needed reality in our discussion. "Tell me a little about *Harry Potter*," I said.

"Well, there's Harry … ," Ricky said, and then stopped.

"You know, that might be a good book for you to listen to on tape, but it's not a just-right-book for you," I stated firmly but calmly.

Next I spelled out what change was needed and why and described a concrete plan of action. "It's important that you choose lots of books that you can really read because that's how you'll grow as a reader," I said. "I'll pick out a variety of books that you can read. I'll put them in a basket, and you can choose books from that basket."

Then I brought up the idea of a reward. "Would you like to read for a reward?" I asked. I told Ricky I would keep track of his reading on a chart, and if he met his goal he would earn a reward. Ricky lit up. I'd never seen him so excited.

Step 3. Set a goal, write it down, and sign it

Writing down your agreements ensures that you'll both have a record to refer to later. I told Ricky that he would earn a reward for reading at least one picture book or one chapter of a chapter book a day. I wrote this goal on a piece of paper. *Ricky will read at least one picture book or one chapter of a chapter book from his basket at each readers' workshop.* I dated the paper and we both signed it. Signing the agreement adds importance for both child and teacher: It's a real agreement, signed and dated.

Step 4. Agree on the reward

I find it effective to reward children for eighty percent success. I told Ricky that he would be working for a weekly reward. He would get a star for each chapter or picture book that he read, and he would need to earn four stars, out of five possible stars, to get the reward each week. "Some rewards that other kids have worked for in the past are helping Mr. Stakel set up for PE or reading to younger kids. Would you like to work for one of these? Do you have other ideas about rewards you'd like to work for?" Ricky chose to help the PE teacher set up on Monday mornings.

Step 5. Talk about which other adults need to know about the agreement and when to revisit it

By then it was time to pick up the rest of the class in the lunchroom. I told Ricky that we'd start our plan next week and come back to discuss how things were going in two weeks. I explained that I'd tell his grand-mother and Mr. Stakel about our meeting.

Implementing the Plan

To keep the child on track and motivated, it helps to:

- Create a grid.

- Offer frequent encouraging reminders and feedback.

- Give the reward promptly.

Create a grid

Any format that efficiently tracks progress toward the goal will do. For Ricky, I created this grid:

Week of _____

Ricky will read at least one picture book or one chapter of a chapter book from his basket at each readers' workshop. Goal: 4 stars

Monday	Tuesday	Wednesday	Thursday	Friday

For each day of the week, I would draw a star if Ricky met the stated goal. Not only does such a grid allow for easy record keeping, but it's an easy tool for giving the child encouraging feedback.

Offer frequent encouraging reminders and feedback

If an individual written agreement is to work, it's important that the child meet his goal during the first two weeks. Encouraging reminders and feedback will make this more likely. Keep in mind, however, the importance of keeping such encouragement as private as possible. We can maintain a low-key tone, quietly whispering reminders and privately showing the student his stars.

It was a Thursday when Ricky and I met to make this plan. We began implementing it the next Monday. At the beginning of readers' workshop I quietly reminded Ricky of his goal by saying, "Remember, one chapter today," and told him that I was confident he could meet it. "I'm sure you can do it," I said. He selected a book from his basket, *Commander Toad and the Planet of the Grapes* by Jane Yolen, and began to read.

Later, as he was completing the first chapter, I checked in and asked him some quick questions to ascertain that he'd really read it. He had. I got out his grid and drew a star in the box for Monday. With an encouraging smile, I privately showed him the star.

The next day I confidentially pointed to the grid before readers' workshop. Later, during the workshop, when I noticed that he was reading, I whispered to him, "How's it going? Will you earn another star today?" He replied by drawing a star on the corner of his reading log and telling me about Commander Toad with a big grin on his face.

As often happens with children on individual written agreements, Ricky was, without realizing it, beginning to practice self-assessment, a skill crucial to growth. Through frequent encouragement, I was creating an alliance with him, building on his budding motivation, even if his motivation at this early stage was simply to earn his reward.

Give the reward promptly

If we hope to help a discouraged child feel encouraged by giving positive reinforcement, the reinforcement needs to be prompt and predictable. Some children, such as kindergartners and first graders, may need a daily reward. Later in this chapter I describe a student who needed a reward every few hours. (See "A student with autism" on page 257.) Children seven and older can usually wait a week.

The Friday afternoon of Ricky's first contract week, I sent home a copy of his completed star chart with a note to his grandmother: "Ricky earned his reward for the week." I emailed our PE teacher to let him know that Ricky would be helping him on Monday. On Monday morning Ricky went straight to the gym to help Mr. Stakel. We were off to a good start.

(To see how Ricky's plan evolved over time, see "Raising the goal gradually" on page 249.)

Keys to Success with Individual Written Agreements

Keep the following in mind to ensure the greatest success with this strategy.

Set specific, easy-to-measure goals

The behavior goal stated in a contract should be specific and measurable. This allows the child to understand exactly what she is meant to do, and the teacher and child to agree easily on whether the goal was met. Steve, a fifth grader, could easily agree with his teacher about whether he had completed and turned in his homework. Sami, a kindergartner, was able to concur with her teacher about whether she had "shared with tablemates."

If there's any ambiguity in the goal, it can be helpful to make a T-chart showing what the goal will look like and sound like. Sami and her teacher made the following chart about sharing materials:

Sami Will Share with Tablemates

LOOKS LIKE	SOUNDS LIKE
Hands in own space	"Could I use that crayon after you?"
Using the green crayon while waiting for the blue one	"Have you seen another blue crayon?"
	"Are you using the brown crayon?"
	"Could I use it?"
	"Would you like to use the yellow crayon when I'm finished?"

Look for gradual improvement, not sudden perfection

We want children to meet their goals. But none of us is perfect, and if we expect perfection, we will surely be disappointed. Rather than 100 percent success, I look for eighty percent, which allows for one off day every week and yet stretches children to make progress.

The eighty percent rule of thumb has worked well for me. You might want to try another percentage depending on the situation. Perhaps eighty percent is too ambitious for a particular child. With Ricky, it felt appropriate for him to earn his reward for meeting his goal four days out of five.

Often children will slack off once they know they've reached their goal for the week. That's okay. We can accept the slacking and celebrate the success.

Another approach is to celebrate after a set number of successes. Marie, in the example later in this chapter, received a reward after five instances of being a friendly worker. She could earn this reward in one day or a week—however long it took her to be a friendly worker five times.

Be absolutely consistent

Teacher consistency is key to the success of individual written agreements. Consistency means giving frequent reminders and feedback day after day. It also means giving a star whenever the child meets a goal, even if she did so with less than flying colors, and withholding a star when she doesn't meet a goal or only partially meets it.

For example, Ricky's goal was to read one chapter. He earned his reward whether he read short chapters or long ones. If he read one chapter, he earned a star. His reading may not have met the other children's standard, but he read. And if Angela started to say, "Yeah, but … ," and cut herself off, she earned her star. She had wanted to argue but she controlled herself. Ultimately she did not argue. She gets her star.

At the same time, if Ricky's goal is to read one chapter, the star has to be for one chapter, not half a chapter. Neither is the star for looking at, but not reading, the chapter. If students see that you're awarding stars for less than the goal, whatever progress they've made could quickly deteriorate.

Consider whether a reward is even necessary

Individual written agreements are about providing motivation for a child to change unproductive behavior. Before automatically assuming that a reward will be necessary, think about what else might motivate this particular child. Will frequent feedback do it? Notice the child. Try giving quiet, positive feedback when she does something well. Is it effective?

Sometimes just receiving a star or having some other visual way to track progress is enough to motivate a child. It's hearing again and again from the teacher, "Yes, you did read one chapter," that's often most effective.

"What do you think? Did you read today?" This brief, private conversation keeps the goal on the front burner for the student.

My colleague Suzi Sluyter tells about a kindergarten student who worked to see a jar fill up with cotton balls. Every time Lorilee followed directions, Suzi put a fluffy cotton ball in Lorilee's jar. Lorilee loved to watch that jar fill up.

My experience is that many students on individual written agreements don't need rewards at all. I advocate trying a behavior chart or some other visual indicator without a reward if you think it might work. You can always institute a reward later if it seems needed.

Think about which rewards are right for this student

If you decide that a reward is needed, limit the choices to those you think are appropriate for the student. What kind of activity does this child need and enjoy? A child who needs a physical outlet might earn extra time shooting hoops with an adult. A child who needs some private downtime might earn a few minutes alone with the puppets or blocks.

Often relationship-based rewards can be helpful to children. For example, many children enjoy visiting or helping past years' teachers. If your colleague agrees, the student's reward might be to help a previous teacher or to lend the art, music, or PE teacher a hand in setting up before class. Helping out in the school office and helping with younger children can also serve as rewards.

I recommend that classroom teachers avoid giving material objects as rewards. Candy can lead to an overweight child with bad teeth and, in some cases, angry parents. And many teachers, once they start giving stickers and small toys as rewards, find themselves giving those things out all year long.

Once you've identified acceptable rewards, let the child pick one. Having some choice often increases students' motivation to meet their goal. You might also ask the child for her ideas for rewards, but only if you feel comfortable explaining why some are not feasible.

Involve colleagues when appropriate

Depending on the child's goal, adults other than the classroom teacher can help encourage progress. Matt, a sixth grader, had a goal of doing his best work in math, so his math teacher was the only person who could give him stars.

But Zoe, a kindergartner who needled other children constantly, was working on being a friendly classmate wherever she went. Therefore, all of her teachers could give her stars. Mr. Jakes spoke with the specialist teachers, showed them a copy of Zoe's goals, and quietly checked in at the end of their classes to see if Zoe had earned a star.

It's important for the child to receive a consistent message from all adults. When you set up the plan, talk with the student about which adults might need to be part of the plan. Explain the plan to the other teachers. Such communication can go a long way toward ensuring that everyone is giving stars for the same level of behavior. You may even want to give your colleagues an example or two of the types of behavior that would earn a star. In my experience, the other teachers want the child to be in control as much as you do and are generally happy to strive for consistency.

Wean children from rewards eventually

Ultimately, we want children to read joyfully, to feel the sense of belonging that comes from being part of a community, and to follow directions because they know that's how to keep school safe and fun. With the intensive structured support of an individual written agreement, Ricky saw that he could read if the books were appropriate, and Angela found that she could do what the teacher told her to do.

To ensure that the child does not continue to work only for a reward, it's important to slowly reduce and then discontinue it. After Angela had spent several weeks participating in classroom activities and following directions without arguing, I met with her. I asked how she thought things were going. We both agreed that she was listening to teachers and following directions. I asked if she thought we still needed the written agreement. She said, "We don't need this thing anymore." Angela had been helping the office secretaries stuff envelopes. I assured her that Ms. Horne and Ms. Smarz would still appreciate it if she visited them on the way into school in the morning.

Questions from Teachers

I'm overwhelmed. I have five students on individual written agreements. How can I keep track of them all?

If you have more than one or two students using an individual written agreement, it might be time to rethink. Have you practiced and modeled expected behaviors with your students? Do students need more practice and modeling? Are you using logical consequences consistently?

In my first year of teaching, my classroom management was a disaster. The following summer I learned about individual written agreements and decided this was the strategy for me. My second year, out of desperation, I put my whole class on written agreements. I was overwhelmed. I don't think I had time to teach that year. It was all I could do to give stars and rewards. Needless to say, I didn't have time for the supports and reminders that might have made the plans effective. A few children earned those rewards every time; some children never did and became increasingly discouraged.

Since then I've realized that having one or two children on written agreements is about all a teacher can handle productively.

If you feel the need to have more than two children on individual written agreements, think about which other strategies you might use to benefit the whole class, such as reteaching and more modeling of expected behaviors, and seeing whether you can use logical consequences even more consistently.

What if the student doesn't want to use an individual written agreement?

First find out why. Perhaps the student is concerned that other children will find out. If so, you can assure the student that you will keep the agreement private. Perhaps she used a similar strategy in another grade and didn't meet with enough success to earn the reward. In that case, you can tell the student that you'll help with private reminders.

Ultimately, however, this strategy is about supplying extra motivation for a student. If the student doesn't feel motivated by this idea, don't insist. Implement logical consequences with renewed consistency and confer with parents or colleagues to see if they can suggest other strategies.

What if the student doesn't meet the goal, or hardly ever meets it?

If the child doesn't meet the goal within the first two weeks, he's not likely to meet it later. See if you can pare the goal down to something more realistic, both for you and the student. Try closely observing the child again. Talk with parents to find out what's working at home or meet with a trusted colleague to bounce ideas around. Weeks of unmet goals build failure, not success.

An individual written agreement is not always the best way to address a student's problem. Suzanne struggled to get her ideas down in writing. We tried an individual written agreement. It was ineffective, so we abandoned it. Weeks later she wrote a quality piece about monkeys. I asked her, "What made you able to complete this piece and do quality writing?" She replied, "I was really interested in the topic. I like animals."

In retrospect, I realize that Suzanne wasn't motivated to write before because she hadn't hit on the right topic. Once she started reading and learning about monkeys, she wanted to tell her classmates about monkeys, and suddenly she was on fire as a writer.

What about having the family give the reward?

Some teachers arrange for the child's family to give the reward when the child meets the goal at school. The teacher sends the behavior chart home with the child, and the family celebrates the accomplishment at home by giving the reward. I have sometimes done it this way myself. It can be a helpful strategy because it can promote the school–family partnership.

Be cautious, however, if you go this route. Early in my career I set up an individual written agreement with a fifth grade student who habitually spread mean gossip about her classmates. I turned the reward part over to her family without a lot of discussion, sending her chart home every Friday.

Nicole's parents promised her a new bicycle if she was kind to classmates for the rest of the year. The reward was too big and too far away. Working for something that would happen at the end of the year wasn't motivating enough. Not surprisingly, Nicole was unsuccessful at meeting her goal. But her parents bought her the bike anyway because they felt bad that they'd set her up to expect it.

Later in my career I worked with a fourth grader, Jordy, who had multiple difficulties both at school and at home. He argued with other children at school and in the neighborhood and avoided both schoolwork and homework. I knew Jordy's parents quite well. I'd taught Jordy's older sister and was confident that his parents would apply the reward system as agreed upon. I called them to discuss the idea of instituting an individual written agreement.

I told them that I could give their child a reward or they could. We discussed types of rewards I might give and types they might give. They suggested that Jordy might like to stay up late on Friday nights to play cards with his dad. Jordy ultimately chose that reward. Playing cards together offered him and his dad a welcome respite from their seemingly incessant conflict around Jordy's behavior. Rather than their regular routine of arguing about multiplication tables and spelling words, they enjoyed laughing together as they played. This relationship building was just what the two of them needed.

If you have a good relationship with a student's family and have been communicating all along about classroom issues, including the problem that made the contract necessary, you'll be better able to judge whether to ask the family to give the reward.

How will other students react to one child's earning a reward?

Fair isn't equal. Some children need things that others don't. If one child needs glasses, we don't all wear glasses. Some children need extra help in reading or math; others need extra help with their behavior.

I find that children can understand this concept if we explain it to

Examples of Rewards

If it seems necessary to give a child a reward for expected behaviors, the reward could be given at school, or, if there is strong teacher-parent communication about the purpose of individual written agreements, it could be given at home. Here are examples of each type of reward.

Rewards given at school

- Helping last year's teacher for fifteen minutes at the end of the day
- Having lunch with the current teacher (you)
- Helping specialist teachers set up or put away equipment and materials
- Helping younger children clean their desks
- Reading to younger children or listening to them read
- Helping the office staff stuff envelopes
- Playing a one-on-one active game with a paraprofessional, administrator, or other adult
- Playing quietly somewhere in the classroom
- Playing a computer game in the classroom for ten minutes

Rewards given at home

- Having a special breakfast with a parent on Saturday morning
- Staying up late one weekend evening to play cards or a board game with a parent
- Wrestling, shooting hoops, tossing a ball, or doing some other activity of the child's choosing with a parent over the weekend
- Having a parent come to school for lunch

them. My experience is that if we talk with the children about how they all might be given different things or be asked to do different things from time to time, they're generally fine with one child's earning a reward for positive behavior.

But it's important to begin this discussion early in the year so that when a classmate is given a reward, the class already has a foundational understanding of its fairness. If this discussion has taken place, then the simple statement "This is something that Steve needs" is usually enough.

Should I try to keep other students from knowing that a classmate has a written agreement?

The classroom is a small and crowded place, and children usually know what's going on. Everyone knew that Steve wasn't doing his homework. Everyone knew that Nicole was spreading unkind stories about classmates. Still, children often prefer to keep their agreements private. One of the ironies of childhood is that sometimes it's the children who act out most publicly who most intensely desire privacy about the solutions.

Ask the student how she feels about other people knowing she has an agreement. Lorilee, the kindergartner mentioned earlier, loved to display her jar with its growing collection of cotton balls. She would cheer as she saw the tangible manifestation of her improved self-control, and her classmates would happily join in with their own spontaneous cheers. Other children might carefully fold over their grid and hide it under a book.

If a child wants to keep an agreement as secret as possible, you can keep the grid in your plan book or another private spot that you use frequently. You can give feedback to the student nonverbally with a wink, a quick thumbs up, or a subtle air-drawing of a star. Ultimately, other children may find out, especially if the reward is redeemed in the classroom, but you can do your best to keep things as private as possible.

My student's goal was to do a certain number of math problems. When I increased his goal, he said no. What should I have done?

I've had that experience myself. I had a student who was meeting his goal of writing two sentences. When I increased it to four sentences, he stopped writing altogether.

I find that this strategy works best if the student feels he is part of the decision making. In retrospect, I should have asked the student if he was ready to increase his goal rather than telling him that I was going to increase it.

Often simply being asked—after getting encouraging feedback about progress made so far—will lead the student to agree to a higher goal. If she still refuses, stay at the current goal a little longer. The student may need a bit more time to build up confidence before taking on another challenge.

Examples of Individual Written Agreements

E X A M P L E   1

Raising the goal gradually: Ricky, the reluctant reader

Sometimes we need to start with minimal goals. Once the child has successfully met those, we slowly raise the standard, eventually helping the child work and learn at his full potential.

December

Ricky and I launched his plan. His initial goal was to read a whole picture book or one chapter of an appropriate chapter book during our daily readers' workshop. Ricky hadn't actually read any books in third grade readers' workshop, so one chapter seemed a realistic start. The world of children's literature is a rich one, and I was confident that once Ricky read material he could comprehend, he would be hooked and want to read more.

His first behavior grid looked like this:

Week of _____

Ricky will read at least one picture book or one chapter of a chapter book from his basket at each readers' workshop. Goal: 4 stars

Monday	Tuesday	Wednesday	Thursday	Friday

January

After Ricky regularly met his goal and earned his reward for a month, I sat down with him to discuss his reading. We both noted what he was doing well and celebrated his success with a resounding high five. I knew it was important that Ricky feel empowered by his success because he was a child who had felt so discouraged. It was also important that he feel able to take on an increased goal that reflected and reinforced his success.

"Look at your reading log now," I said. "You've read ten books and we both know that you understood them. You've shared with me and with your reading partner."

Then I asked, "Do you think you're ready to increase your reading? Are you ready to read more than one chapter during readers' workshop?"

Ricky happily suggested two chapters.

So we amended his contract to this:

Week of _____

Ricky will read at least two chapters of a chapter book from his basket during readers' workshop. Goal: 4 stars

Monday	Tuesday	Wednesday	Thursday	Friday

February

By now Ricky was reading with enjoyment and good comprehension. I thought his reading would improve even more if he began to read at home (a daily assignment for all third graders). I called his grandmother and explained that I was going to discuss with Ricky the idea of adding homework reading to his agreement. Then I met with Ricky, sharing the results of a recent reading assessment and congratulating him on his progress.

"You've grown so much as a reader," I said. "Good readers read a lot. That's how you've learned to understand your reading, by reading a lot. Starting to read at home will help you understand even more books."

I asked if he thought he was ready to earn stars for at-home reading. I would make sure that he had an additional copy of his current independent reading book to keep at home until he'd finished it. He would check in with me each morning and tell me about his reading the night before. This would be a quick check-in, just a couple of minutes of chatting about his book.

Ricky agreed. He seemed pleased that he would be doing what the other kids were doing.

Ricky's third contract looked like this:

Week of _____

Ricky will read at least two chapters of a book from his basket during readers' workshop. He will read at least one chapter at home each night. Goal: 8 stars

	Monday	Tuesday	Wednesday	Thursday	Friday
Reading at school					
Reading at home					

March

Ricky and I built on his love for animals. He read about wolves and about guinea pigs. His reading log was full of lists of books he'd read. By March I thought he was ready to be challenged to improve his written responses to his reading.

I met with him. First we celebrated his successes by talking about what we had each noticed about his improved reading. Then we looked at his weekly written responses to literature, which at that point were just a few words each week.

"You're reading and understanding now," I said. "You're sharing thoughts about your reading with your reading partner. I believe you could show some of that thinking in your written work. I bet you could write a response with a main idea that shows your thinking and two supporting details from the story. What do you think?"

Ricky, proud that he was now working on skills that other students were working on, quickly agreed.

So we adjusted his contract again to look like this:

Week of _____

Ricky will read at least two chapters of a book from his book basket during readers' workshop. He will read at least one chapter at home each night.

When Ricky writes his weekly written response to literature, he will:

Write at least three sentences.

Write one main idea about what he read.

Support this idea with two details from his reading.

Goal: 20 stars

	Monday	Tuesday	Wednesday	Thursday	Friday
Reading at school					
Reading at home					
Written response to literature (one star for each sentence)					

Ricky grew as a reader in third grade, with the support of a carefully implemented individual written agreement. By the end of the year, he was engaged with his reading, laughing at the funny parts and happily recommending books to classmates.

As I wrote his year-end report card ("Ricky needs to read during the summer") I knew it was possible he'd take some steps back during the summer. I also knew I had some successful strategies to share with his fourth grade teacher.

> **THINGS TO NOTE** about Ricky's plan

- *Understanding the child:* I recognized Ricky as a discouraged child and encouraged small, positive steps.

- *Incremental progress:* We started with minimal goals and increased them as Ricky was ready.

- *Frequent feedback:* I gave Ricky reminders about this contract at the beginning of readers' workshops, checked in briefly during the workshops, and showed him the star I drew at the end of the workshops.

- *Student choice:* Ricky had a choice of rewards. I let him choose between helping the PE teacher and reading to younger children, two activities I knew he would enjoy.

- *Eighty percent success:* Ricky was rewarded for earning eighty percent of the possible stars.

EXAMPLE 2

Frequent feedback throughout the day: Vanessa, a first grader

Vanessa was a first grade student whose family life was more chaotic than many children's. Her older sister, and de facto role model, had a degenerative brain disease that caused her to be out of control most of the time. Vanessa's parents' relationship had crumbled under the strain of raising three children, all with challenging behaviors. Both parents were homeless and the children were in and out of relatives' homes and foster homes. Vanessa was a sweet and affectionate child who wanted to be close to someone. She would often lean up against me in our Morning Meeting circle.

Vanessa had multiple academic challenges as a result of inconsistent school attendance. She didn't know the names of the letters or the sounds they made, nor could she recognize high-frequency words. In math, without one-to-one correspondence, she couldn't match sets of plastic teddy bears to the correct numerals.

When school demands became overwhelming to her, Vanessa crawled on the floor, made animal noises, and chewed on other children's feet.

Faced with children like Vanessa whose school problems stem at least in part from deep, complex family issues beyond our control, it's easy to become paralyzed, to throw up our hands and declare there's nothing we can do.

But although one teacher cannot solve a child's family problems, it is possible—and necessary—for a teacher to address, one piece at a time, the child's school behavior. This incremental approach can make a difference to the child's success.

My first step with Vanessa was to modify her school work. I spent as much time as I could working with her, playing simple letter and word games, buddy-reading books with a few repeating words and lots of picture support.

As those strategies began to help Vanessa, I assigned her a student buddy for partner reading. I found a retired teacher looking for volunteer work to sit with Vanessa during math three days a week, providing friendship and academic support.

I also used some strategies to help Vanessa maintain control. I used "proximity," situating her next to me when the class gathered in a circle and having her do independent work nearby when I met with other readers. I used positive time-out as a reminder when she did begin to lose control. I built my relationship with Vanessa, checking in with her frequently during the day.

As Vanessa began to feel more successful in school, her behaviors in the classroom improved, but she still had some rough moments. She was frequently out of control in specialist classes, on the playground, and in the lunchroom. It was time for an individual written agreement.

I met with Vanessa and noted the things that were going well in the classroom: She read, did her math work, and was often in control of her body. I told her it was important that she be in control of her body outside the classroom, too, so that she and other children could learn. We looked at the classroom rules together, and I reminded her that our rules followed our class wherever we went.

I told Vanessa that I was going to give her a reward for maintaining control throughout the day. I had already prepared a grid, showing our schedule and the goal *Vanessa will control her body* at the top. I made a separate grid for each day of the week so the grids would be visually simple. Here's what Monday's grid looked like:

Vanessa will control her body:	
M O N D A Y	
	Morning Meeting
	Reading
	PE
	Math
	Lunch
	Recess
	Read aloud
	Social studies
Possible total stars for one day: 8 Goal: 6	

For scoring purposes, I included times when Vanessa was in the classroom so as to build on her current success. I also included the trying times such as lunchtime and recess as well as all of the specialist classes.

I showed Vanessa the resulting eight boxes for each day. I told her that if she controlled her body during a time in the schedule, I would draw a star in that box. She would then earn a reward if she got at least six out of the eight possible stars. This way, she could receive a reward if she was in control during times in our class and one of the out-of-the-classroom times. This goal seemed realistic to me. If she earned six stars on Monday, she'd get her reward on Tuesday. If she earned six stars on Tuesday, she'd get a reward on Wednesday, and so on throughout the week.

Vanessa was excited about earning a reward. Together we came up with a few possible ones. She could quietly play with the puppets or the Legos® during ten minutes of reading or math time. She could have extra computer time. She could play a game with the school psychologist one day a week. Or she could read a book to a kindergartner.

Vanessa chose playing with the puppets for her Monday, Tuesday, Thursday, and Friday reward and playing a game with the school psychologist for her Wednesday reward.

Vanessa and I discussed, modeled, and practiced what "stay in control" would look like and sound like in the library, the gym, the music room, the lunchroom, and on the playground. Together we made a T-chart delineating what "stay in control" would look like and sound like at lunch, one of her most challenging times, taking care to put each item in positive terms.

Stay in Control in the Lunchroom

LOOKS LIKE	SOUNDS LIKE
Eat your food (food is only for eating)	Inside voice
Eat own lunch	Kind words
Stay in chair	
Hands in own area	

To further ensure the success of this plan, before the children left for a specialist's class or for lunch, I confidentially reminded Vanessa about the specific behaviors we discussed. Before PE, I'd whisper, "Personal space," and before library class I'd whisper, "Gentle with the books." Sometimes I'd whisper, "I know you can do it" or "Remember, stay in control."

I explained Vanessa's behavior system to the specialist teachers and the lunch and recess supervisors so we'd all be on the same page. For example, when I picked up the students from their specialist classes, I'd quietly ask the teacher whether Vanessa had earned her star and then give Vanessa a quick thumbs up if she had. After lunch and recess, the adult who walked the children back to the classroom reported on Vanessa's behavior during lunch and recess, using the same standards I was using.

Vanessa was able to control herself most of the time and earned her reward on many days. The system did not resolve all of Vanessa's challenges, but it did help her move another step toward being a more successful learner and community member.

> **THINGS TO NOTE** about Vanessa's plan

- *Starting with other strategies:* I modified Vanessa's work and provided extra academic support first. Then I added an individual written agreement when those strategies didn't bring enough improvement.

- *Building on previous success:* Vanessa had guided practice and success in the classroom before being asked to attempt new behaviors in other areas of the school.

- *Encouraging teacher language:* I chose words such as "personal space" and "gentle with the books" that helped Vanessa envision appropriate behavior.

- *Explicit teaching of expected behaviors:* We practiced and modeled what expected behaviors would look and sound like in various places in the school.

- *Eighty percent success:* Vanessa was rewarded for earning six out of eight possible stars, approximately eighty percent success, each day.

- *Student choice:* Vanessa was able to choose between a few rewards that I suggested.

- *Frequent reminders:* I gave Vanessa frequent private reminders about her chart.

EXAMPLE 3

A student with autism: Marie, a second grader

Marie, a second grader with a diagnosis of autism, was a bright girl who was having difficulty finding meaning in school activities. She often seemed disconnected during lessons. Listening and paying attention to lessons that didn't interest her felt too demanding. When called on, she didn't know what we were discussing. She was disengaged during Morning Meeting, confused about activities that had been carefully modeled and practiced. She cried when I told her it was time to read or write.

Marie had an IEP that a team of adults (including the school psychologist, a special education teacher, Marie's paraprofessional, and me) were working together to implement. But Marie was unable to successfully use some of the tools and methods spelled out in her IEP.

Marie's paraprofessional, Ms. Cole, for example, used checklists and graphic organizers to help her understand what was expected, but Marie simply cried more. Marie took frequent motor breaks, walking up and down the hall with Ms. Cole, but then was reluctant to return to work. Marie's speech therapist, Ms. Kale, helped her practice social interactions during speech class. Marie's IEP included giving her positive reinforcement when she used appropriate social behaviors, but we didn't yet have an effective way of doing that.

The team knew we needed to figure out a way to motivate her, to tap into her potential for learning.

Marie's special education teacher and our school psychologist attended a conference about motivating children with special needs. While at the conference they realized that many of our expectations may have felt negative and unachievable to Marie: We wanted her to listen to lessons that didn't interest her and complete work that felt too hard. The two returned from the conference excited about giving Marie some positive motivation to pay attention and learn in school.

The team met to review and modify Marie's IEP. We began by naming a new expectation for Marie, one that would feel positive and achievable to her. We decided on the expectation that she be a "friendly worker." A friendly worker would be a student who raised her hand and answered questions during lessons, who did her school work cheerfully, and who was friendly to classmates during Morning Meeting.

Dr. Babich, the school psychologist, met with Marie to discuss this expectation. They made a list of what a friendly worker would do:

A friendly worker smiles when she greets her neighbor in Morning Meeting.

A friendly worker says "good morning" to teachers and classmates.

A friendly worker listens carefully and pays attention to how to participate in the Morning Meeting activity.

A friendly worker raises her hand and answers a question during a lesson.

A friendly worker writes at least two sentences during writers' workshop.

A friendly worker reads at least one chapter during readers' workshop.

A friendly worker solves at least two problems during math.

Then Dr. Babich and Marie made a list of rewards she would like to earn. All of Marie's ideas involved quiet play alone, a sign that Marie needed some respite from the interaction of school. Some of Marie's ideas were:

Play with the puppets in her regular education classroom

Play with the blocks in her regular education classroom

Play with the train in the special education room

Play a game on the computer

We created the following grid and made multiple copies. This simple grid helped Ms. Cole and the other adults working with Marie keep up with her progress toward each reward. Marie could also check her chart to see how she was doing as she worked toward each set of five stars.

Marie's stars			Date_____	

Every time a member of the team saw Marie being a "friendly worker," she or he would draw a star on her grid. Once Marie had earned five stars, she could choose one of the activities on her list of rewards and do it for five minutes.

Marie was motivated. The first day she greeted her Morning Meeting partner with a great big smile, raised her hand to answer questions twice during math, read a whole chapter in her independent reading book, and wrote without crying at writers' workshop.

With the reward system in place, Marie began using the checklists and graphic organizers we'd created for her, which had not helped her before.

As she wrote, for example, she used her checklist of "Marie's steps in writing" effectively.

She'd earned her first reward by 11:30 and happily played with the puppets in a corner of the classroom for five minutes.

As the year progressed, Marie frequently earned her five minutes for an activity of her choice. The team added to her list of what a "friendly worker" might do as she learned new skills. For example, Marie earned stars for greeting a friend without a reminder as she entered the classroom in the morning and for asking a friendly question such as "What would you like to play?"

The skills were beginning to carry over and Marie was applying them outside of the support of her school reward system. One day Marie's mother called me, tearfully, to say that Marie had gotten in the car at the end of the day and asked her, "How was your day, Mommy?" That was a first in their relationship.

THINGS TO NOTE about Marie's plan

- *Tailored supports:* The team created support systems that made Marie's goals feasible, such as graphic organizers, checklists, and motor breaks.

- *Encouraging language:* For example, the term "friendly worker" was one that motivated Marie.

- *Measurable goals that Marie understood:* The goals we named ("A friendly worker smiles when she greets her neighbor in Morning Meeting," "A friendly worker says 'good morning' to teachers and classmates," etc.) were clear, measurable, and easy for Marie to understand.

- *Frequent and immediate feedback:* Marie's plan included feedback as soon as she used one of the behaviors we had identified as the behaviors of a "friendly worker."

- *Student choice:* Marie was allowed to choose from among an array of possible rewards.

- *Consistent feedback:* Marie got consistent, frequent reinforcement from many adults.

- *Teamwork:* An adult team collaborated to meet Marie's needs.

EXAMPLE 4

No reward needed: Donnie, a fifth grader

Donnie, a fifth grader who would turn ten in December, irritated and frightened other children with his rough behavior. He swung his partner too hard during practice for the fifth grade Hoe Down, mowed children down in recess football, and knocked classmates off their chairs as he crossed the room. His fourth grade teacher had described him as "out of control," and his mother complained that the teachers in school didn't like him.

I met with Donnie and pointed out that I'd noticed he was rough with his classmates. In a matter-of-fact tone I mentioned that students were complaining about the way he swung them during Hoe Down practice. I told him that I wanted him to have friends in the class and that the other students would be more willing to work and play with him if he were gentle with them.

Donnie and I discussed what "gentle" might look like. Even though he was a fifth grader, I thought it was important that he receive a little explicit instruction in this area. What would a gentle swing look like? How might he walk across the room so that he could avoid collisions?

Donnie was motivated to have friends. There was no need to offer him an extrinsic reward because he already had a powerful built-in intrinsic reward in the making—friendship with the other fifth graders. He was eager to accept my feedback and help in changing his behavior. I wrote down *Donnie will maintain self-control. He will be gentle with his body*. We both signed the agreement.

Because Donnie's rough behaviors were ingrained and habitual, I thought he might benefit from some system of showing his progress toward becoming gentle with classmates. I asked him if he would like me to create a chart to keep track of how he was doing. Donnie agreed and I created the following:

Week of _____

Donnie will maintain self-control. He will be gentle with his body.

Monday	Tuesday	Wednesday	Thursday	Friday
Before school	Before school	Before school	Before school	Before school
Morning Meeting	Morning Meeting	Morning Meeting	Morning Meeting	Morning Meeting
Readers' workshop	Readers' workshop	Readers' workshop	Readers' workshop	Art
Walking to & from PE	Math	Math	Walking to & from PE	Readers' workshop
PE	Music	Music	PE	Math
Recess & lunch	Recess & lunch	Recess & lunch	Recess & lunch	Recess & lunch
Walking back from lunch	Walking back from lunch	Walking back from lunch	Walking back from lunch	Walking back from lunch
Writers' workshop	Science	Science	Writers' workshop	Writers' workshop
Read aloud	Read aloud	Read aloud	Read aloud	First grade buddies
Dismissal	Dismissal	Dismissal	Dismissal	Dismissal

Possible total: 50 stars   Goal: 40 stars

Donnie and I established a goal of eighty percent to help make his progress visible.

I reminded and encouraged Donnie many times a day. Often our communication was nonverbal. I'd give him a quiet pat on the shoulder and whisper, "Remember, gentle body." I'd point to our classroom rule "We will be kind." I'd silently smile and draw a star in the air with my finger.

Of course, the salient marker of his progress was the other kids' growing comfort with him. As children began to accept Donnie's invitations to play after school, we could both see that Donnie was learning to be a gentle friend.

THINGS TO NOTE about Donnie's plan

- *No need for an extrinsic reward:* Donnie was motivated to have friends. His classmates' willingness to play and work with him would be his greatest reward.

- *Positively stated goals:* Donnie's goals were stated in the positive using encouraging language, such as "gentle with his body."

- *Clear and specific goals:* We discussed "gentle" together and practiced collision avoidance to make sure he understood what it would look like and feel like.

- *Frequent private feedback:* I sometimes gave reminders and encouragement as often as ten times a day.

- *Connection to classroom rules:* I referred to our rules, especially "We will be kind," when giving him reminders.

Making it work for you

INDIVIDUAL WRITTEN AGREEMENT PLANNING SHEET

Student's name:_____ Date:_____

Thinking about the problem

What is the problematic behavior? (Pick one behavior that is both problematic and potentially changeable.)

What are some possible reasons for this behavior?

What other strategies have you tried?

Modifications to academic work:

Support to help the child meet academic expectations:

Proactive strategies such as referring to classroom rules and interactive modeling:

Other problem-solving strategies such as a problem-solving conference:

What behavior do you hope to see the student adopt? (Make sure these behaviors are specific, easy to measure, and limited in number.)

Contacting the child's parents

How will you talk about this issue? What words will you use?

Meeting with the student

Reminder: Make sure you're feeling collaborative!

When and where will the meeting take place?

How will you state the problem, remind the student of expected behavior, and connect it to classroom rules?

> **Steps in introducing an individual written agreement to the student·**
>
> 1. Invite the student to a private meeting.
>
> 2. State the problem and describe the plan.
>
> 3. Set a goal, write it down, and sign it.
>
> 4. Agree on the reward.
>
> 5. Talk about which other adults need to know about the agreement and when to revisit it.

What's some language you will use to express your desire to help? How will you suggest having an individual written agreement?

Will you suggest working for a reward? If so, what are some appropriate rewards for this student? (Remember, a reward is optional.)

How will you and the student keep track of progress? (Possibilities are a chart or other visual system such as Popsicle sticks or a cotton ball jar.)

How often will you check in and record progress? (Pick a manageable schedule that will provide the student with enough encouragement. Possibilities are every time the student uses the behavior, every academic period, or four times a day.)

Which other adults will be involved in implementing this agreement? (Consider special educators, administrators, behavior specialists, specialist teachers, previous teachers, and parents.)

How concerned is the student about keeping the agreement confidential?

When will you and the student meet again to evaluate progress?

CHAPTER SEVEN

Using Strategies in Concert: Paulina's Story

This book has offered a variety of strategies for teachers to try when things don't go well for students socially or academically. Often, the use of one or two strategies resolves the difficulty, and it's never an issue again. For example, after a class meeting, small group work becomes productive and satisfying for everyone. Or after a teacher-student problem-solving conference and an individual written agreement, a student who was resisting doing hard math problems comes around to attempting them with focus.

Sometimes, however, a child's difficulty surfaces, resolves, and resurfaces, perhaps manifesting itself in a different way each time. In such cases, we may need to use several of the strategies in this book over the course of the year, each time choosing the strategy that's appropriate for that particular occurrence.

Used in concert this way, problem-solving strategies not only help that individual child, but can create valuable learning experiences for the entire class. Paulina's story is an example.

Role-Playing Inclusiveness at Recess

Paulina was a student in a third grade class I taught. In September, I gathered the children to do some role-plays on including everyone at recess. This is something I do every year because inclusion during lunch and recess is a predictable beginning-of-the-year concern.

This was a new group, but like most elementary school groups, it was one with some interpersonal history. Several students had prior friendships. A few had prior conflicts and resentments. My goal was to maximize the chances that these students would become a community in which everyone was included and accepted.

"We've agreed on our rule to be kind," I said. "Yesterday we did a role-play about how to notice who might be alone and ask them to play. Today we're going to look at this situation from another point of view. What if you're the person who's alone and you want someone to play with? What might you do to join your classmates?" Using the students' ideas, we acted out ways to ask someone to play and ways to join a game.

In the days following, many children tried the skills we had practiced. I saw lots of variety in students' choice of playmates.

A Problem-Solving Conference

After a while, however, I began noticing that Paulina was often alone on the playground. In the classroom she appeared to be easygoing and friendly. She worked smoothly with assigned partners, listening as well as sharing her ideas. She participated in the give and take of the classroom, doing her part in setups and cleanups. But on the playground she seemed to have trouble. I wondered what was going on.

I looked back at the parent/guardian questionnaire that Paulina's mother had filled out at the beginning of the year. "Paulina had a hard year last year. Her good friend started rejecting her, and then moved away before they could make up," she had written. I tucked that away as interesting information that might or might not be relevant.

In late October, Paulina's mom called me. "I'm worried about Paulina," she said. "I was picking up my younger son after kindergarten, and I noticed that Paulina was sitting by herself on the playground. She doesn't get phone calls from other girls and doesn't talk about friends in school. Is she always alone?"

"She seems fine in the classroom," I responded, "but I share your concerns about the unstructured parts of the day. Let me talk with Paulina, think about this, and get back to you." I find it's often best to give myself some time if a parent calls with a concern. In this case, I wanted to have a problem-solving conference with Paulina and spend some time thinking about the situation overall.

I invited Paulina to join me for lunch. She was delighted. I suspected that she was lonely in the lunchroom as well as on the playground.

Paulina and I sat down together at the reading table. "Paulina," I began, "I've noticed that you contribute to your math group in such a friendly way. You listen to other people's ideas and help them with their work."

"I like to help kids," Paulina replied brightly.

"I've also noticed that you're alone a lot on the playground," I continued.

"Yup," she answered, as a cloud passed over her face. "I play by myself."

In the ensuing conversation, it came out that the previous year Nanette, Paulina's once best friend, had gotten mad at her and told the other girls not to play with her. Even though Nanette had moved to another city and no longer went to our school, Paulina was still living with the pain of that incident and was having trouble approaching the girls in the class. She would play with the boys, except they were all into football, which she didn't like.

By the end of this conference, Paulina and I came up with an idea for finding a playmate at recess: Rosalea, a new student at our school, also needed friends. Paulina would ask Rosalea to play.

The next day was my weekly recess duty day. I saw Paulina and Rosalea happily playing hopscotch together.

Small-Group Conflict Resolution

Things went smoothly for a while. With Rosalea's support, Paulina expanded her group of friends. Perhaps some feelings of resentment from Paulina's incident with Nanette had crept into our group's year together; if so, they now seemed forgotten. On Fridays, when I was on the playground for recess duty, I observed Paulina running and playing with Oliver and Cody, playing Four Square with the big group in the corner of the blacktop, or shooting hoops with the line-up in the middle of the playground.

But one sunny Friday in February, when we were outside for a much needed outdoor recess, I noticed Paulina alone and close to tears. "What's happening?" I asked Paulina.

"I asked Moira and Rosalea if I could play. They said yes but then they walked away. They don't want me to play with them."

"Do you want me to help you talk with them?" I asked.

"Yes," Paulina replied, and we went in search of Moira and Rosalea.

The four of us sat down at a picnic table for a conflict resolution meeting.

Paulina started with an I-statement. "I felt so sad when you just walked away from me. I thought we were playing together." Paulina was getting a much needed chance to practice assertion, a big step toward finding a solution to her intermittent social isolation.

As the two other girls followed the protocol for paraphrasing and offering I-statements of their own, Rosalea also found her stride in asserting that she wanted to play with Paulina, too, even though Moira was claiming Rosalea for herself. It was important for Moira to hear Rosalea state her wishes clearly and boldly. In the end, the three girls agreed to all play together.

As I drove home that night, I thought about Paulina. She had solved each individual problem that came up around lack of playmates, but I wondered why she kept having difficulties with friends every so often. She had so many positive qualities. She was friendly and open-hearted, consistently ready to help a classmate. She had a great sense of humor, always quick to laugh. Why did her peers keep rejecting her?

Often I find it helpful to think about the whole picture—the child as a member of a family and the family as a member of the community. I know I have no control over family matters, but thinking about them sometimes helps me tease out things that I can control.

I thought back to a strange incident the day before school started. One of my new students' moms had dropped by to meet me. She'd looked at the class list, noticed Paulina in the list, and said, "That one's mom!" as she rolled her eyes.

This inappropriate comment and body language made me so uncomfortable that I'd promptly forgotten the incident. Remembering it now, I started to think about Paulina and her family. I thought about how, at conference time, Paulina's mom had told me that Nanette's mom had been her best friend but they'd had a falling out.

Apparently, Nanette's mom had gotten angry at Paulina's mom, and thus Nanette had gotten angry at Paulina. I wondered if Paulina was struggling with making and keeping friends because other parents had sided with Nanette's mom. If a distrust and disdain of Paulina's family had indeed trickled down to the children of this class, then it made Paulina's problem a whole-class issue.

Although I couldn't control how students' parents treated each other, I could affect how the students treated each other. I decided it was time for a problem-solving class meeting.

A Class Meeting

I thought carefully about how to begin the meeting. I needed to start with a statement that would allow the students to feel safe expressing their feelings and that would inspire them to kindness.

"We are all a community," I said. "When we created our rules, we agreed to be kind to each other. I've noticed that some members of our class still don't always have friends to play with at recess, even when they want someone to play with," I continued. "What have you noticed?"

We went around the circle, each student contributing what they had noticed, without naming any names. Then we went around the circle again, this time looking for solutions. Ideas included asking recess teachers to lead a big game for everyone who wants to play and making a rule that if someone asks to play, you have to say yes. Another idea was to designate Duck, Duck, Goose as an "open to everyone" game. One student issued a standing invitation to everyone in the class to build snow forts with her.

Using the thumbs up, thumbs in the middle, or thumbs down consensus method, the class agreed unanimously to the snow forts and the Duck, Duck, Goose ideas. Having to say yes if someone asks to play got a number of thumbs up, a few thumbs in the middle, and no thumbs down. Clearly, student awareness had been raised about how hard it was to be told "no" when asking to join a game.

On Friday, my recess duty day, I observed the students all building snow forts together with great interest and absorption.

Other Strategies

Besides using these problem-solving strategies that involved students, I took a couple of other steps to address this recess inclusion issue.

Restructuring recess

I could see that if a whole-group game was always available at recess, children like Paulina who might be isolated would have something to do. I made a point of teaching my own class a game during the week. I then led that game for anyone to join on my Friday recess days.

After I explained this to my colleagues, some of them started leading big group games at recess as well. The availability of a whole-group game provided a safety net for many children.

Promoting a positive parent community

Although I knew I couldn't "fix" all the problems among the parents of the class, I did think it was within my power and responsibility to help encourage a feeling of community among family members when they interacted for school-related reasons. This could only help promote good relationships among their children.

One month, all the third grade classes had a project to create a "museum" so the classes could share knowledge about the Native American community they'd studied. This was something that parents traditionally helped with at our school. I asked Paulina's mother to take a major role, making sure other parents who came in for the activity interacted with her and saw the positive way she worked with their children.

As the parents worked together to help the children prepare the museum, I could see connections among parents developing. Parents who hadn't known Paulina's mother so well were getting to know her, and the parent group alignments were shifting. This added feeling of community among the parents may possibly have added to the success of the other strategies I'd used to help Paulina's social situation in the class.

The End of the Year

It was the last day of school. The children had left, and I was looking once more at snapshots of our year together and notes the children had written to me. I saw a photo of Paulina, grinning and happily posing arm in arm with the other girls. I looked at a note from Moira. "I hope next year you get a class that works as well as a community as our class does," it said.

Then I got to Paulina's note. "The most important thing I learned this year was friendship and if it's broken you can fix it."

Like every year in school, this one was full of ups and downs. Sometimes children did mean things, but I had strategies to help them fix their mistakes, and they grew in kindness. We built a community together.

Morning Meeting

A Powerful Way to Begin the Day

Morning Meeting, a *Responsive Classroom*® practice I have used for many years, helps build the safe, caring classroom climate that makes successful problem-solving possible. This article, adapted from *The Morning Meeting Book* by Roxann Kriete and originally published in the *Responsive Classroom Newsletter* in Winter 1999, summarizes key points about Morning Meeting.

In the spring of my first year as a secondary school teacher, I got a letter from a student for whom I had a particular fondness, letting me know that she was dropping out of school. School wasn't making much sense to her, and little that she was being asked to learn held much interest for her.

She wrote, almost apologetically, that school just wasn't a place she felt she belonged. More than twenty years later, her words still seem profoundly sad to me:

I will always remember how you said "Hi, Sue" as I walked into eighth period. It made me feel like it really mattered that I came.

It touched and pained me to know that something that seemed so small to me, an act I hadn't even been aware of, had meant so much to her. I vowed to learn something from it and became more intentional about greeting my students.

I stationed myself by the door and tried to say a little something to each one as the children entered, or at least to make eye contact and smile at every student, not just the ones like Sue for whom I had an instinctive affinity.

Gradually I realized how much I was learning at my post by the door. I observed who bounced in with head up and smile wide, whose eyes were red-rimmed from tears shed in the girls' room at lunch, who mumbled a response into his collar and averted his eyes every day for an entire semester. I didn't know what to do about much of it, but at least I was learning how to notice.

I have learned a lot since then. It is good for students to be noticed, to be seen by their teacher. But it is only a start, not enough by itself. They must notice and be noticed by each other as well.

Years after I taught Sue, I joined the staff of Greenfield Center School, Northeast Foundation for Children's K–8 lab school. There, I saw teachers teaching students to greet each other, to speak to each other, to listen to each other. I saw students start each day together in Morning Meeting, where noticing and being noticed were explicit goals.

Today, many children in kindergartens and elementary and middle schools around the country launch their school days in Morning Meetings. All classroom members—grown-ups and students—gather in a circle, greet each other, listen and respond to each other's news, practice academic and social skills, and look forward to the events in the day ahead. Morning Meeting is a particular and deliberate way to begin the day, a way that builds a community of caring and motivated learners.

The Format

Morning Meeting is made up of four sequential components and lasts up to a half hour each day. The components provide daily opportunities for children to practice the skills of greeting, listening and responding, speaking to a group, reading, and noticing and anticipating. These are the four components:

- *Greeting*—Children greet each other by name. Greetings often include handshaking, clapping, singing and other activities.

- *Sharing*—Students share some news of interest to the class and respond to each other, articulating their thoughts, feelings, and ideas in a positive way.

- *Group Activity*—The whole class does a short activity together, building class cohesion through active participation.

- *Morning Message*—Students develop language skills and learn about the events in the day ahead by reading and discussing a daily message their teacher writes for them.

Teachers and students alike crave a certain amount of predictability and routine in the school day, especially at the start. The format of Morning Meeting offers both predictability and plenty of room for variation and change. Meetings reflect the style and flavor of individual teachers and groups. They also reflect the ebb and flow of a school year's seasons— September's new shoes and anxious, careful faces; December's pre-holiday excitement; February's endless runny noses; April's spring-has-sprung exuberance. Its mixture of routine and surprise, of comfort and challenge, make Morning Meeting a treasured and flexible teaching tool.

Morning Meeting Sets the Tone for Learning

The way we begin each day in our classroom sets the tone for learning and speaks volumes about what and whom we value, about our expectations for the way we will treat each other, and about the way we believe learning occurs.

Children's learning begins the second they walk in the doors of the building. It matters to children whether they are greeted warmly or overlooked, whether the classroom feels chaotic and unpredictable or ordered and comforting. If they announce, "My cat got hit by a car last night, but it's gonna be all right," they may find an interested, supportive audience or one that turns away. Every detail of their experience informs students about their classroom and their place in it.

When we start the day with everyone together, face-to-face, welcoming each person, sharing news, listening to individual voices, and communicating as a caring group, we make several powerful statements. We say that every person matters. We say that the way we interact individually and as a group matters. We say that our culture is one of friendliness and thoughtfulness. We say that hard things can be accomplished and important discoveries can be made when we work and play together. We say that teachers hold authority, even though they are a part of the circle. We say that this is a place where courtesy and warmth and safety reign.

To learn, we must take risks—offering up a tentative answer we're far from sure is right or trying out a new part in the choir when we're not sure we can hit the notes. We can take these risks only when we know we will be respected and valued, no matter the outcome. To risk, we must trust, and Morning Meeting helps create a climate of trust.

Morning Meeting Merges Social and Academic Learning

Morning Meeting provides an arena where distinctions that define social, emotional, and academic skills fade and learning becomes an integrated experience.

Teachers have long known and researchers are now confirming that social skills are not just something to be taught so that children behave well enough to get on with the real business of schooling. Rather, they are inextricably intertwined with cognitive growth and intellectual progress. A person who can listen well, who can frame a good question and has the assertiveness to pose it, who can examine a situation from a number of perspectives—this person will be a strong learner.

All those skills—skills essential to academic achievement—must be modeled, experienced, practiced, extended, and refined in the context of social interaction. Morning Meeting is a forum in which all that happens. It is not an add-on, something extra to make time for, but rather an integral part of the day's planning and curriculum.

A Microcosm of the Way We Wish Our Schools to Be

The time teachers commit to Morning Meeting is an investment repaid many times over. The sense of group belonging and the skills of attention, listening, expression, and cooperative interaction developed in Morning Meeting are a foundation for every lesson, every transition time, every lining-up, every resolution of every upset and conflict, all day and all year long. Morning Meeting is a microcosm of the way we wish our schools to be—communities full of learning, safe and respectful and challenging for all.

Rules Children Care About

The Responsive Classroom® *Approach to Creating and Teaching Classroom Rules*

I like to swim laps at a local pool. One day, while waiting for swim lessons to end, I started reading the "Swimming Pool Rules" for the first time. *No running, No shouting, No babies without diapers, No using the pool equipment.*

Some of these rules, such as *No babies without diapers*, are useful.

Some, such as *No shouting*, are not terribly important. And some, such as *No using the pool equipment*, are downright counterproductive. I'd been using the pool for the past two months, and I'd seen that nearly everyone who comes uses the pool equipment—the kickboards and noodles. It's safe to say that these are rules everyone ignores.

Traditionally, there have been two types of rules in school: the type children resent and the type children ignore. Both are introduced by an adult (a teacher or an administrator) when school opens in the fall. Created by some faceless authority, the rules, usually a long list of them, tell children what they can't do: "No talking without permission," "Don't get out of your seat," "No dangerous objects allowed in school," "No fighting," "No hitting," "No pushing," "No cursing."

The rules I remember from my own schooling are type one, the rules we resent. My teachers would invoke the rules throughout the year to keep order. "No talking," my teachers would tell me as I again indulged in my penchant for chatting with friends during endless lessons. "The rule is you stay in your seat," the teacher would say when the student next to me, overcome with restlessness, stood up and moved around.

In many cases such rules do maintain order, but they do so by constricting the children's movement or speech or sometimes even their thought. The children don't get to be themselves or to think for themselves. Moreover, the children have had nothing to do with the creation of the rules, so they have no investment in following them. It's easy to see why most children resent these rules.

In type two, the rules are displayed on the wall and then largely ignored for the rest of the year, much like the rules at the pool where I swim. This was my approach to rule creation when I began teaching. In these classrooms, the children may behave positively or not, but the rules have nothing to do with it, because neither the children nor the teacher looks much at the rules or talks about them. When children misbehave, the teacher may or may not deal with the situation effectively, but again the rules play no role. No one even seems to remember that the class has any rules.

Imagine instead a third type of rules—rules created by the children themselves, rules that say what children will do rather than what they're not allowed to do, rules that embody the children's ideals for working and playing together as a community.

Imagine rules that children actually live by in their daily classroom life. Imagine children caring about their classroom rules, even if at times they wish they didn't have to adhere to them.

Rules like this may sound too good to be true, but I and thousands of teachers throughout the nation have learned how to turn this vision into reality in our classrooms. Part of the *Responsive Classroom* approach to teaching, this positive approach to rules builds on children's intrinsic desire to belong and do well, fosters an orderly and caring classroom community, enables academic learning, and allows for successful problem-solving.

In the *Responsive Classroom* approach, creating and teaching students the rules consists of three key elements:

- Involving children in rule creation

- Modeling what following the rules looks and sounds like

- Referring to the rules frequently

Involving Children in Rule Creation

We all feel greater ownership in what we've had a hand in creating. If children participate in creating their classroom rules, they feel more invested in following them.

I begin rule creation during the first days of school with everyone, students and myself alike, reflecting on and stating our hopes and goals for the year. Children's goals often have common threads such as wanting to learn and to have fun together. "I hope to use the computer a lot," "I hope to make new friends," and "I want to read long chapter books," students say. I add, "I hope our classroom will be a safe and caring place so all of you can learn." These hopes and goals establish the context for our rules, the reason we need rules in the first place.

Next, the students, with my guidance, generate a list of rules that might help us achieve these goals. Typically children generate a long list of edicts such as "Don't yell at anyone" and "Don't push or fight in line." They've had previous experiences with such rules.

As children contribute the don'ts, I say, "If we aren't going to yell, what *will* we do?" Together we turn the negative statements into positive ones— "Don't yell" becomes "Speak quietly," for example, and "Don't push or fight" becomes "Be safe and friendly." By stating the rules in the positive, we create a vision for what we want our class to be rather than what we don't want it to be.

Finally, we consolidate the long list of rules into a few general ones that encompass all the specifics named. Usually these global rules cover care for ourselves and our learning, care for each other, and care for the environment. To help with remembering, I make sure we craft rules that are general enough so that we need only a few (not more than five). But I also make sure the rules aren't so general that they're confusing to the children. "Be respectful," for example, is usually too abstract.

Here's a typical set of rules for a fourth grade class:

We will be safe and kind to all classmates.

We will do our best work.

We will take care of our environment and everything in it.

Modeling What Following the Rules
Looks and Sounds Like

It's not enough to establish the rules. It's also important to teach children what following the rules will look like and sound like. An important way to do this is through interactive modeling.

In interactive modeling, the teacher names a behavior and shows the children how to carry it out. The children notice and name what the teacher did. Next, a few students show the class the same behavior, and classmates name what they saw. Then the entire class practices the behavior while the teacher coaches.

For example, on the first day of school, I might say, "In this class, so that everyone will be safe, we will line up for lunch in a careful way." I ask the students to watch closely while I show them what this looks like. I go to the line spot, moving carefully.

"What did you notice?" I ask. Students might say, "You walked" or "You stayed away from the bookshelf while you stood in the line spot."

Next a few children take a turn. They get in line in a safe and careful way while classmates watch. Classmates tell us what behaviors they saw. "Toby kept his hands down by his side" or "Jenni walked," they might say. Then the whole class lines up while I coach, telling them the positive behaviors I saw.

For me, interactive modeling has been one of the most effective practices for improving classroom climate. I use it frequently—to model how to get work out and put it away, how to sharpen a pencil, how to keep the independent reading book safely in its pouch.

I also repeat the interactive modeling throughout the year as needed, especially right before or right after vacations, when students' self-discipline tends to get a little ragged.

Interactive modeling is even necessary—and works—for older elementary students. One time, I was in a fifth and sixth grade class as an instructional coach for a colleague. Eager to show the use of math manipulatives in teaching key concepts, I neglected to model the safe and careful use of these materials. The children flung the manipulatives across the room, grabbed favorites away from each other, and built towers after I had begun instruction. When I started using interactive modeling, the behavior improved. These older students developed a clear understanding, some perhaps for the first time, of the behavior standard for using materials during lessons.

In all grades, I've found, the more use of interactive modeling, the safer, more peaceful, and more caring the classroom becomes.

Referring to the Rules Frequently

I've learned through experience that if everyone in the class is to live the rules, I need to keep them front and center in students' attention by talking about them frequently, even after we've modeled them.

For example, we're about to have peer writing conferences. First we talk about how we can follow our rules "Be kind" and "Help each other learn." Or, we're getting ready for lunch. We discuss what our rule "Take care of our environment and everything in it" would look like in the lunchroom. These reminders help children keep their behavior on track. I know this consciousness-raising is working when a visitor arrives in our classroom and one of the students says, "Let's tell him about our rules."

I also refer to the rules when our classroom life inevitably hits bumps in the course of the year. "One of our rules says 'Be kind,'" I might say. "How can we solve this problem in a way that's kind to everyone in the class?" By referring to the rules in this way, I give the children a compass to use in the sometimes complex business of problem-solving.

The *Responsive Classroom* approach to creating and teaching rules works. It helps teachers manage classrooms, and it helps the children create a community in which everyone feels safe and everyone can learn. It's no wonder children care about rules created and honored in this way.

Beyond the Classroom Walls

Solving Problems that Involve Children from Different Classrooms

The problems described in this book, such as children's excluding a classmate or refusing to do hard work, are problems confined to one classroom.

Many problems at school, however, occur in areas such as the lunchroom, the playground, and the school bus, where children from a variety of classrooms interact. Because these areas of the school are often less structured, they may become breeding grounds for conflict, unsafe behavior, and emotional upset. Can the strategies in this book be used to address problems like these that involve children from different classrooms?

I have found that the answer is yes—if a teacher has extensive experience with the strategies and feels confident facilitating their use with colleagues and students who don't have much experience with them.

As this book makes clear, the effective use of these problem-solving strategies requires that students have significant foundational skills, skills that their teacher must teach explicitly, sometimes over several weeks or months. A teacher experienced with these strategies, however, may be able to adapt them or borrow elements from them when addressing problems across classrooms. The issues would then be handled in a way that fosters responsibility and investment in all parties involved. In addition, colleagues and their students who are unfamiliar with collaborative problem-solving strategies would gain an introduction to them.

Following are two examples of such cross-classroom problem-solving. One uses the conflict resolution protocol described in Chapter Three. The other uses the class meeting format described in Chapter Five.

E X A M P L E   1

Conflict Resolution: Fifth Grade Name-Calling on the Bus

The fifth grade teachers were eating lunch in the teachers' room. "Ella's mom called me yesterday," said Ms. Shaw. "She says there's a boy named Jack who's picking on Ella on the bus, bus seven. Whose class is Jack in?"

"I have a boy named Jack in my class. He's on bus seven. He must be the one," responded Ms. Lesser.

Conflicts on the bus come in all shapes and sizes. Jack might be "picking on" Ella, Ella might actually be "picking on" Jack, or they might be teasing each other in equal measure. The teachers decided to research the problem.

Talking with each student individually to learn more

Ms. Lesser started by speaking with Jack. "What's going on with you and Ella on the bus?" she asked.

"She teases me all the time. She calls me 'Shorty' and you know how I hate being teased about my height," Jack replied.

"She says you're bothering her. I think you two need to talk."

Meanwhile, Ms. Shaw talked with Ella. "What's going on with you and Jack on the bus?" she asked.

"He bugs me every single day."

"We need to all get together and talk about this," said Ms. Shaw.

Teachers plan together

Ms. Lesser had been using the conflict resolution protocol described in Chapter Three with her students. She felt very comfortable with the format, and her students were grasping it well. She therefore knew that at least one of the children, Jack, would understand the intent of their conversation and would be able to stick to the protocol. She felt confident that she could guide Ella sufficiently for the conversation to have a good outcome.

Ms. Shaw had heard about student-to-student conflict resolution but had never used it with her students. She appreciated its emphasis on respectful listening, however, and was open to trying the format as a possible way to solve this problem.

The two teachers agreed that both should be present for the conversation with Ella and Jack. This would communicate that a solution was important to both teachers. Because Ms. Lesser was the one with experience in this conflict resolution format, they decided she would take the lead. She reviewed the steps with Ms. Shaw so they could work together to keep the process on track.

One child begins with an I-statement

The two teachers and two students met in Ms. Shaw's room at lunchtime. Both children brought their lunches, but neither showed the slightest interest in eating.

"Who would like to begin with an I-statement?" Ms. Lesser asked.

"I will," said Jack. His class had been practicing I-statements and he felt comfortable offering one. "Ella, I feel really bad when I hear you call me 'Shorty' because I'm already self-conscious about my height. I also feel bad when I hear you call me 'Waffle Boy' just because I eat my waffle on the bus. I want you to stop calling me names like 'Shorty' and 'Waffle Boy.'"

Ella, less experienced with the conflict resolution format, started to interrupt. "But I didn't…"

"Wait, Ella," said Ms. Lesser. "First tell Jack what you heard."

Second child states his or her understanding of what was said

"I heard him say he doesn't like it when I call him 'Shorty' and 'Waffle Boy,'" said Ella.

In the simple act of repeating what Jack had said, Ella let go of the need to insist that she hadn't called him those things.

Second child states his or her point of view

"Ella, now it's your turn," said Ms. Shaw. Having gone over the steps with Ms. Lesser, she knew the protocol.

"But he called me "E" for "Idiot," said Ella. Both Jack and Ella thought "idiot" was spelled with an "e."

The two teachers glanced at each other briefly. Ms. Shaw made a mental note to review the sounds of the vowels "e" and "i" with Ella's spelling group. Ms. Lesser proceeded. "Say it to Jack," she told Ella calmly.

Turning to Jack, Ella said, "When you called me 'E' for 'Idiot,' I was embarrassed. I want you to stop calling me names, too."

First child states his or her understanding of what was said

"You don't want me to call you names either," summarized Jack.

The children reach a solution

"Let's gather some ideas for solutions," Ms. Lesser suggested.

"We could both stop calling each other names," recommended Jack.

"That's okay with me," Ella chimed in.

In this case, there was an obvious solution, so there was no need for further brainstorming or discussion. The value of the conversation was in the children's telling each other directly how they were feeling and respectfully listening to each other. They shook hands and headed off to the lunchroom to finally eat their lunches.

The entire conference had taken about five minutes.

The teachers discuss the outcomes

The two teachers spoke briefly about the conference and agreed that it sounded like a conflict between two equally matched children calling each other names, possibly even flowing from predictable fifth grade attempts at flirting. They both agreed to check in with the students regularly to see how their interactions were going.

THINGS TO NOTE about Jack and Ella's conflict resolution

- *Both teachers present:* Both participated in the conversation. This conveyed to the children that they both felt it important for the children to resolve this conflict.

- *Teachers stayed objective:* The teachers remained open-minded and didn't take sides. They didn't offer solutions, letting Jack and Ella arrive at a solution themselves.

- *An experienced teacher and student:* Ms. Lesser's and Jack's skill with the conflict resolution format, and Ms. Lesser's reviewing of the steps ahead of time with Ms. Shaw, helped ensure the success of this conversation.

EXAMPLE 2

A "Class Meeting": Chaos in Third Grade Recess

"Recess is out of control," announced my colleague Ms. DiStasio as she entered the teachers' room. Heads nodded. All the third grade teachers supervised recess one day a week, and we all shared her feeling.

"So, what does 'out of control' really mean?" I wondered aloud.

"Let's all observe recess this week and see if we can come back with some specifics," suggested Ms. Harrison.

With all of the children in one grade out on the play yard at the same time, any solution to the chaos of recess would need to be a collective decision. We needed to work together to make changes, and the first step was to define the problem. A problem well defined is a problem half solved.

A week later, the third grade teachers gathered for an early morning team meeting. Our agenda included looking at our students' writing samples, discussing district-wide math scores, and sharing what we'd noticed at third grade recess.

Ms. Harrison started the recess discussion. "There's a group of boys who play football together. They choose teams according to who's friends with whom, and then proceed to race up and down the field, bashing each other. When someone falls down, everyone piles on top of him. It's unsafe."

Ms. Phillips reported next. "I watched the blacktop area. There aren't any supplies, so kids just race around, trying to tag someone. They bump into each other. It's dangerous."

Ms. Carey volunteered to talk with the PE teacher, Mr. Viesselman, about putting out some simple supplies at the blacktop area: jump ropes, chalk for drawing on the pavement, a ball for shooting baskets. Mr. V. also agreed to teach the rules of touch football during PE classes so the football players would be able to play a fair and safe game.

A week later, the blacktop area had calmed down, but football was still chaotic. The children had learned the rules of football but were continuing to form teams on the basis of friendship groups and then to play roughly.

First step: A logical consequence to stop the hurtful behavior

The team of teachers decided that we would close football at recess until we'd found a way to make it safe. We took the football away, explaining to the children our concern about the game's physical and emotional safety. We told them that play would resume once we had a solution to the problem.

Next, a "class meeting"

To search for some solutions for making the football game safe and fun, we decided a class meeting format would work well.

Among the five third grade teachers, two, Ms. Harrison and I, were using class meetings regularly with our own classes. The other three teachers had never used it. Ms. Harrison and I both felt comfortable with the format. We were confident that between the two of us, and with the help of our students, who were also experienced with the format, we could lead an effective cross-classroom "class meeting."

Even if the meeting didn't resolve the issue once and for all, it would be a forum for the children and adults to discuss ways to play safely and develop a shared set of expectations about the football game.

We decided that all of the teachers would participate, because the problem involved all of our students, and that Ms. Harrison and I would facilitate.

The next morning, we each announced in our classroom the upcoming meeting about football safety for anyone who played football at recess, used to play football at recess, or wanted to play football at recess. The meeting would take place first thing during our school's Morning Meeting time.

Our principal supported our effort by providing adults, including herself and the assistant principal, to run Morning Meeting for the nonparticipating students.

On the day of the meeting, we gathered on the stage in the auditorium, a space large enough for all participants. We had a big turnout that included boys and girls. Apparently the teachers weren't the only ones concerned about the rough football games. We sat in a big circle, students and teachers together.

Going over ground rules for the meeting

One of my students began by reading our class guidelines for class meetings: "Listen to each other. Work to solve the problem."

A teacher states the reason for the meeting

Ms. Harrison began with a statement of the problem. "We teachers have noticed that football isn't safe. It isn't safe for people's feelings or their bodies. What have you noticed?"

Students each state what they've noticed about the problem or say "Pass"

My job was to keep us to the format of class meeting. Our time was limited and not everyone was familiar with the protocol, so I stated clearly, "We'll go around the circle. You may share what you've noticed about this problem or you may pass. We'll discuss possible solutions after that."

Lots of people had things to say. Paul said that the teams were unfair, that the guys who played football after school were all on the same team.

J.T. said, "Kids who play a lot only pass to each other, and some kids never get the ball."

Shoshanna said that girls would like to play, too, but the boys didn't let them.

José said that he used to play but he stopped because he kept getting hurt. He'd like to play if football was safer. "I think a teacher should be at the football game all the time," he added.

"José, save your solutions for the next time around," I interjected.

Ms. Phillips shared that she'd heard that Mr. V. had reviewed the rules for touch football in PE, but it didn't look like anyone was following them.

Matt, one of the informal captains, passed. He could hear that other kids were concerned about the way the game was going.

Each student suggests a solution or says "Pass"

Now, I announced, we'd go around the circle again, with suggestions for solutions. Once again, everyone would have a chance to speak in turn.

José suggested that players tag instead of tackling. That was what Mr. V. required them to do when they played football in PE.

Jay said he thought teachers should help pick fair teams.

Ms. DiStasio suggested random teams, using Popsicle sticks marked "1" and "2."

Matt shared his idea: There should be the same captains every day, and the captains would pick the teams.

Alyssa said everyone who wanted to should be able to play.

Ms. Phillips pointed out that hurting each other was against our school rules and that we also had a school rule saying that if you hurt someone during recess, you would need to sit out for the rest of the period.

Students comment on the solutions suggested

There was a lot of discussion about picking teams. Matt wanted captains who would pick their teams. Phong wanted the teachers to pick the teams. Shana said she didn't think there should be captains.

The group reaches agreement on a solution to try, using "thumbs up, middle, or down"

After everyone had a turn in commenting on the solutions named, I announced that we would use the thumbs method to pick some strategies to try. Demonstrating, I said, "You put your thumb up for solutions you think would work, thumb in the middle for solutions you can live with, and thumb down for solutions you absolutely can't live with, something you think would make recess no fun at all for yourself and the other football players."

Some students had used a consensus process in their classrooms, but many hadn't, so I explained what consensus meant in practical terms: We wouldn't use a solution that had any thumbs down. I reminded the students that football was closed and would remain closed until we came up with a solution for making it safe, so it was important to put your thumb down only for something you really couldn't live with.

I told the children that as Ms. Phillips had pointed out, hurting each other at recess was against our school rules, so we wouldn't be showing thumbs for tagging instead of tackling. It would be a given that anyone who tackled or knocked down a player would sit out for the rest of recess.

We then proceeded to work toward consensus on the items we *could* decide on, items that fit into our school rules. "Thumbs up, thumbs in the middle, or thumbs down for regular captains who will pick their teams," I stated. Matt, Ted, and Jerome, the football stars, put their thumbs up. Everyone else had thumbs down. No one had thumbs in the middle. There was no middle ground here.

"Thumbs up, thumbs in the middle, or thumbs down for having the teachers help pick fair teams," I continued. The majority of the children put their thumbs up for this one, with a smattering of thumbs in the middle. Matt had his thumb down.

"Thumbs up, thumbs in the middle, or thumbs down for random teams using Popsicle sticks," I said. Even more students put their thumbs up for this choice. Ted and Jerome had their thumbs in the middle and Matt had his thumb down.

"Matt," I said, "we won't be able to have football again until we can reach agreement."

"But I only want one choice," Matt argued, "the one where I can be captain and have my own team."

"Everyone else has been able to agree on the Popsicle sticks method," I stated. "Lots of kids would like to have the football back and be able to play again." I glanced at my colleagues, making eye contact with each of them. Understanding my nonverbal question, each nodded her assent. "If you're not ready to work with the group, the other kids will be able to play but you'll need to find something else to do at recess."

"Okay," Matt agreed reluctantly. "I'll put my thumb in the middle for the Popsicle sticks way."

With a show of thumbs, we continued to work through the suggested solutions, reaching agreement on the following:

- Everyone who wants to may play.

- There will be no captains.

- Players will pass to everyone.

A teacher sums up and compliments the group on their collaboration

Ms. Carey read our new agreements aloud, and Oliver agreed to make a reminder poster to put near the door to the playground. Ms. Harrison complimented the group, saying "I noticed you listening to each other carefully. We came up with some solutions that should make recess fair and safe for everyone."

We had used up our half hour. The teachers and children returned to their classrooms.

Teachers follow through to ensure success

At lunchtime, the teachers agreed to make sure the football game had constant adult supervision. We agreed to be consistent about taking children out of the game as soon as they started to get rough. And Ms. DiStasio volunteered to make the numbered Popsicle sticks for team selection.

THINGS TO NOTE about the football "class meeting"

- *Clear definition of the problem:* The teachers began by defining the problem on the basis of careful observation of the children.

- *Restructuring the environment:* The teachers arranged for recess equipment to be available and for the children to learn football rules. This solved part of the problem.

- *Administration's support:* The principal and assistant principal made the meeting possible by providing supervision of nonparticipating students.

- *Leadership by the experienced teachers:* The teachers who had used class meetings with their own classes facilitated the meeting, stating its purpose and keeping the group on track.

- *Full teacher participation:* All the third grade teachers came to the meeting. Those who had never used class meetings nonetheless participated in the discussion, sharing information about school rules and contributing ideas for solutions. This powerfully conveyed to the children that all the teachers thought this was an important issue to solve.

■ *Supportive school rules:* A rule about keeping everyone safe at recess was already in place. This supported the solutions to the problem at hand.

■ *A format that encouraged compromise:* The class meeting format helped children focus on a solution that everyone could live with, not just their own favorite solution.

■ *Teacher follow-up:* To support the solution, the teachers followed up with supervision and made sure the Popsicle stick method for selecting teams was being used.

Collaboration Beyond Classroom Boundaries

The strategies in this book will help you work with students in your classroom to solve their interpersonal or academic problems. Once you're skillful with these strategies, you can also use or adapt them to address students' problems that stretch beyond your classroom walls.

These strategies then become not only a way to address the difficulty at hand, but a vehicle for building a habit of collaborative problem-solving in the wider school community. Just as children in one room learn more richly and deeply when they work together, children from different rooms learn more richly and deeply, and teachers from different rooms teach more richly and deeply, when we all work together.

REFERENCES

Brown, L.M., & Gilligan, C. (1992). *Meeting at the Crossroads: Women's Psychology and Girls' Development.* Cambridge, Massachusetts: Harvard University Press.

Cosden, M., Gannon, C., & Haring, T.G. (1995). Teacher-control versus student-control over choice of task and reinforcement for students with severe behavior problems. *Journal of Behavioral Education,* 5: 11-17.

Deci, E. L., & Flaste, R. (1995). *Why We Do What We Do: Understanding Self-Motivation.* New York: Penguin Books.

Dyer, K., & Dunlap, G. (1990). Effects of choice-making on the serious problem behaviors of students with severe handicaps. *Journal of Applied Behavior Analysis,* 23 (4): 515-524.

Jablon, J.R., Dombro, A.L., & Dichtelmiller, M.L. (2007). *The Power of Observation.* (2nd ed.). Washington, DC: Teaching Strategies, Inc.

Jensen, E. (1998). *Teaching With the Brain in Mind.* Alexandria, Virginia: Association for Supervision and Curriculum Development.

Levine, M. (2003). *A Mind at a Time.* New York: Simon and Schuster.

Nelsen, J. (1981). *Positive Discipline.* New York: Ballantine Books.

Saphier, J., & Gower, R. (1997). *The Skillful Teacher: Building Your Teaching Skills.* Acton, Massachusetts: Research for Better Teaching.

Simmons, R. (2002). *Odd Girl Out: The Hidden Culture of Aggression in Girls.* New York: Harcourt.

Webster's New World Dictionary, Second Concise Edition. (1982). New York: Simon and Schuster.

FURTHER RESOURCES

From Northeast Foundation for Children, developer of the Responsive Classroom® *Approach to Teaching*

Books

20 Articles from 20 Years: Timeless Selections from the Responsive Classroom Newsletter. 2008.

99 Activities and Greetings: Great for Morning Meeting … and Other Meetings, Too! by Melissa Correa-Connolly. 2004.

Classroom Spaces That Work by Marlynn K. Clayton. 2001.

The First Six Weeks of School by Paula Denton and Roxann Kriete. 2000.

Habits of Goodness: Case Studies in the Social Curriculum by Ruth Sidney Charney. 1997.

Learning Through Academic Choice by Paula Denton, EdD. 2005.

The Morning Meeting Book by Roxann Kriete. Second edition. 2002.

Morning Meeting Messages K–6: 180 Sample Charts from Three Classrooms by Rosalea S. Fisher, Eric Henry, and Deborah Porter. 2006.

The Power of Our Words: Teacher Language That Helps Children Learn by Paula Denton, EdD. 2007.

Rules in School by Kathryn Brady, Mary Beth Forton, Deborah Porter, and Chip Wood. 2003.

Teaching Children to Care: Classroom Management for Ethical and Academic Growth, K–8 by Ruth Sidney Charney. 2002.

Yardsticks: Children in the Classroom Ages 4–14 by Chip Wood. Third edition. 2007.

DVDs

Creating Rules with Students in a Responsive Classroom (companion to the book *Rules in School*). 2007.

The First Day of School in a Responsive Classroom (companion to the book *The First Six Weeks of School*). 2007.

Morning Meeting Greetings in a Responsive Classroom (companion to the books *The Morning Meeting Book* and *99 Activities and Greetings*). 2008.

Morning Meeting Activities in a Responsive Classroom (companion to the books *The Morning Meeting Book* and *99 Activities and Greetings*). 2008.

Time-Out in a Responsive Classroom (companion to the book *Rules in School*). 2007.

Since beginning her teaching career thirty-seven years ago, Caltha Crowe has taught a range of elementary grades and preschool in a variety of settings, including schools in inner city New Haven, Connecticut, in the Chicago suburbs of Winnetka and Glencoe, and in Westport, Connecticut. Caltha has been involved with Connecticut's Beginning Educator Support and Training (BEST) program since its inception more than twenty years ago, serving as a mentor to new teachers, helping with mentor training, and serving on program advisory groups. A *Responsive Classroom®* consulting teacher, Caltha travels around the country to present workshops and coach teachers on using the *Responsive Classroom* approach. Caltha has a BA from Smith College, a master's degree in early childhood education from Goddard College, and a master's degree in educational leadership from Bank Street College of Education.

The *Responsive Classroom* approach to teaching emphasizes social, emotional, and academic growth in a strong and safe school community. The goal is to enable optimal student learning. Created by classroom teachers and backed by evidence from independent research, the *Responsive Classroom* approach consists of classroom and schoolwide practices for deliberately helping children build academic and social-emotional competencies.

At the heart of the *Responsive Classroom* approach are ten classroom practices:

Morning Meeting—gathering as a class each morning to greet each other and warm up for the day ahead

Rule Creation—helping students create classroom rules that allow all class members to meet learning goals

Interactive Modeling—teaching children expected behaviors through a unique modeling technique

Positive Teacher Language—using words and tone in ways that promote children's active learning and self-discipline

Logical Consequences—responding to misbehavior in a way that allows children to fix and learn from their mistakes while preserving their dignity

Guided Discovery—introducing classroom materials using a format that encourages independence, creativity, and responsibility

Academic Choice—increasing student motivation and learning by allowing students teacher-structured choices in their work

Classroom Organization—setting up the physical room in ways that encourage students' independence, cooperation, and productivity

Working with Families—involving them as partners and helping them understand the school's teaching approaches

Collaborative Problem-Solving—using conferencing, role-playing, and other strategies to resolve problems with students

More information about the *Responsive Classroom* approach is available through:

Publications and Resources

✱ Books, videos, and professional development kits for elementary school educators

✱ Free quarterly newsletter for elementary educators

✱ Website offering articles and other information: www.responsiveclassroom.org

Professional Development Opportunities

✱ One-day and week-long workshops for teachers

✱ One-day workshop for administrators

✱ Classroom consultations and other services at individual schools and districts

✱ Annual conference for school leaders

For details, contact:

Northeast Foundation for Children, Inc.
85 Avenue A, Suite 204, P.O. Box 718
Turners Falls, MA 01376-0718

800-360-6332   FAX: 877-206-3952
www.responsiveclassroom.org
info@responsiveclassroom.org